Sacred Place: Ch _

Religion, Culture and Society

Series Editors:
Oliver Davies
Gavin Flood
Department of Theology and Religious Studies,
University of Wales, Lampeter

Religion, Culture and Society is a series presented by leading scholars on a wide range of contemporary religious issues. The emphasis throughout is generally multicultural, and the approach is often interdisciplinary. The clarity and accessibility of the series, as well as its authoritative scholarship, will recommend it to students and a non-specialist readership alike.

Sacred Place: Chosen People

Land and National Identity in
Welsh Spirituality

DORIAN LLYWELYN

UNIVERSITY OF WALES PRESS
CARDIFF
1999

British Library Cataloguing-in-Publication Data
A catalogue record for this book is available from
the British Library.

ISBN 0-7083-1519-4 (paperback)
ISBN 0-7083-1520-8 (hardback)

The right of Dorian Llywelyn to be identified as author of this work has
been asserted by him in accordance with the Copyright, Designs and
Patents Act 1988

Typeset at the University of Wales Press
Printed in Great Britain by Dinefwr Press, Llandybïe

Cyflwynaf y gyfrol hon er diolchgar gof am fy nhad,
Cymro, cenedlgarwr a Christion,
ac i genhedlaeth ddiweddaraf fy nheulu crefyddol –
Gwenllian, Siôn a Twm

Contents

Introduction

The origins of this book lie quite as much in personal reasons as intellectual concerns. The theme of the search for unity within a coincidence of opposites runs through this book, and it has distinct personal resonances. The American theologian Sandra Schneiders points out that spirituality is a 'self-implicating discipline': we bring our own particular hermeneutic to the material we study, which means that the teller and the tale are inevitably part of each other. I am a Catholic priest and a Welsh-speaking Welshman, standpoints which inevitably affect my own intellectual interests and thought-patterns, my cultural and theological preferences, and my own way of telling the story contained in this volume. As a priest in a Church in which concerns for Welsh national identity and its relationship with faith and mission have sometimes been invisible or else considered as marginal, eccentric and even dangerous, and as a Welshman who has espoused a faith which has often been perceived as un-Welsh, my position is something of an anomaly on both counts. All Welsh-speaking Catholics are members of two worlds – those of largely anglophone Welsh Catholicism and of mainly Protestant Welsh-speakers. Many of us experience the richness and tensions which such dual loyalties create: unconventional insights, the daily task of negotiating a way through potential incompatibilities, and the perennial vocation of being simultaneously permanent outsiders and cultural and theological ambassadors.

Writing this book has also been a mid-life journey of self-discovery. I find it particularly easy to identity with the proverb *Gorau Cymro, Cymro oddi cartref* – the best Welshman is a Welshman abroad – since I have spent large periods of my adult life outside Wales, having made my home at various times in France, England, Egypt, Indonesia, Spain and the United States. The theme of exile which appears in this book therefore has particular poignancy for me. Whilst studying at the Graduate

Theological Union and the University of California at Berkeley, I began to develop an interest in spirituality and the natural world and the spirituality of creation. My Welsh approach to landscape was notably very different from that of my American classmates, most of whom were white, middle-class, and none of whom had the experience of awareness of ancestral belonging to place which so typifies Welsh consciousness. Many of them sought a sense of roots in two directions, looking for inspiration to the worlds of 'Celtic spirituality' or to the religion of indigenous American peoples. In both cases, my religious and political instincts were firmly sceptical about the desirability or even possibility of wholesale exportation or appropriation of models of spirituality belonging to other places and peoples and times.

In investigating spirituality of place, I was puzzled not to be able to recognize on first inspection anything amongst the classic phenomenological descriptions approaching a twentieth-century Welsh experience of place. As a nation which has been largely Protestant for the last 400 years, Wales possesses few sacred sites, none of which could possibly fit Eliade's *axis mundi* model of sacred space, and yet a sense of place is very much part of Welsh instincts. In much of that peculiar middle-class piety which describes itself as 'Celtic spirituality', I was – and remain – unable to recognize much that corresponds to my own personal experience. Two elements in particular seemed to be missing in these considerations: first of all, any theological insights which could do justice to a Protestant spirituality of place, and secondly, any sense of political awareness attached to a sense of place. The element of nationality is common to both these elements, and my instinct was that they were intimately connected together. One of the aims of this book has been to investigate the theological roots of a Welsh sense of place.

In the Welsh-speaking Baptist tradition in which I was brought up, national and religious characteristics were inseparable and sometimes identical with each other. As a child growing up in this ethnic Protestant Welsh religiosity, I equated Welshness with religiosity and righteousness. To worship God anywhere else than in a chapel, and in any language other than Welsh, was both alien and wrong – and that wrongness was as much a cultural as a religious sin. The other strand of this book – the connection between nationality and religion in Wales – arose in a need to identify the roots and developments of my own ethnic spirituality, to place it in a wider theological spectrum, and to evaluate its values and counter-values. In this way, by finding out the theological roots of my cultural traditions, I hoped to be able to identify their connections with the theological convictions I now espouse, and to use these insights pastorally, within the Catholic Church in Wales. And lastly, I hoped also to bring this research to bear on the field of cultural politics in Wales in which I have been actively interested for all my adult years. The theological traditions I identify in these pages are still strong in many different strands of Welsh life.

What is unique, I believe, about this spirituality is a sense of nationhood *and* of belonging to the land. A Welsh sense of holy place is inseparable from a sense of belonging to a specific community of people – both those who, synchronically, are part of the same culture, and those from whom, diachronically, the tradition has been inherited. This is a spirituality experienced by modern speakers of a Celtic language, and whose mix of the religious with the political, the aesthetic with the ethnic means that it is not easily included if at all in 'Celtic spirituality'. It continues to live, often unperceived on England's doorstep, and even within its own homeland, its rich story is not well known. I am convinced, however, that, despite my initial inability to recognize Wales in universal descriptions of sacred place, this story is an interesting element in the wider patrimony of holy place. In the development of wider spiritualities of place and of nationhood, Wales has a valuable part to play.

Limitations on the length of this book mean that it can, at best, only hope to raise the most basic of issues. For the Welsh-speaking reader, I hope that it will furnish something of interest, and that the insights of other disciplines such as social geography or the echoes of other cultures may serve to delight – and occasionally also to challenge. I hope that English-speaking Welsh readers may be helped to understand their own roots. The non-Welsh, non-specialist reader will discover within these pages only the glimpse of an introduction to Welsh literature. At an early stage, I had to make the painful decision to include only a small selection of those writers who were most theologically eloquent, with the consequence that I have not been able to discuss much of the tradition of poetry of place in Welsh. I am currently engaged on another study in which I hope to repair some of these lacunae.

There is one colophon to this story. Most of this book was written before the referendum of 18 September 1997 when, with the thinnest of margins, the people who live in Wales reversed a theological trend of many centuries, and voted to accept the proposal of an elected Welsh Assembly. An understanding of national identity as a spiritual state, beginning in the sixth century, and compounded by the Reformation, yielded significant ground to the establishment of a material and politically separate national identity. Much of what I describe therefore in this book was challenged by that decision. Whether Welsh national identity will continue to be informed by religious values, or whether it will be a purely secular reality is yet to be known. It was certainly possible to read the referendum campaign of both sides as a conflict in theology. But that will be another book.

Acknowledgements

This book could not have been written without the help of a large number of people. My thanks are due to Sister Mary Ann Donovan SC, my supervisor at Berkeley, for her unfailingly perceptive comments, guidance and interest; to Revd John Baldovin SJ and Revd Arthur Holder, for allowing me to talk at them at great length and clarify my ideas; to my teachers at the Graduate Theological Union, Dr Douglas Burton-Christie, Dr Sandra Schneiders IHM, and Br William Short; to Philip Sheldrake, whose article on Christian spirituality of place spurred me to consider this theme; to Peter Lord, Revd Enid Morgan, Revd John Fitzgerald O.Carm. and the Rt. Revd Rowan Williams, all of whom have given me valuable insights and leads; to my Bishop, the Rt. Revd Daniel J. Mullins, for sending me to Berkeley to study spirituality; and to the Claretian Community there, who put me up and put up with me during the research and the writing of the thesis which gave birth to this book. I thank my friend, colleague and editor Dr Oliver Davies for all his interest and work, and Mrs Gwendraeth Morgan for her help with the chapter on Waldo Williams. A diolch o galon i deulu Crud yr Awel am roi i mi wir le.

1

Mapping the terrain: problems and paradigms in nationality, land and spirituality

> Man's days are like those of grass
> like a flower of the field he blooms;
> The wind sweeps over him and he is gone
> and his place knows him no more. (Psalm 103)

A search for roots and a 'sense of place' are common experiences for late twentieth-century Westerners, a longing for a 'pure place, a place of extraordinary import found among all that is common and profane'[1] as an answer to existential crisis. The expression of such needs in territorial terms is part of the universal human patrimony: Rowan Williams notes that in both Celtic myth and Christian spirituality, we find 'spatialized time' – a landscape with figures which responds to human existential needs, and which is essentially ahistoric, responding to the hope that salvation not yet gained in the here-and-now can be gained elsewhere.[2] Two species of this soteriological landscape exist – the other-worldly, extra-historical heaven, and the intramundane sacred place. It is this latter – and its connections with the former – that this book explores. In the psalm quoted above, the Psalmist conceives of death as a situation in which one is no longer in intimate relationship with one's 'place': the fullness of life, in the biblical world-view implied here, involves a relationship with place. 'Land' is one of the series of renunciations which Jesus places as a condition for discipleship (Mt. 19: 29), indicating the relativity of land, but also its importance, since in this *logion* land is placed on the same level of significance as those family relationships which function as providers of a sense of identity. Central to this book is the belief that a relationship to place, a sense of belonging to one specific landscape, is one of those dimensions of life which render us truly and fully human, in both individual and social aspects.

There are other relationships which are similarly foundational of a full human identity: a sense of belonging with others, with specific individuals and with a specific community. These are more of those necessities without which we risk losing a sense of ourselves. One of the communities which provide us with that sense of belonging is the nation, the other object of study of this volume.

Much Christian anthropology holds that all those things which make us more truly and fully human may also be considered, in the widest sense as spiritual categories. But what are the specifically *spiritual* imports of a sense of place and nationality? And is there any essential connection between land and national identity? It is questions such as these, in their manifestations within the spirituality of Wales, that this book seeks to explore. Both a sense of place and of nation are capable of expressions which are positive or destructive, superficial or profound, transient or enduring, humane or inhumane, sacred and profane. The theoretical and practical issues which are involved in these expressions are based on a large number of potentially irreconcilable polarities.

The first of these is *the relationship between the particular and the universal:* how do particular, local places relate to the whole? Does God show himself in particular places, and if so, how can we begin to describe that event or presence? If a particular place, such as a temple or a forest glade or a city, is felt to be holy, what are the implications of that for places outside that aura of holiness? Is a strong and particular sense of nationality compatible with universal brotherhood? When divine election is predicated of one particular nation, what is the spiritual import of all other nations? And what are the practical – including the political – implications of divine election of one nation for the non-elect remainder of humanity? Is national territory exclusively reserved for members of one particular community only, or is it open and available to be universally disposed of and used at will?

Related to this polarity is the question of *individual and social experience*: what connection, if any, is there between particular, individual experiences of place and a wider social dimension, and does either of these two levels have greater significance? What is the import – on both purely human and religious levels – of an individual's belonging to a particular community such as a nation, and vice versa? Is a community such as a nation merely the sum of its constituent parts, or can it have some corporate identity and thus be considered as a moral being?

Questions such as these already invoke the challenging and ancient riddle of *the relationship between the sacred and the profane.* In Christian – or to be more precise, in Catholic – terms, this problem is historically expressed in the tension between nature and grace, creation and salvation, a tension which exists in the attempts to explicate the different ways in which the divine is present or acts in the world and in human history. In the Judeo-Christian version, the story of salvation happens within time, in a dramatic pattern which has its ups and downs; the struggle of the writers of the Bible and Christian tradition has been to try to explain the question of the relationship of human history and human will with the divine: is time merely a secular reality, or is it coextensive with salvation? Does revelation happen merely within or by means of history? If the world is divine creation, to what extent and how is God present in his creation, and is that presence the same in all parts? Possible answers to this question will give us a patchwork of holy sites, or a world which is uniformly holy. Is God immanent – present within the material world, and within time? Or does divine transcendence mean that the world of time through which we travel at speed throughout our lives has no connection with the world of the eternal? Within a secularized Western culture, to attribute any divine origin or spiritual significance to the nation probably appears by now an antiquated stance. Nevertheless, for many peoples throughout history the nation has been understood essentially as a religious reality. To what extent can this be true?

Human responses to divine actions exist in tension between two potential polarities: understanding life, on the one hand, as divine gift, an aspect which will tend to stress being, contemplation, the static and the aesthetic, and on the other hand as task, or responsibility, stressing morality (as human response to God's gift), the dynamic and the temporal. The classic Christian summary of these polarized aspects are faith and works. There are secular analogues of these questions: a concentration, on the one hand, on human responsibilities and, on the other, on human rights, along with varying interpretations of the relationship between the individual human person and the collective.

The many theoretical attempts by Christians to wrestle with these questions generally show preferential options for one or other polarity, in various constellations, emphasizing either the world of creation or the world of salvation. These are theologies which derive from and in their turn create practical, lived spiritualities, with political implications: the historically important problem of the relationship between state and Church, and between national and religious identities, is at heart a practical working-through of this theological issue. As we will see, the concept of place may also be expressed in purely secular ways – the modern secular state, the understanding of social geographers of place *inter aliis* – or in a religious version, under the species of holy place, sacred space, epiphany, *axis mundi*. Even within a purely secular mind-set, the problem of the sacred and the secular continues, sometimes disguised as the relationship between the conceptual and the concrete. How, if at all, is it possible to reconcile these different realities, and how may the different intellectual attempts to harmonize and reconcile the apparently irreconcilable themselves be brought together?

Amongst the theological attempts to provide some intellectually rigorous answers to these questions is the Catholic understanding that grace does not destroy nature, but requires its presence in order to build on and perfect it. The insight that the intramundane, temporal and material realities of this world have a spiritual, divine and eternal remit contains many practical implications. That this is true of the human person, summit of creation and image and likeness of God is obvious, within a Christian mind-set. The problem remains, however, of the relationship between the various levels of humanity – individual and social – and the created world. If, as I have stated, a sense of place is part of what it is to be human, then this raises such universally applicable questions as 'What is my relationship with my place, and our relationship with our particular places, local and national?'

Christian anthropology understands the human person as a bipolar reality, a union of the material, temporal and specific (the body) with the divine-created and eternal (the soul). Deriving from this are spiritualities which will be more partial to one or another of these aspects. In the person of Jesus Christ, son of God and son of Mary, orthodox Christianity has seen the supreme example and model of such union, in which *quod non assumptum non salvatum:* all that is constituitively human and natural is included in the person of Christ, the perfect human being, in whom the human is united with the divine. Only after several centuries of Christian theology was the emerging Church equipped with the necessary intellectual tools to elucidate the relation of Christ's humanity with his divinity. The bishops meeting at the Council of Chalcedon sought to tackle the theological problem of the nature of Christ – a direct and urgent question, given the need to combat a number of heresies, and their immediate practical implications for the way Christian life was understood and lived. The dogmatic definition declared that Christ was to be understood as one person with two natures, human and divine, joined together in a hypostatic union

> perfect both in his divinity and in his humanity . . . We declare that the one selfsame Christ, only-begotten Son and Lord, must be acknowledged in two natures, without any commingling or change or division or separation; . . . the distinction between the natures is in no way removed by the union, but rather the specific character of each nature is preserved and they are united in one person and one hypostasis; he is not split or divided into two persons, but that there is one selfsame, only-begotten Son, God the Word, the Lord Jesus Christ.

These four adverbs – *inconfuse, immutabiliter, indivise, inseparabiliter* (without any commingling or change or division or separation) – also served to define the nature of the Christian life, fully incorporating the life of nature into the life of grace. But for our immediate purposes, they provide us with a more detailed description of a union of realities, in which X and Y meet and are united: not mixing to produce a third reality which is neither divine or natural (*inconfuse*), X not being subsumed by or identical to Y or vice versa (*immutabiliter*), the whole of X and of Y being included in the union (*indivise*), and X and Y being only fully realized or apprehended when in union with each other (*inseparabiliter*).

The Chalcedonian model of association of different ontological realities provides us, I believe, with a central hermeneutical paradigm for the union of such polarities as I have described above. This book studies the development and expression of several such unions within Welsh spirituality: the relationship between the divine and the natural in the understanding of the land of Wales and of the Welsh people; the connection between the individual and the collective in the nation; and the relationship between religious and national identity – as we will see, a concern which typifies Welsh spirituality from its most ancient roots up until the present day. It is from the Welsh philosopher J. R. Jones that this book borrows its second hermeneutical paradigm: interpenetration. Seeking to elucidate the intimate importance for a nation – in this case, the Welsh – of its own language and land, and exactly how these elements relate to each other, Jones talks of 'the interpenetration of language and land', offering us this definition: 'Substances interpenetrate when one runs as it were totally through the other; when one goes as it were into the other, without merging, but rather creating an interior relationship which does not come about when substances are merely joined together.' At the heart of interpenetration is relationality. A synthesis of Chalcedon and interpenetration allows us not only to propose but also to describe the mechanics of a spirituality in which secular and the sacred elements are united in a healthy and mutually enhancing relationship. Negatively, one can begin to glimpse the potential anti-models of relationships between these two polarities, those in which the sacred and the secular are commingled, changed, divided or separated.

Whilst Chalcedonian hypostatic union expresses the unchanging nature of relationship between polarities, there is a third hermeneutical paradigm which helps us to understand the element of movement and dynamism which is part of any healthy relationship. In Trinitarian theology, the interpersonal relating of the three persons is conceived of as a movement known as perichoresis, a term which suggests that the union and differentiation within the Godhead is a dynamic process of unity in which the ontological differences between persons or spheres are actually strengthened, rather than dissolved, by their uniting. Within the Trinity, unity does not involve uniformity, but unified plurality. That this technical term was applied originally to the divine and human natures of Christ suggests that the union of the human and the divine, the physical and the spiritual is similarly involved in a dynamic internal economy. As a hermeneutic for understanding the unity between potentially inimical realities, this concept then allows us to see such relationships as creative tension or dynamic balance between two poles. The named themes of this book, the spiritualities of place and of national identity, themselves offer such a polarity. As will become evident, place as a concept is far more than a material description of territory, since it involves relationship with the divine, with particular societies and with individuals, all of whom have a temporal, intrahistorical aspect. Nevertheless, in the consideration of the concept of place in its sacred and secular versions, the element of time has tended to receive diminished attention. On the other hand, the nation is most often considered – at least in the modern period – primarily as a temporal, non-substantial and ideated reality, its connection with place being seen as only one of many elements in its composition. What most clearly tends to define an identifiable and strong strand of Welsh spirituality is not so much a sense of sacred place per se, as a sense of nationhood *and* of belonging to the land: there certainly exists a sense of holiness of specific place, but this localized holiness is interpenetrated by and inseparable from a sense of belonging to a specific, transtemporal, community of people. Biblical data alone suggests that a rigid separation of time (involving history, politics and community) from place cannot do adequate justice to a Christian notion of spirituality of place, neither in Wales nor anywhere else. Place and identity – individual, communal and national – relate to each other intimately, and any attempt to describe an ethnic Welsh spirituality must include both. What this book seeks to explore is the connection and mutual co-implication between two expressions of the fundamental existential planes of space and time, along with another two theological considerations, namely the human (both individual and the social) and the divine. God, man, place and nation are then the four actors of this drama, played out on the stage of Welsh history and land.

Operative typologies

The constellation of possible interactions between the universal and the particular, the individual and the social, the divine and the secular, the human and the natural, is infinite. The history of Welsh spirituality, however, shows a number of typical configurations – some of which are truly interpenetrative and balanced, and models of healthy spirituality. Others however show tendencies towards blurring of boundaries, ignoring necessary and complementary balances, or theological schizophrenia.

Perhaps the basic common insight in much of Welsh spirituality is the importance given to the social insertion of the individual: whatever the formally espoused belief of Welsh Christians, Welsh spirituality is often experientially posited on an instinct that the individual quest for identity can only be resolved when the individual is inserted in a community, be it a local one or a national one. This spirituality is therefore fundamentally communitarian, based – at its best – on an interpenetration between the social and individual aspects of what it is to live life in its fullness. Whilst there is ample scope for the individual, individualism (as a vitiated sense of individual identity, one which is not in healthy interpenetration with one's social identity) does not seem to be a tendency of this tradition.

For J. R. Jones (see Chapter 3) the nation is the community which provides meaning for the individual. This insight, which I refer to in this book as the 'Wales-Israel tradition', has its roots in late Antiquity. It was consequently taken up by Protestant traditions within Wales, and continues to inform Welsh attitudes. Taking Israel as its model, it has I believe tended towards a certain spiritualization. Political expression of a distinctive Welshness being difficult, national identity was translated to a separate spiritual sphere, national spiritual eminence being interpreted sometimes as national election along the lines of Israel. This tradition carries the tendency to turn Wales into an idea, and national identity, rather than a concrete, embodied reality, into a moral way-of-being, in which the Welsh are considered as a nation which has existed in the past, and which may possibly exist in the intrahistorical future, or which may only find its fulfilment beyond time. In this model, space, as the arena of God's presence in the world, yields chronologically and in terms of ontological density to time, understood as the arena of history, which in its turn is conceived of as human action and God's condemnation and salvation in response to this and vice versa. The key divine attribute in this model is transcendence: the invisible world of grace is felt variously to be more evolved than and so to ignore, abandon, or even to destroy the world of nature – a theological tendency against which 'change', the second Chalcedonian concept, warns. One practical result of this has been a compensatory and pietistic spirituality which gives little credence to secular realities. Another highly significant tendency has been constantly to commingle national and religious identities in Wales (the first Chalcedonian practical heresy), making the nation into a quasi-church. Insofar as the Church of the New Testament is conceived of as Israel of the spirit, a Welsh use of typology has sometimes diverted the Old Testament typology of Israel and applied it to the nation of Wales, resulting in a related but different paradigm, Wales-as-Church. In the understanding of the Wales-Israel tradition, the holiness of the land of Wales derives from or is felt to be conditional on the sanctity of the elect who inhabit it. In this quasi-ecclesial model of national identity, the material reality of the land sometimes takes on a sacramental function, not so much reflecting as guaranteeing the sanctity of the people.

A characteristic note of much of Welsh spirituality has been the interplay of religious notions with political implications. A stance which derives from Old Testament prophecy was firmly taken by Gildas, the founding-father of the Wales-Israel spiritual tradition, and by his spiritual descendants, the preachers, divines and hymnists of Wales. But influenced partly by the notions of German Romanticism which based nationalism on language and on the rights of that language, this sense of national identity has also issued into modern Welsh nationalism, based on the notion of rights and deriving from the theological consideration of the nation as a moral person.

The model of Wales-Israel is intimately related to another strand, the biblical roots of which are in Abraham's election, perceived not so much as a separating out, but rather as a destiny, a vocation, and a sign or promise of universal election and salvation: 'All nations will be blessed in you' (Gal. 3: 8). The understanding of this model of place and national identity is *pars pro toto:* the specific place and nation of Wales have the task of being signs and creators of universal understanding, national distinctiveness being the guarantor of true universal unity. Behind this consideration lies the understanding of the community of nations as a church, individual members of that church being the different nations. In the *pars pro toto* model, the emphasis is placed on a nation's responsibilities rather than on its rights. It is for the sake of the whole of humanity that Wales, like Israel, is an elect nation, with its own holy land functioning to signal the destiny of all the earth. Politically this typology has also fed into modern Welsh nationalism. National distinctiveness is understood not so much as separation from the world (as in the Wales-Israel model) but as engagement with it, difference being the prerequisite for union.

The history of Wales, constantly under threat of cultural extinction, and in internal psychological exile, explains the congeniality of the spiritualizing and the militant tendencies of the Wales-Israel model, and the significant attention paid to the nation in Welsh spirituality. But the notion of place is also a notable part of the spiritual tradition. There is, I believe, within the traditions of Welsh spirituality a tension between *brogarwch* (the love of one's own native area), and *gwladgarwch* (patriotism), between on the one hand specific places and on the other, the whole place of Wales. The Wales-Israel model predicates time as its centre of interest, and divine transcendence as its preferred modality. Within this model of Wales as sacred place, individual places have less currency, and the whole of Wales is considered as a holy land. In this model it is purely human interaction with places which renders them holy: there is arguably nothing particularly sacred about such places as Bethlehem, Nazareth, or Bethesda in Wales (although it is also true that ancestral contact with such places is part of the process through which a place becomes considered as holy). In this spirituality, specific places tend not to be considered as mediators of the divine, and the holiness of the land of Wales is largely a derivative of the social, religious and political identity of the nation. As a result, in this model, since significance or holiness is only derivative of a specific group of people, place tends to become a *purely* social reality. In the event of the diminution or disappearance of a people and its culture, places therefore may lose any transcendent or universal significance, a result which allows for the desacralization of the sacred, one people's holy place becoming a commodity to be appreciated merely aesthetically, bought, sold or invaded by others.

There has also been however, a tradition – less well-known and often unperceived or ignored – which is interested in divine presence in specific places in Wales, places which mediate holiness: this is the world of the traditions and places of the early saints, of folklore and medieval legend, and of pre-Reformation, Catholic Wales. It seems appropriate to refer to this tendency or typology as Catholic-local spirituality,[3] and as such, it is also related to the Wales-as-Church model. Here, the key divine attribute is immanence, and the role of place is as mediator or sacrament of the divine. In this tradition, Welsh holy places do not differ much from any other holy places: this spirituality finds echo in a wider anthropological context – in ancestral Celtic civilizations, the world of Australian Aborigines, or amongst Native Americans, and the experience of place of primal indigenous religions described by the typologies of phenomenologists of religion, in which divine action is believed to have happened in specific places, rendering them holy. In Wales, this pattern is often unconsciously subscribed to in both religious and secular versions by poets, in their poems of praise to their own homelands – signally so by Gwenallt and Waldo Williams (see Chapters 5 and 6). This tradition is sympathetic to the *pars pro toto* understanding of community and nation. However, within it, specificity, the local, the singular, the peculiar, and the national, are not seen as the enemy of the universal, but rather as its precondition, guarantor and material incarnation. In terms of sacred place, this tradition tends toward attributing universal and transhistorical sacrality to places, with the practical result that perception of sanctity is not conditional upon membership of a particular social group.

Both the Wales-Israel and the Catholic-local traditions consider the human element in place: in both cases, with differing emphases, the human significance is essential. And in both cases, it is the social, rather than the individual aspect of a sense of place which tends to be given greater prominence.

There are other possible reactions towards place, which find little direct echo in the Welsh tradition, but which are silent adversaries against which the tradition reacts. The first of these is to consider place under its material reality alone, devoid of any meaning or human associations. This attitude ignores – or chooses to ignore – the interpenetration of social identity with land in the concept of place, denuding it of any social associations, and thus finds little place for moral or political considerations regarding place. The practical corollaries of this attitude include the political heresies of imperialism and colonialism, the anti-models to which Welsh spirituality is often in reaction. Since imperialism can only be undertaken by those whose identity is not interpenetrated with a relationship with particular land, we would not expect to find this as a type of Welsh attitude, at least not toward the place and places of Wales.

If Welsh spiritual traditions generally are historical, politicized, communitarian and tend towards the moral, there also exists an aestheticist-individualist attitude towards place, one which finds almost no echo in Welsh understandings of land. The work of the art historian Peter Lord shows how Welsh landscape was 'discovered' in the late eighteenth century by English painters, and portrayed as a 'beautiful empty place', largely ignoring any social reality which the land carried and portraying its inhabitants largely as picturesque primitives. This colonialist and romanticizing attitude towards Wales – and indeed to many other places inhabited by small nations of indigenous peoples – continues to thrive, and is strongly present in many strands of neo-Celtic spirituality. As in the case of imperialism, this model fails to incorporate fully the social aspect of place, reducing it to its appearance only. Where the holy enters into consideration of place, here it is generally as an individual and an individualist experience only, and if the social is integrated into this model, then it is largely under the aegis of past, rather than present experience. However, holiness necessarily implies social – and I would argue, political – relationships. A spirituality of place based on an unadulterated aestheticism is reductionist. Rowan Williams offers a twofold corrective to a purely aesthetic stance towards place: 'The aesthetic in respect to landscape does not involve ideas. Setting up the model of the holy without the moral aestheticizes it.'[4] Whilst aestheticism may often present itself as an 'apolitical', or universalist, attitude towards land, it is necessarily a political stance, and more than frequently a thinly disguised cultural or territorial colonialism, and a spiritual self-idolatry. Both these stances have analogues in practical political questions: whose interests are served by different perceptions of geographical locations: as 'land of the fathers' or as 'a beautiful place', as keeper of identity, or as a commodity to be bought and sold? Since the aestheticist and colonialist models of place ignore social realities, the practical result of these two models is the same: the destruction, whether sought-for or not, of place as place, and the levelling of necessary local distinctivenesses. Within these pages then, the reader will find a study of both the theological and practical implications of place and nationality, expressed in a rich and ongoing history. Now that I have outlined the deep theological issues which the questions of spirituality and place and nationality involve, a brief description of the journey through this book may help the reader.

Although place and nation have often lent themselves to religious understandings, they also have well-developed secular versions, and as such are studied by a range of secular academic disciples. Bearing in mind that grace builds on nature, that one begins with the anthropological and the psychological before one can consider the specifically Christian and spiritual, Chapter 2 offers an overview of concepts of place and holy places, then proceeding to examine the biblical data concerning place and national election, and concluding with some modern understandings of the nation and nationalism. Moving from the general to the specific, Chapter 3 provides an overview of the intellectual understandings of nationality in Wales and, with the concept of interpenetration of J. R. Jones, investigates the connection between identity, both national and local, and specific place. The rich development of the Wales-Israel tradition, from its very beginnings to one of its twentieth-century manifestations, is traced in Chapter 4. The following two chapters introduce us to poetic manifestations of a spirituality of place and national identity. In the poems of Gwenallt, several different aspects of spirituality coexist in tension: the local and the national, a nationalism which shifts between rights and responsibilities, the sacramentality of both nation and church. The work of Waldo Williams weds tradition with innovation and deep insight: in his poems on Wales the polarities I have outlined above are reconciled in a true and harmonious interpenetration of universal import.

In sympathy with the *pars pro toto* school of national identity, it is my firm conviction that Wales has a challenging and specific contribution to make to this developing field of study. Aware now of the deeper tectonic plates of the theoretical issues, and armed with a map of the immediate intellectual landscape, it is time to proceed with our journey.

2

Laying the firm foundations[1]

Although the concepts of both place and nationality have been much studied by other disciplines, they have enjoyed scant specifically *theological* attention. Sandra Schneiders describes the academic discipline of spirituality, considered as the theological examination of human religious experience, as a 'field-encompassing field'. A cross-disciplinary approach to a theological understanding of place is both necessary and enriching: social geographers and landscape historians, amongst others, provide valuable concepts concerning the relationship of humanity to place, while to phenomenologists of religion and anthropologists are owed the notion of specifically sacred space or place. Political scientists and historians are an obvious source for theological reflection on nationality. Literature too is another source for spirituality, especially in Wales, where the theological endeavour has often been carried out by poets, hymnists, and essayists. But an examination of the specifics of Wales demands an appreciation of wider understandings of place and nation, both secular and religious.

Terminologies and typologies

Writers on place and space, sacred place and sacred space, evidence a widely diverging use of terms and typologies, and a commonly held terminology represents a horizon rather than an established reality. Differences in terminology reflect a diversity of academic backgrounds: geographers, historians of various hues, philosophers and theologians all write on this subject, each with their own intellectual traditions, concerns and viewpoint. But, diversity apart, there are a number of historical and philosophical factors why the study of place is a fairly new theological discipline, including the assumptions of a certain kind of metaphysics which holds that truth is the same in all locations, and therefore that physical context has no effect on its content, and the Cartesian idea that what most typically defines the human is the ability to think. This latter credo is underpinned by a certain historical Christian undervaluing of the significance of the human body, originating in a body–soul dichotomy found in Western philosophical and theological traditions, the corollary of which is that the proper concern of spiritual matters is the disembodied (and therefore the unlocated) and the hereafter. These are, admittedly, crude caricatures of a certain world-view, but they go some way to explaining why a concern for place and space is a comparative newcomer to the academy, at least in the English-speaking world.

Authors are quick to point out, however, that the importance of place is an anthropological constant: in traditional societies, the individual is defined, among other things, by his or her belonging to a specific place. Only in modern, Western, industrialized society is such a relation absent, and it is perhaps Wales's rural and generally conservative society which has allowed the sense of place to survive there. For many writers, this absence of 'home place' is both witness to and partial cause of the existential *anomie* of twentieth-century Western humanity.

Mircea Eliade's work famously uses the term 'sacred space'. What Eliade refers to as 'space'[2] seems to fit into a number of authors' concept of 'place', which they counter-distinguish from 'space'. The Australian theologian Geoffrey Lilburne[3] points out that the classical geometric concept of space, as an infinite, empty and homogeneous expansion, is a comparatively new concept; in this geometric conception, any one location in space is felt to share the same, homogeneous qualities as any other. Discoveries in quantum physics have revealed the partialities of this Newtonian conception.[4] Importantly for the theological discussion of place, this materialist conception of space as being geometrically homogeneous has proved to be reductive: clearly, to think of a space in purely physical terms is inadequate as a descriptive model for the human experience which any spirituality of place must treat. Anthropology and social geography provide more useful tools for the study of place, both holding that what defines a place as being place is some peculiar, specific quality. Significantly, authors generally mean by this the quality of experiences with which such places are associated. Lilburne's work implies that places may have of themselves some *inherent* quality, which may be perceived by anyone, regardless of their cultural or religious background: his argument seems to be that it is therefore – or should be – possible in some way for Christian, white Australians to partake of the same experience of place as do the Aboriginal peoples. This would be a highly problematic contention on theological grounds, as it would make a large number of assumptions about the nature of the relationship between Christianity and Aboriginal religions. It would also deny the specific nature of Aboriginal society, and would be politically offensive to Aboriginal land-rights activists. To attribute a sort of inherent, unconditional and essential holiness to a place is also in contradiction to the biblical data on Israel's relationship to the land of Israel, where as we will see, holy place is intimately related with the idea of an elect people.

For the sake of clarity, I would like to propose two basic attitudes to geometrical or geographic locations, and two words which describe those attitudes: by 'place' I refer to locations which are charged with human significance and positive values and associations. In the widest sense, this is a religious sphere, and so it seems only sensible to refer to 'sacred place'. In contrast to 'place', 'space' is a location whose boundaries are generally not defined; it is devoid of meaning and of any specific quality. And since relationships with a group of people constitute, in Christian anthropology, one of the central features of what meaningful human life involves, then space must represent a sort of existential vacuum, a location which is devoid of truly human society. In this way, 'space' is also a kind of 'anti-place' connoting a certain existential emptiness, a non-being, anti-value or chaos: such was the attitude for example of the Israelites towards the wilderness. (We should note, however, that in the expanses of the desert space, the Israelites also discovered the presence of Yahweh: in this way, what was felt initially to have been 'space' was revealed by the salutary experience of encounter with Yahweh as being 'place'.) The experience of exile is the substitution of space for place. The polarity of place and space also describes the human tragedy of invasion, imperialism and colonialism, one people's 'place' being seen by another people as their 'space', empty of any recognizable human value, and therefore occupiable: the political implications of land are as old as the occupation of land itself.

Insofar as it is a social reality, place implies an ineluctable moral aspect, since the presence of a number of people involves the questions of relations between them. A moral – and indeed political – understanding of place is one of the keystones of Welsh spirituality, where both the Wales–Israel and Catholic-local tendencies are based on what I have categorized as 'place', a location associated with positive values of meaningfulness, security, and identity. These human values are also religious values. Insofar as, in Christian anthropology, grace builds on nature, what is conceived of as 'place' can easily become perceived as being 'sacred place'. For some writers, phenomenologists of religion in particular, sacred space is the source and measure of all other understandings of place.

A typology of sacred places

Mircea Eliade proposes his concept of sacred space as being *axis mundi*, or sacred centre of the world: his world of religions functions on a cosmic model of two totally separate spheres – the realm of the gods, of grace, of the transcendent, and the realm of the world of humanity, of nature, of the immanent. However, the membrane between the two is not wholly impermeable: sacred place happens where there is a breach in the wall, precipitating leakage of the divine into the world. Such a place is held to be the sacred centre of the earth, a belief which arises in response to the need of the religious person to organize the profane, potentially chaotic and meaningless world into a *kosmos*, a world of intelligibility, order and meaning. The irruption of the sacred into the sphere of the profane renders the place of meeting consecrated by contact, so that it becomes extraordinary, gifted with being to such an extent that to the religious person, only sacred space and those who inhabit it can truly partake of the fullness of reality.

The American theologian Belden Lane, in his *Landscapes of the Sacred*, proposes a rather different phenomenology of sacred place, in the shape of

four self-evident assertions that underlie the way in which landscape is molded in the religious imagination, four phenomenological categories:

1. *Sacred place is not chosen, it chooses* . . . It is a construction of the

imagination that affirms the independence of the holy. God chooses to reveal himself only where he wills.

2. *Sacred place is ordinary place, ritually made extraordinary.* It becomes recognized as sacred because of certain ritual acts that are performed there, setting it apart as unique.

3. *Sacred place can be tread upon without being entered. Its recognition is existentially, not ontologically discerned.* The identification of sacred places is thus intimately related to states of consciousness.

4. *The impulse of sacred places is both centripetal and centrifugal, local and universal.* One is driven to centredness, then driven out from that centre with an awareness that God is never confined to a single locale.[5]

Lane's description usefully illuminates various strands of Welsh spirituality: the Catholic-local tradition involves liturgical celebration of and at specific places, ritually making them holy, while the existential nature of place describes well the nationalist understanding of the land of Wales. Lane's third point underlines the difference between 'place' and 'space' and explains the perceptual roots of colonialism against which Welsh spirituality reacts. And as we will see, the local and the universal (a *pars pro toto* understanding of place) find strong resonances in the work of Waldo Williams.

Ellen Ross[6] provides another very useful typology of sacred places which acts as a corrective to overgeneralized assertions: (1) *Land as sacred presence,* in which the community's relationship with the divine happens through its interaction with geographical space as such, where the concept of land in general symbolizes God's presence. (2) *Historical place as sacred presence,* in which specific geographical locations that have gained recognition within the Christian tradition's concept of salvation history function to connect believers with the divine. (3) *Created space as sacred place,* in which human-made ecclesial structures are invested with sacrality. (4) *Landed eruptions of the sacred,* in which the divine manifests itself to communities or individuals through the land in a spontaneous and occasional fashion. (5) *Space as apocalyptic presence:* the features of this geography are not physical or territorial, but spiritual categories of bondage and freedom.

Ross's typology is useful and innovative. She differs from most authors in her assertion that sacred place can be made: both Belden Lane and Eliade specifically deny this possibility.

However, there is I believe a way in which the patina of generations' experience of the sacred in one particular location may render that place sacred, perceived as being open in some special way to the transcendent: the great pilgrimage centres of medieval Catholicism fit comfortably into this mould, but it also describes Welsh social experience of place. I would also wish to argue that Ross's fifth category is in fact a spiritualization of place, in which the physical is subsumed out of existence, as in the spiritualizing tendencies of the Wales-Israel model. Generally, for the purposes of Welsh spirituality of place, Ross's is a most useful and complete typology: Welsh notions of the land of Wales fit comfortably into her first category – land as a symbol or maker of the nation's relations with God, in the Wales-Israel model. Ross's second and third categories describe the Welsh Catholic-local tradition of holy place. Her fourth category – in which God appears in a people's history, in its land – applies well to the experience of Israel, and this is of importance for Wales also: in Chapter 4 we will examine the historical identification of Wales with Old Testament Israel.

Significantly, each of Ross's categories emphasizes the importance of time, and therefore of history, in varieties of sacred place. Both Eliade's and Lane's typologies suffer from a certain essentialist atemporality in their consideration of sacred space or sacred place. Classical Newtonian space is conceived of as a sort of endless, featureless warp and weft, and this is also true for a Newtonian concept of time. But this attitude towards time will not do justice to a *theological* description of history: time is not devoid of quality, since it contains events which are of universal significance, the most important of which is the Incarnation, centre of all time, all meaning – and therefore of all place and places.

Although theologians of this century have concentrated on the temporal aspects of Christian theology – the salvation history tradition – the American evangelical Walter Brueggemann's *The Land*[7] points out that place is a central category of the Bible, and that place and time are intimately and inseparably connected. I would like to suggest therefore, that what *all* comprehensive concepts of 'place' involve is time. Just as there is no history without a physical and geographical context, neither is there a complete experience of place which does not take into account the human *history* of that place: using Chalcedon and perichoresis as our model, place cannot be separated from history. History and place co-implicate each other, political considerations being an essential component of history.

No typology of sacred place can be any more than provisional: there is still much human experience of the divine as mediated through the experience of specific sacred places which will not fit easily into any single one of Ross's or any other categories. Rather, it is probably wiser to consider all such categories as possible aspects of sacred place. As an 'irruption of the sacred' or place of encounter between different cosmic planes, sacred place obviously involves the divine, ineffable and irreducible mystery.

However, if the divine aspect of sacred place escapes our grasp, we can at least say something of the human nature of sacred place, and indeed of place in general. Many writers on place from other disciplines ascribe numinous or spiritual qualities to place, not necessarily invoking a transcendent referent. Eliade's grand scheme of two oppositional spheres of the sacred and the profane is far from universally accepted: the religious phenomenologist's 'sacred space' may well turn out to be the social geographer's 'special place'.

The concept of place

Almost all writers on the concept of place treat it as an anthropological category: not so much as something which might possess in and of itself a number of inherent qualities, but rather as something which invites a particular set of human relations with it – an understanding sympathetic to the Wales-Israel experience of place. The doyen of social geographers, Yi-Fu Tuan, coins two neologisms to describe human attitudes towards place: *topophilia*, which he describes as 'the affective bond between people and place or setting',[8] and *geopiety*,

> a special complex of relations between man and nature. 'Geo' . . . is the soil and by extension land, country and nation. Piety means reverence and attachment to one's family and homeland and to the god who protects them . . . Geopious feelings are still with us as attachments to place, love of country and patriotism.[9]

The note of familiar intimacy is included in almost all attempts to define place. The French philosopher Gaston Bachelard employs a descriptive method of aesthetics in his definition of place and places, demonstrating by the use of images the close link between the places we live in and the development of individual human identity. His *Poetics of Space*

> seeks to investigate the human value of the sort of space that may be grasped, that may be defended, the space we love – eulogized space . . . Space that has been seized upon by the imagination . . . cannot remain indifferent space subject to surveying mathematically. It is always lived in – with all the artificiality of the imagination . . . it nearly always exercises attraction . . . for it concentrates being within limits that protect.[10]

For Bachelard, place is a location charged with associations and values. We are able to gauge its value and significance for us through the poetic images which are coined to describe it.[11] He asserts that 'the house is our first universe, a real cosmos. All really inhabited space bears the essence of the notion of home.'[12] The constellation of these intimate associations means that place is a provider of shelter and protection, and of meaning, identity and memory: the spheres of body, spirit and soul meet and intermingle in the category of place.

Bachelard's aesthetic meditations, however, all bear the mark of an individual's – and an individualistic – reaction towards place. But a Welsh spirituality of place is typified by a stance which is resoundingly communitarian: the neighbourhoods of Wales are social and geographical realities, and the land of Wales is the land of a particular nation. An aestheticist-individualist response towards the place of Wales is noticeably more typical of non-Welsh writers on Wales than of Welsh writers, whose interests tend markedly towards the moral or the political. Yi-Fu Tuan defines the aesthetic as one of several possible reactions towards place, being generally that of the visitor, noting that a visitor's experience of the same place may invoke reactions and associations entirely different from that of the inhabitants: it is possible to be in a place without realizing its significance for the groups of people who have historically inhabited it. Belden Lane also notes that 'moving into an allegedly sacred place does not necessarily make one present to it. Being bodily present is never identical with the fulness of being to which humans can be open in time and space.'[13] In contrast to Bachelard, most writers on place tend to stress the social aspect of human relations with place. As a provider of meaning and identity, place is largely a social, rather than an individual concept. Both immediate and transtemporal, historical social aspects are involved in the rich matrix of significances of place. Given that the extension through time of a society strengthens its sense of identity, then a sense of history is also involved in a sense of place.

If social experience is involved in the interpretation of place, place is also reciprocally involved in the interpretation of social experience. One's place – the setting in which we are rooted, by our belonging to a specific group of people whose existence is more than just those individuals who constitute it right now – reveals itself as a hermeneutic of human experience. For Brueggemann

> place is space which has historical meanings, where some things have happened which are now remembered and which provide continuity and identity across generations. Place is space in which important words have been spoken which have established identity, defined vocation and envisioned destiny. Place is space in which vows have been exchanged, promises have been made, and demands have been issued.[14]

I have stated that the consideration of place is a comparatively new field for Christian spirituality. Many people in modern Western cultures – Wales is something of an exception in this – express a loss of an organic sense of place. It is not surprising therefore that people in search of a sense of place have sought to learn from the attitudes towards land of peoples amongst whom a signal sense of place survives, Native American and Australian Aboriginals *inter aliis*. Studies note the fact that for many Native American peoples, place is a more important category than time: the *location* of a story is of greater importance than when it happened. Since the story attached to particular places tells one how one should behave, the landscape functions as a moral mnemonic,

> [Quoting an Apache elder]: 'Even if we go far away from here to some big city, places around here keep stalking us. If you live wrong, you will hear the names and see the places in your mind. The names of all these places . . . make you remember how to live right, so you want to replace yourself again.' The claim . . . that the land occupied by the Western Apache 'makes the people live right' . . . becomes

understandable as a proposition about the moral significance of geographical locations as this has been established by historical tales with which the locations are associated. [There exists] an association of place names with a belief in the power of historical tales to discourage forms of socially unacceptable behaviour. Losing the land is something the Western Apache can ill afford to do, for geographical features have served the people for centuries as indispensable mnemonic pegs on which to hang the moral teachings of their history.[15]

The link between Australian Aboriginal peoples and their places is even more intimate: not only does their tribal and individual totemic identity depend on their place of origin, but the ritual action, of song and pilgrimage, described in Bruce Chatwin's *The Songlines*,[16] is believed to be necessary to the perpetuity of the landscape and to the survival of the people: the liturgy not only celebrates place by remembering what happened there in the 'Dreamtime', but also makes the Dreamtime ritually present in the here-and-now, the sphere of the sacred irrupting into the secular world. The sacramental aim of the ritual is, however, not a commemoration of the past, but the keeping of the place, preserving it from degenerating into 'space', and the keeping of the ordered present as a *kosmos*, lest it fall into chaos. So close is the connection between people and place that trespassing on or destruction of land is tantamount to physical aggression or genocide. Geoffrey Lilburne, while attempting to learn from Australian Aboriginal attitudes in his search for a Christian theology of the land, offers a timely and serious warning to those engaged in a search for a sense of place:

> We may be tempted to look at traditional cultures such as the Aboriginal with rose coloured spectacles. It is possible to project our own lost innocence to the aboriginal peoples and be blinded to the realities of their struggle for existence. . . . Arrogance and romanticism have for too long coloured the relations between the European and . . . indigenous peoples.[17]

Physical, emotional and spiritual well-being has often been projected on to more geographically rooted peoples by people unsure of their own identities, sometimes with imperialist methods and undertones.[18] The current Western fascination with Tibetan or Native American cultures, or with 'Celtic spirituality' of various hues, are but the latest in a long series of enthusiasms for other places and other times, which locate the holy anywhere other than the here-and-now. Yet Belden Lane recognizes that

> a modern hermeneutics of suspicion has called for a . . . stringent criticism of all easy mysticism, all naive tendencies to enshrine the holy in water tree and stone, . . . it is no longer possible or perhaps even desirable to reach back to a renewed sense of Paleolithic wonder. Yet for the mass of twentieth-century Americans the landscape remains mute, its mystery unavailable to the modern spirit . . . The problem is that the path has been lost that goes back to the burning bush.[19]

Yet in offering descriptions of historical and religious reactions to several American landscapes, Lane provides a very useful contribution towards an understanding of place: 'it is the experience of meeting which gives meaning to place, not the attributes of place which are able of themselves to occasion meaning. Hence ordinary landscapes – those least expected to offer entry onto any mystery – can sometimes prove the most profound.'[20] That the ordinary place may sometimes prove to be the most profound suggests the *potential* sacredness of all places. This understanding avoids a pan-sacrality which would deny or ignore the autonomous secular reality of places. It recognizes, however, the relationship between the sacred and the secular as one of exemplarity or vocation: in a *pars pro toto* dynamic, holy places are a reminder of the holiness which may be created or discovered in all places; insofar as they represent the partial achievement of universal holiness, they provide a motive for hope; and the fact that the divine mystery can be experienced where it is least expected is a call to a spirituality of place which is engaged in the concrete circumstances of each individual's existence.

As we have seen, Eliade's theory of binomial opposition and separation between the sacred and the profane is not always easy to apply to reality. Jonathan Z. Smith is one of a younger generation of theoreticians of religion who criticize Eliade's narrow cultural focus into which non-Indo-European models of place have been squashed and distorted. Smith proposes instead an anthropological dichotomy, not between sacred and profane, but rather between 'locative' and 'utopic' (= no-place) visions of the world,[21] the former being 'typical of early Near-Eastern urban, literate agricultural hierarchical slave cultures'.[22] This scheme has the benefit of providing us with a useful anthropological point of departure for understanding ancient Israel's idea of the Holy Land – and for Welsh spirituality's replay of the Israelite experience. For Smith, as for Bachelard, the idea of place – in this case the holy place of Israel – is to be understood in terms of the images used to describe it. He notes that Israel is variously conceived of as 'strategic hamlet', as land fought for and won, as being the fruit of a primordial charter in which the security of the blessing – and of the boundaries – must be ceaselessly laboured for. Only at a later point in Israel's history does the whole land itself become a centre, most notably when it is longed for in the pain of exile. Smith reads the Hexateuch as a form of creation myth, from which emerges the point that

> in order for this land to be my land, one must live together with it. It is man living in relationship with his land that transforms wasteland into homeland, land into the land of Israel, it is that one has cultivated the land, that one's ancestors are buried in it, that rituals have been performed in the land, that one's deity has been encountered there . . . that renders the land a home land, a land-for-man, a holy land. History makes a land mine. The shared history of generations converts the land into the Land of the Fathers.[23]

And at this point it might be worth reminding non-Welsh readers that the Welsh national anthem is entitled 'The Old Land of My Fathers'.

A careful rereading of Eliade's ideas reveals that, despite Smith's rejection of Eliade, the two authors tend in some ways to complement each other. For Eliade,

> in the view of archaic societies everything that is not 'our world' can be made ours only by creating it anew, that is by consecrating it . . . to settle in a territory is in the last analysis, equivalent to creating it . . . Settling in a territory is equivalent to founding a world. As 'our world' was founded by imitating the paradigmatic world of the gods, the cosmic unity, so the enemies who attack it are assimilated to the enemies of the gods, the demons. Any destruction of a city is equivalent to a retrogression to chaos.[24]

Likewise, Yi-Fu Tuan observes that

national territories are usually taken to be secular entities, yet are they not also types of sacred space? As a thing becomes holy, it is cut off from surrounding place. Amongst the most ancient of the known forms of the man-made sanctuary was the enclosure.[25]

Later in this book, we will encounter Gildas, describing the fragile civilization of the Christian Isle of Britain under the threat of the pagan Saxons who will reduce that civilization to chaos, turning place into space. Another constituent element of place begins to emerge: place, whether sacred or secular, as provider of shelter against the forces of destruction. It is through its being a centre of all that is life-giving, a safeguard against physical, psychological and spiritual chaos, that one's place is a centre of the world – one's own world. Each place is a *kosmos*, an enclosure of order amid encircling chaos, a concept repeated in J. R. Jones's ideas on the value of specific places as having the value of being whole worlds in themselves. Through a history of continued inhabiting, a place becomes a stronghold of social and individual identity, meaning and orientation, which endures across the generations.

In the Wales-Israel paradigm, the whole of the land of Wales is felt to be not only place but also – if only by implication and contact – specifically sacred place.[26] In Wales as in Israel: the model of place that Smith derives from ancient Israel – land as enclave, place of fragile blessing and insecure borders, as historied land and Land of the Fathers – finds many echoes in historical concepts and images of Wales.

Biblical notions of land

In the field of biblical theology, the nineteenth and twentieth centuries witnessed a tendency to undervalue the category of place in favour of time. This pattern derives from a consensus that the Bible has primarily to do with history rather than nature or land. Brueggemann's *The Land* traces the reasons for this view: the influence of existentialist philosophy and the predominance of the theology of salvation history (the idea that God reveals himself primarily through acting in mighty deeds); a reaction against the fascist conflation of religion, nationalism and land ownership; a post-war existentialist concern for the individual search for meaning and purpose which tended to neglect the social aspects of a sense of place. Brueggemann seeks to offer a corrective to such views, and since he places land as *the* central biblical hermeneutic, it will be useful to explore briefly his exposition of Old Testament land theology.

The Bible, Brueggemann argues, is primarily concerned with the issue of being displaced, and of yearning for place, an issue which is played out in three great dramatic sweeps in the Old Testament: (1) To the Land (the period leading up to the settlement of Canaan); (2) In the Land (the period of judges and kings prior to the exile); and (3) From Exile to Land. In all cases, the land of Israel is used as a multivalent term, involving both symbolic and real historical senses. The symbolic, psychological and spiritual value of land is that it gives meaning and identity to the people of Israel, while the historical meaning includes their physical well-being and shelter against the forces of destruction. All of these values are expressed in the historical enterprises of the Israelite nation. The Bible may be understood as the Israelite reflection on what it means to belong to the land before God. The land is in itself the content, the sacrament and the embodiment of Yahweh's covenant with his people (a relationship involving land, people and God which we may now recognize as Chalcedonian perichoresis, or interpenetration). Faithlessness to the terms of the covenant leads inexorably to landlessness, and fidelity to blessing. Only under conditions of recognition of radical contingency and dependence on God's providence is it possible for the nation of Israel to continue to receive the blessing of the land of Israel.

In the Exodus experience, Israel is purified from the tendency to divinize land, or to attribute to it any essential, intrinsic properties. Life does not come from the land itself, but only from God. As God's gift, land is only the mediator, not the maker of the covenant. As Israel enters into Canaan, the land is seen to be a life-giving embodiment of the life-giving word (Deut. 6: 10–11), and as *sola gratia*. It is in the land and through the land that Israel will now maintain (or neglect) the covenant:

> Israel's involvement is always with land and with Yahweh, never with Yahweh as though to live only in intense obedience, never only with land, as though simply to possess and manage [it] . . . Israel had a

particular notion that land is not natural setting, but historical arena, place not just for satiation, but also for listening.[27]

According to Brueggemann, the practice of Old Testament faith is therefore located, incarnate in one specific place. Israel is called to avoid the two extremes of a spiritualized religion which pays no attention to physical, here-and-now realities, and a purely material way of life. Land is material, but not only material; it is symbolic of spiritual realties but not only symbolic. In the meeting of symbolic and material aspects lies the uniqueness of the covenant. It is an intense relationship between people and place, at once immanent and transcendent.

Brueggemann makes clear that Israel's history in the land reveals time and time again that apparently guaranteed security in the land has in itself a seductive power to urge Israel to secede from the covenant (where land is Yahweh's gift), effectively secularizing land by depending on it as 'space', a location where there is no history nor moral commitment, and which also possesses within itself unconditional – and exploitable – gifts of life and fertility. For Israel, the chief resource against such infidelity is history, evoked in acts of national remembering which are in fact statements about her present. As with the land of the Western Apache, the land of Israel takes on the function of mnemonic, reminding the nation of its collective duties.

Brueggemann sees the episode of Ahab and Naboth's vineyard in 1 Kings 21 as emblematic of different attitudes towards land. For Naboth, the vineyard represents the traditional covenantal understanding in which the land is not owned in a way that would permit its free disposal. The vineyard is 'inheritance', held in trust from generation to generation, beginning in gift and continuing as gift. Inheritance as a land ethic directly contradicts Jezebel's royal notions of land ownership which know no limitations. It affirms the religious base of those enduring networks of meaning and relationship, symbolized by and present in place, and the belief that these networks are fundamental to the shape of society[28] and give to the individual human being identity, purpose and meaning: belonging to others and belonging to one specific place involve each other.

We have seen Yi-Fu Tuan's idea that national territories tend to become perceived as religious realities. Since place and people are intimately tied to each other, then this pattern must inevitably involve a similar tendency for nations to take on a religious tonality. Naboth's vineyard, divine inheritance from God passed on through generations of ancestors, is a concern which must necessarily involve social issues, and as emblem of Israel involves the whole of the nation. Here the issues involved are equally ones of human rights (given by God) and of human responsibilities and duties towards God. We will come into Naboth's vineyard again in the next chapter, with Gildas, with Charles Edwards's *Y Ffydd Ddi-Ffuant* (The Unfeignèd Faith), and most famously in the 'Vineyard' speech of Saunders Lewis's *Buchedd Garmon* (The Life of St Germanus).

Brueggemann notes that, among the pre-exilic prophets, it is Jeremiah who is most concerned with the issue of land: the religious and political crisis of the years around 587 is expressed as a crisis of land. Already in Jeremiah 2, the prophet senses the oncoming dislocation of Israel. The following chapter applies marital imagery to the land: the land itself suffers as a result of the action of the nation. Jeremiah 12 presents a picture of the land made wilderness, place become space, the dramatic images of disinheritance providing the background to the incredible promise of restoration glimpsed in Jeremiah 32. It is well known that in post-exilic Israel much of the imagery previously applied to the whole of the land became progressively centred on Jerusalem and then on the temple. Brueggemann notes, however, the continuation of a concern with the land. The land under covenant requires holy separateness of its people: in the face of the threat of dilution, Ezra and Nehemiah proclaim the call to continue and foster national and religious distinctiveness. Wisdom literature, notably Ben Sira, still aims at maintaining a consciousness in which Yahweh's intervention in history is to be expected, in which land is still gift, still open to transformation: place is the possibility of history, conceived of as Yahweh's action in time, in the land.

Most writers agree that the importance of the land of Israel wanes significantly in New Testament theology, and find a corresponding difficulty in establishing a specifically Christian theology of land or place based on scriptural sources alone. For Brueggemann the New Testament repeats the experience – or at least the memory of the experience – of landlessness as a *sine qua non* for gift: in the theology of the Magnificat and the Beatitudes, it is the disinherited who will inherit the earth. For landlessness, the New Testament substitutes the scandal of the Crucifixion and for restoration, Resurrection. Underlying the Pauline dialectic of law and grace, Brueggemann identifies the issue of dispossession and possession. Yet in the application of his land hermeneutic to the New Testament, Brueggemann comes close to dematerializing his concept of land, reducing it to mere symbol and thus denying the very premiss of his own argument of the united symbolic and historical meaning of land.[29]

Lilburne[30] contends that, in the books written during and after the exile, the issue of land already fades in importance, and that by the time of the New Testament the theme has practically disappeared. He suggests that this was partly because the changing circumstances of the Jewish people had led them to discover that God could be known in places other than the promised land; large-scale migration from rural to urban centres meant that land took on an increasingly symbolic, disembodied meaning; the influence of Hellenistic thought led to a relativizing of notions of locality and particularity in favour of a cosmopolis. Finally, apocalypticism relocated the fulfilment of divine promises in the sphere of the transcendent, diminishing the sense of Jewish holy places: this earth is a passing reality, and all that it contains has relative value only.

Lilburne notes that the spread of Christianity broke open the territorial limitations of Judaism, literally christifying holy space. The history of the religion of Israel shows a progressive centralization of holiness, from the land of Israel to the city of Jerusalem, and then to the temple. Christianity intensified this process, locating the source of all holiness in Jesus. The Abrahamic and Davidic promises having been fulfilled in Jesus, what could the significance of the land of Israel, or indeed any land, now be for Christians? The Epistle to Diognetus famously states that

> Christians are distinguished from the rest of men neither by country nor by language nor by customs . . . For nowhere do they dwell in cities of their own; they do not use any strange form of speech or practice a singular form of life . . . They pass their days on earth, but they have their citizenship in heaven.[31]

W. D. Davies's *The Gospel and the Land* provides us with a more nuanced treatment of the idea of land as it appears in the New

Testament. Davies notes that the various New Testament strata portray differing attitudes towards the land. In Acts 7, for instance, the spiritual significance of land is rejected outright. In other places, it is spiritualized or eschatologized. But the historical reality of the Incarnation demanded an attention to the *realia* of Jesus' life, which included a particular country and particular places. In Luke, Davies finds the beginnings of the transformation of Palestine into the Christian 'Holy Land', consecrated by its contact with Jesus.[32]

Davies holds that the territorial aspect of the Abrahamic promise is totally ignored by Paul. In Romans and Galatians, the Law, with its connection to land, is seen as being peculiar to Israel. Holy place has become relocated in the community of persons who are the Body of Christ, centred no longer in the temple nor in the Torah, but in the spirit. Davies's view contrasts decidedly with that of Brueggemann, who sees the stress on Abraham's paradigmatic faith, and the passages (Rom. 8: 12–25; Gal. 3: 37–9; 4: 1ff.) as implying some sort of relationship involving land.

The theological difficulty of establishing an understanding of place seems compounded by the differing theologies of Scripture. Brueggemann's reference to the land of Israel as 'sacrament' provides a signpost to how we might begin to look for New Testament foundations of a spirituality of place. In a sacrament, different orders of being meet intimately, and the ordinary is made holy in a process of consecration by contact. A reading of St John's Gospel, and to a certain extent Hebrews shows a diffused sacramentalism at work. In this understanding, the Incarnation is the model and source of the way in which grace is made available through the physical realities of life. The cosmic christology of Colossians and Ephesians sees the Redeemer as reconciling all things (*ta panta*) to himself, all matter now being filled with his salvific power. In this proto-sacramentalism, all matter has been transfigured by the Incarnation, and is thus potentially a means of grace. This is especially true of those places where the Jesus of history had been, the holy places having been made sacred by contact with his earthly body. This sacramentalist attitude persists in Eastern Christian and medieval theology, at once subordinating all places to Jesus, but also affirming the *potential* christification of all spaces, the potentiality once again avoiding the practical heresy of pan-sacrality. The insight of Gregory of Nyssa is that wherever Christ is experienced that place is holy: all places may represent Jerusalem.[33] Importantly for a Christian spirituality of place, it focuses this holiness not so much on the physicality of the places themselves, but rather on what humans experience there, individually but especially collectively.

We have seen that Brueggemann seeks to locate the experience of grace – the New Testament analogue of Old Testament landedness – in the collective experience of the disenfranchised. Similarly Lilburne locates the Kingdom within the Christian community: 'The Kingdom is present where Jesus is present. It is not so much that the cosmic Christ is present universally, rather the Spirit of the risen Christ is present wherever communities gather in Jesus' name.'[34] For these Protestant theologians it is human contact with a location that renders it sacred, and such sacredness is derivative. Likewise, most phenomenologists hold that any qualities possessed by places are not inherent ones, rather, they gain those associations only attributively, through historical human contact. Brueggemann's thesis demonstrates that outside of the covenant, the land of Israel has no inherent meaning. It is a divine gift, but the covenant also needs to be humanly ratified. The existence of a holy, promised land, in order that it be a place, demands its historical habitation by a particular, chosen people.

Land then provides a people with a national identity founded on a geographical reality. But if place tends towards a potential sacrality, the same may also be said of national identity. The differences between religious and national identities, nation and church, have often been unclear for many peoples. As in the Israel of the Old Testament, within the Welsh spiritual tradition the concept of holiness of the land of Wales is largely derivative from a belief in a divinely given, specific vocation of the Welsh nation to sanctity: the idea of particular election has led many Welsh people to consider, if unconsciously so, that the foundations of *their* national identity are at heart religious, land and religion interacting in national consciousness in complex and subtle ways. Writings of place and sacred place have now provided us with a wide canvas on which we can find Welsh attitudes towards the place and places of Wales. The understanding of the spiritual import of the nation within Welsh spirituality also demands that we consider the wider theological issues of this contentious issue.

Nation and election

In a century which has seen so many wars caused by the various manifestations of the potentially explosive mixture of nation and religion, it might seem surprising to some readers that Christian theology can still talk of nationality and nationalism, let alone take seriously the divine election of particular peoples and nations. There are many good reasons for wariness towards questions of nationalism, and also for a lack of theological interest in nationality. The history of Christian spirituality shows a movement towards a certain individualism in religion. Perhaps more accented in certain forms of Protestantism – the spirituality of Jesus as one's *personal* Lord and Saviour – it is also part of the Catholic tradition, for example, in the spirituality of St Ignatius Loyola's Spiritual Exercises. Deeply engrained Cartesian and secular notions of freedom tend to abhor any notion of election understood as predestination (in the sense that it would represent a limitation on the individual's action). Clearly Christians believe that each individual human person is an image and likeness of God, and few would quibble with the idea that God calls individuals to specific actions and paths as the embodiment, *pars pro toto*, of a generalized call to sanctity. For Christians, God created the Church, and calls it to holiness, but does Christianity teach that God creates nations? If so, does he call them also to a particular vocation?

Many modern thinkers understand the nation as being an exclus-ively secular reality. Arguing against such assumptions, Wolfhart Pannenberg essays a theology of election which suggests that the nation is an essential Christian reality. Meticulously differentiating between the nation and the state (as the particular political ordinance of a nation or nations) and studiously avoiding any proposal or suggestion of redivinizing the state, Pannenberg proposes that all aspects of human endeavour – including the nation – should be seen and judged against a background of transcendence:

> Against pietism or Catholic fideistic supranaturalism, Christian theology must insist that the world of universal human experience is

the creation of God . . . and therefore that no phenomenon of the finite reality of this world, including human beings, is appropriately understood so long as it is seen apart from its relationship to God.[35]

Pannenberg notes that Western society has over the last four or five centuries effectively suffered a radical secularization. The classic view of Christian history, as laid out in Augustine's *The City of God*, has been effectively replaced by a doctrine of political sovereignty in which human nature has come to occupy the place previously assigned to religion. Public and political life are felt to be essentially secular spheres, and religion has been demoted to the arena of the personal.

Against such deviations in the notion of history, he offers a revitalized version of the notion of election, applied primarily to whole peoples rather than to individuals. Pannenberg argues that the Old Testament notion of election, a notion based on the idea of covenantally ordered history, applied originally to the entire people of Israel: God has made a covenant with *one* people, consecrated, separated and chosen out of all others, and is active in all aspects of their life. It is the radical contingency, the ups-and-downs of this relationship which makes history. Yet election is not unconditional, for implicit in the notion of election is the principle of judgement, a principle which for Pannenberg is the guarantee of fidelity, a safeguard against any national idolatry which would seek to locate unconditional holiness in the nation itself. Pannenberg recognizes the possibility of idolatry: the nation, just as much as the land of Israel, has the potential to become an end in itself. The notion of covenant is the safeguard against land-idolatry, and divine judgement against worship of the nation: divine favour can be withdrawn if the nation does not fulfil the contract, and the election passed on to another people. Pannenberg also notes however within the post-exilic books of the Old Testament something of a sea change in the notion of election, a new tendency towards individualization and detemporalization. In this essentially pessimistic world-view and especially in its apocalyptic elements, God is felt to be absent from the times and places of this world. In this latter vision, it is individuals rather than the nation, who are chosen, predestined in an election made before time, to take part in a covenant which will be fulfilled only eschatologically.

As Pannenberg notes, both these notions – the collective-presentist and the individual-atemporal – exist in the New Testament, but the calling of the Twelve may be seen as combination of both: they are called in time but in reference to eternity, called individually yet made into one body. Following the resurrection, election and vocation are extended to all who accept the Gospel – an action in time which makes history, but which gains eternal significance. In Romans 11, Paul maintains the chosenness of the people of Israel despite their rejection of the Gospel, but in 1 Peter 2 it is the Christians who are now the chosen people of God. For Pannenberg, this ambiguity regarding the object of election persists in early Christian theology, in the tension between judaizing influences and more universalizing ones.

Pannenberg traces the persistence of the atemporal and individualistic notion of election, through Aquinas and Calvin. It continued especially under the vitiated subspecies of predestination, the theory in which certain individuals are believed to be destined, exclusively by divine mandate before time, to salvation. He notes however, that the corporate, concretely historical notion of election survived in the idea of the 'people of God'. The second–third-century bishop Eusebius provided theology with the idea that the Christians are 'a new people . . . the most numerous and pious of all peoples, indestructible and pious of all peoples, because it lives under the protection of God forever'.[36] In Eusebius' theology, Pannenberg identifies the first stages of laying the ground for the Byzantine solidarity of church and empire: God acts in harmony with the empire, creating a new history with a new people.[37] The sack of Rome threw this theory of history into crisis. The concept of history which Augustine proposes in *The City of God* states that the Kingdom of God is neither identical nor intrinsically connected with any one form of political government on earth: the chosen individuals are the community of the chosen, the City of God as opposed to the secular city, the state. The nature of the City of God is therefore primarily spiritual, existing at the moment in the form of the Church. Pannenberg identifies in Augustine's work the roots of the secularization of public life:

This is a dualistic political thesis, the vision of a paralleled development of the two kingdoms or cities . . . based on his abstractly individualistic doctrine of double predestination, constituting different groups of people and thus providing the basis for their paralleled developments in history. The consequence was a retreat of the Christian faith from all political structures of society. The Kingdom of God is now said to be manifest only in the Church. This dualism cut into the life of every Christian because they had to participate in the political and economic order in addition to membership of the Church . . . [T]o identify the Church with the Kingdom of Christ was ambiguous and dangerous . . . depriving the organization of society of its religious meaning.[38]

A side-product of this process was the growth of various forms of 'civil religion', filling the vacuum left by the reduction of religion to the merely personal and private. Amongst the forms of such civil religion Pannenberg includes the imperial ideal of the Holy Roman Empire and modern forms of nationalism. Whereas many historians claim that the origins of modern political nationalism lie in the French Revolution and in German Romanticism, Pannenberg discovers older roots based in the notion of divine election being applied to one particular nation to the exclusion of others:

> The religious idea of a peculiar national calling that culminated in England during the Cromwellian period can be traced back to the rivalry between France and Germany that developed after the end of the Carolingian period. This sense of chosenness which is characteristic of civil religion belongs to the very heart of nationalism as it developed in the history of Western Christianity.[39]

Gildas will show us that, at least within the Isle of Britain, the story is older by far.

Religious nationalism based on the idea of divine call to a particular nation has been found in many forms and in many ways, especially amongst the nations of Europe; as a result of the disintegration of the Christian empire, each nation felt a particular call to reintegrate the peace, to create order out of chaos. English nationalism and sense of national identity in particular were characterized by a notably close relationship to the Old Testament, deriving from the pervasive biblicism of the Reformation. John Foxe's *Book of Martyrs* proposed English religious distinction and incidentally served as one of the models of Welsh religious and national pride which we will meet in Charles Edwards. In the late sixteenth century John Lyly praised God for taking special care of England 'as of a new Israel, his chosen and peculiar people'.[40] And interestingly we find Gildas, almost a thousand years previously, referring to the Romano-Celtic Christian Britons as *praesens Israel.*

The typological application of Israel to other nations appears at many points in history, but was highly compatible with the principles of Protestantism. Dutch Calvinism, exported to South Africa, provided the Boers with a theological justification for their presence and political creeds there until the late twentieth century: apartheid has roots in the notion of national election. Puritan religious sensibilities and profound biblicism meant that as a group, they too were particularly fond of seeing themselves as a chosen people, a quasi-nation. Their biblical interpretation easily lent itself to a typology of history in which God is seen to continue to work amongst his people in the same patterns with which he had acted in the history of ancient Israel. For the Puritans the Bible was not only an expression of the past: in the workings out of their own lives they saw the renewed fulfilment of Old Testament prophecy. The emigration of English Puritans to America gave new expression to the idea of their being a new Israel, journeying to a new Canaan. Henceforth the chosen people would live in a land which was chosen for them. Belden Lane's *Landscapes of the Sacred* contains a chapter on Puritan attitudes towards land which usefully illuminates some Welsh attitudes. The Puritan myths of destiny, closely tied to Puritan symbols of place, meant that geographical proximity of people was also an expression of social and theological proximity. As in ancient Israel, spiritual purity and social identity are together contained in an enclave, within a surrounding arena of potential hostility:

> To belong to the people of God was to live within the boundaries of the proclamation of God's love . . . God's people were expected to dwell in proximity to the place of meeting. These boundaries of grace always lay in tension with the foreboding and tempting landscape beyond the camp.[41]

Pannenberg seeks to value seriously the American Puritan expression of covenant and pledge, as an expression of a mentality which makes the policies of a nation accountable to God. History is the arena of divine judgement. The essential freedom granted to a nation by dint of its covenantal election is divine gift, to be used responsibly. Thus responsibility is an essential element of election, a relationship with God which is conditional, not absolute. Responsibility means applying divine values to each element in the life of a people.

The chronicles of history recount the frequent use of religious principles to legitimize what is essentially irreligious political rhetoric and action. Pannenberg warns that the conflation of nation and church is potentially as dangerous as the unilateral and simplistic identification of the Kingdom with the Church. He founds his theology of history on the idea of election, defined as 'the definitive intention in the corporate experience of the vocation of a people. Thus the act of election constitutes the unity of that history, since it provides a continuous direction to the course of events'.[42] This notion of election provides a basis for understanding statements which assert that God is at work in a people's history. Election is not to be understood exclusively, as a setting apart of a nation in a sphere of religious superiority: rather each people is called to its own specific election, its own incarnation of God's will, as a service to the whole of humankind. In this, the paradigm is the universalistic reference in the election of Abraham: God makes him an oath for the sake of 'all the families of the earth' (*pars pro toto* again). Also linked is the Pauline idea of charisms, particular gifts or callings to individual members of the church for the sake of the whole body. The logical development of this is the suggestion that the relationship of any one nation to the whole of humankind is analogous to any member of the Body of Christ to the whole of the Church: inseparable and indivisible from it, with its own unique contribution to make, its own duties and responsibilities.

Although election in Pannenberg's understanding is something that a nation does rather than receives, his work also suggests that peoples and nations are divinely ordained. He does not make explicit exactly how this divine ordinance happens:

> The notion of election indicates that it was the initiative of God . . . which constituted the social world and the basically religious identity of a people . . . The notion of election imports primarily the religious

qualification of historical experience of basic foundational social experience . . . God's intentions are concerned with the establishment and reservation of a social order as a condition for the continuous existence of a people . . . overcoming the evil powers that threaten their survival.[43]

Pannenberg is sympathetic to the idea of chosenness which so many nations have expressed. Though fully aware of its possible deviations, he lauds the idea as a restoration of a more public and less individualistic religious sensibility, a reintegration of God into notions of history and society:

One should take seriously the claim to peculiar chosenness in its many forms throughout Christian history, without being obliged to accept the overstatements of national pride and exclusivism . . . The consciousness of chosenness expresses and articulates a specific awareness of special historical opportunity and responsibility, related to the God of Israel and Jesus Christ . . . That religious sensibility enabled some men to appraise their own situation in terms so highly accurate should be considered admirable.[44]

He continues his argument:

In relating such an awareness of historical particularity to the God of the Bible I cannot discover an element of idolatry . . . [T]his phenomenon expresses the quite sincere piety of people who experience the concrete course of their own history in relation to the God whom they see as acting still in history. There is nothing unbiblical in listening to the call of God in one's own personal and social history as long as one remains conscious of one's own possible judgement.[45]

Pannenberg's view goes some way to providing a theological justification for the existence of the nation, as a form of social organization appropriate to the call of election, and as one which fits the original, biblical conception of the public and social spheres as being the most appropriate arena where divine action in history may be discerned. And in its insistence on the responsibilities rather than the rights of the nation, his theology provides a building-block for healthy nationalism.

Welsh theology, particularly of the twentieth century, is characterized by a notable interest in the role of the nation. Such an emphasis on the nation (rather than the individual) as the sphere of human and divine history inevitably presents us with the question of what particular type of social and political order best corresponds to or prepares the way for the Kingdom of God. There are many Christian commentators who are prepared to allot to the nation if not a divine, elected value, then at least a contingent one. Fewer can find Christian justification for the forms of social order described as nationalism, and nationalism of any sort is anathema to many. A full account of the phenomenology and history of nationalism is beyond the scope of this study, but an awareness of some typical reactions from modern commentators on political nationalism will help us to see the distinctiveness of the ideas and concerns of Welsh theologians.

Nationalism and reactions to it

The fact that the twentieth century has witnessed one major manifestation of the worst of nationalism, namely the Third Reich, has inevitably coloured the reactions of many people towards all forms of nationalism. Writers of the left have dreamed of the Internationale, while those of the right have tended to shy away from explicit nationalism after Auschwitz. Enlightened thinkers have predicted the imminent demise of nationalism. Yet the history of the world, following the progressive emancipation of peoples from colonialism, and especially since the fall of communism, has shown that as a political ideology, more often than not with a religious tinge, nationalism continues to thrive and attract.

Reactions towards all forms of nationalism are sometimes as monolithically vituperative as that of William Pfaff:[46] the unnuanced anger of his statements is well worth quoting. For Pfaff, nationalism is not an ideology in that it is not universal; rather, it is a manifestation of what Pannenberg has called 'civil religion', an ersatz faith that 'occupies the moral and emotional ground otherwise held by political ideology and often that which has been yielded by religion. It promotes a worship of the nation which is implicitly, if not explicitly, blasphemous.'[47] Pfaff's essay does not clearly differentiate between state and nation but, in opposition to what Pannenberg has to say, asserts that there is a political duty to secularize the state, to react against any redemptive or eschatological assumptions which nationalism may place upon it, and to fight for democracy, to which Pfaff believes nationalism to be inherently inimical. It is, he holds, a religious duty to deny the blasphemy which would make of the nation any more than what it is, namely 'a historical community like any other'.[48]

Pfaff points out the difficulty of defining the nation, quoting Seton Watson to the effect that 'no scientific definition of a nation can be devised . . . A nation exists when a significant number of people in a community consider themselves to form a nation. When a significant number hold this belief, it holds "national consciousness".'[49] Neither ethnic nor territorial considerations are sufficient descriptors of national identity. For Pfaff, religion may enter into the definition of a nation only in the form of the quasi-religion of self-worshipping national idolatry. Clearly, Pfaff is correct in identifying the danger of national idolatry which is potential in national consciousness. But is national self-worship the *inevitable* outcome of national pride? Love, surely, is not identical with worship.

Other writers are more cautious. Isaiah Berlin[50] locates the origins of nationalism in the break-up of Christian religious unity. For him it is essentially a Romantic, nineteenth-century movement, inspired by the German writer Herder. Berlin distinguishes carefully between consciousness of national identity – which he believes is a primordial instinct -- and nationalism, whose gospel is the need to react against the universalizing and centralizing forces of history, a concept based on rights. Berlin's evaluation of nationalism is generally negative:

> Nationalism is an inflamed condition of national consciousness which can be and on occasions has been tolerant and peaceful. It usually seems to be caused by wounds, some form of collective humiliation . . . The response to being the object of contempt or patronizing tolerance is a pathological exaggeration of one's real or imaginary virtues and resentment and hostility toward the proud, the happy, the successful.[51]

Berlin notes that religious motives may be among the grievances which fuel nationalism, particularly where ethnicity and religion combine. The Marxist historian Eric J. Hobsbawm cites Holy Russia – the Russia portrayed by Dostoevsky – as paradigm of the potent mix of national and religious identities, noting that the popular sense of Holy Russianness may or may not correspond to the real facts of the modern nation. It is, he notes, the popular image and the national myth, rather than the historical facts, which have power to shape people's lives – an insight which complements the phenomenological approach to place via imagery of Tuan, Smith and Bachelard. The truth of Hobsbawm's insight has been illustrated tragically over the last thirty years in the social chaos of the Northern Ireland troubles and the Balkan wars, where the potent admixture of ancient grievances, cultural myths and religious differences has exploded into seemingly endless cycles of hatred and violence.

I have pointed out that the principles of Protestantism have sometimes taken flesh in strident nationalisms: the ethnic cleansing and the mass immigration caused by the settlement of the Thirty Years War in Germany established identification of state with religion. But mention of the Balkans and of Holy Russia suggests that Orthodoxy, with its ancient roots in Byzantine theology and solidarity of church and state, can also easily lend itself to various shades, both dark and light, of nationalism: the resurrection of national churches following the break-up of Soviet communism is witness to this. Catholicism too has bred its own nationalisms, Franco's 'national Catholicism' being just one of the manifestations of this shadow side of the Catholic Church.

One interesting Catholic phenomenon is the association of various forms of Marian devotion with national pride or even identity: the figure of Our Lady of Guadalupe, reputed to have appeared to Juan Diego, a Mexican peasant in the sixteenth century, was put to political use from its very origins. In our day, the supposed manifestations of the Virgin Mary as Queen of Peace at Medjugorje have distinct political ramifications. Perhaps the prime example of this political Marianism is Poland, a nation whose 'place' was subsumed for several hundred years, but whose religious allegiance, along with its language, was the major factor in keeping alive a sense of national distinctiveness. In the Virgin Mary's title as 'Queen of Poland', nationalistic and religious elements come together. Not for nothing was the Mother of God invoked as patroness of the Solidarity movement!

All these examples show the inseparable interplay of political and religious themes, and the potential power of image and myth.

Like Pfaff and Berlin, Hobsbawm identifies the 'icons' of nationalism – those symbols and rituals or common collective practices which may be the only incarnation of the dreamed-for reality of the nation – with what Pannenberg calls 'civil religion', a form of national idolatry or communal narcissism. It is not a total surprise, therefore, that Hobsbawm's overview of the nationalist movements of the late twentieth century is likewise generally negative: nationalism is at heart a surrogate for lost or declining religious identity.

Conclusions

We began this chapter with sacred place and have ended with nationalism as an ersatz religious identity. Nevertheless, the thread which connects the alpha of this chapter with its omega is the aim to provide the background to a consideration of a Welsh spirituality of place and national identity. So let us pause for a moment here and review the ground covered.

From phenomenologists of religion we have gained some insights into the nature of the various types of holy place, which will help us to see an image of Wales as arena of God's action in history, a 'strategic hamlet' or enclave, a place both set apart and under siege, under threat of internal exile. Philosophers of place, landscape historians and social geographers have alerted us to the *human* value of place and to the fact that human experience of all 'place', in its fullest sense, tends towards the spiritual. Moreover, in a synthesis of the insights we have gained on place, we can see that *pace* aestheticist-individualist responses, 'place' as an anthropological concept is one which is essentially social, moral, historical, and therefore political. The rich constellation of all these meanings is involved in a Welsh spirituality of place, in which place is an intersection or interpenetration of different orders of reality: timelessness meeting history, geographical location meeting people. In the concept of sacred place, land, the transcendent and social experience are intimately united.

The question of the specificity of *Christian* holy place, and what constitutes that objective holiness, remains a difficult matter for Christian theology. Neither Brueggemann's *The Land*, Geoffrey Lilburne's *A Sense of Place*, nor W. D. Davies's *The Gospel and the Land* find a satisfactory or commonly agreed New Testament basis for a theology of place. The questions remain: what makes a holy place holy? What sort of holiness is that? The advantage of a Catholic spirituality of place is that it need not be limited to purely scriptural sources. Belden Lane's *Landscapes of the Sacred* ends with a short section on possible further approaches to the subject. Among the possible imports of theology, he names incarnation and, as derivatives of this, the concepts of icon and sacramentality.

Icon and sacrament provide us with some of the adequate and necessary theological underpinnings of an authentic Christian spirituality of place. Both function by bringing together the sacred and the profane. Although descriptions of place as experienced by Australian Aborigines and Native Americans may usefully illustrate Welsh experience, it is Israel's land experience which is the closest and most influential comparative model for Wales. In the experience of place of Old Testament Israel, all Christians see some paradigm. But given the transcendent significance of the Bible in Wales, and the deep-seated impact of Calvinism on the psychology of the Welsh, the biblical background is essential to an appreciation of how the Welsh have understood themselves in relation to their territory, to God – and also to the English. A major element in the foundations of Welsh spirituality of place is found in Old Testament Israel's relationship to the land, where holiness is seen as both divine gift and call to the nation, in a spirituality involving rights and responsibilities. Both the land and the nation of Israel function in a sacramental manner, the land mediating God's relationship with his people, and the elect nation mediating the divine dispensation by being an icon showing what all nations are called to be. Given that paradigmatically in Israel, land and nationality are inseparable, land may also be understood to take on the role of being elect, of being an example of what all places may become. Associating these ideas, we begin to see some of the theological and scriptural roots of Welsh spirituality, in the image of the place and land of Wales understood as being charged with the responsibility of being a window on to the world of the divine, charged with the unique election of being themselves for the sake of all places and peoples.

As for Israel, Welsh national identity has been bound up since the beginnings of the Welsh nation with the question of religious identity, and in both nations, religious identity has been intimately linked with the problem of political and cultural survival. The most salient specific form to which national consciousness and Christian convictions have led in twentieth-century Wales is political and cultural nationalism. In the same way that the boundaries between place and holy place are not always clear, religious and national identities are often confused. A similar permeability exists between national consciousness, geopiety, topophilia, and political nationalist separatism, both for those who are sympathetic to nationalism and those who are not. All the writers on nationalism whom we have considered in this chapter are by birth or adoption members of large, culturally dominant nations, and so their opinions serve, by contrast, to illuminate the Welsh experience. Members of a nation which has often felt itself to be simultaneously religiously distinguished and politically besieged, Welsh Christian writers of the twentieth century, as the next chapter will now show us, differ notably from non-Welsh writers, in their understanding of the universal human and religious import of a sense of nationality and in their positive evaluation of nationalism.

3

Standing in the breach[1]

With the broader brushstrokes of the spiritual import of place and nation now in place, we can explore with greater objectivity and detail how these questions are considered in the Welsh spiritual tradition. The most salient point is that an abstract consideration of place is completely absent from Welsh theological consideration. Most of the writers we will meet here are Christian ministers, and their theologizing reflects the practical needs of people: in technical terms, this is pastoral theology rather than fundamental theology or systematics. And for these writers, a significant part of their pastoral concern is for their nation. Twentieth-century Welsh spirituality is notable for its interest in issues of nationality in Wales, and as a derivative of this, in wider questions of the spiritual import of national identity and of political nationalism. If place arises at all as a theological issue, then it is as a function of social issues. The vast majority of Welsh theologians write within Nonconformist traditions, which find no theological place for mediations of holiness other than the person of Jesus Christ. Among such writers, if holy places in Wales are discussed at all, it is generally only as a derivative of the religious nature of national identity. Of the writers with whom this chapter deals, only one, the philosopher J. R. Jones, deals explicitly with the issue of place, in the form of his category of 'interpenetration' of land (in our case, the specific place of the land of Wales) with language. As we will see, both nation and place are treated by Welsh writers primarily in terms of their role in the life of the human person, understood as *homo culturalis*. Despite their theological preferences, in the works of many of these thinkers concerning what it is to be fully human, an interest in place is evidenced by the particular emphasis they attribute to the historical and geographical context of social insertion. In the Welsh mind as it appears in these writers, one's place and one's society play a significant part in who one is as an individual. Place

– understood as a social and geographical reality – defines, shapes and guides each human being.

Religion, language and nationality in Wales

The theology of nationality and the theological justification of nationalism have been very minor concerns for most theologians and spiritual writers in the European and American continents. For Welsh theologians of this century, however, they have been central issues. That many of the writers in Welsh on nationalism in general have been clergymen and academics is not surprising, for the particularities of Welsh history have meant that these social classes have tended to be the only ones sufficiently literate in Welsh to be able to write theology and political philosophy in it. Educational factors apart, there are other, more complex reasons: the instinctual feeling, idea or assumption that in Wales Welsh, rather than English, is the language better suited to writing of religion, and the underlying instinct that Welsh nationality is essentially religious. Before proceeding further, we must take an *excursus* to explore the reasons for this phenomenon.

Religion, sense of national identity and language have related to each other in complex ways throughout Welsh history.[2] This associative complex is the background against which the writers we will examine in this chapter express their ideas, and against which they must be understood. A knowledge of a minimal amount of Welsh history is called for.

With the formal political union of Wales and England in 1536, a centuries-long process of conquest and political assimilation was sealed. Henceforth, Wales was to be governed from England together with England, as one political unit. The 'Act of Union' recognized, however, that significant cultural differences remained between the two countries, most evidently in the fact that the vast majority of the Welsh spoke Welsh alone. In the hope that eventually linguistic homogeneity would produce cultural union, the terms of the Act prohibited all 'sinister usages' of the Welsh language henceforth, in any public sphere. Developments in religious history – the rise of Protestantism and the consequent establishment of the Church of England – provided the ground for one exception of transcendent significance for the subsequent history of Wales: persuaded that a Welsh Bible would greatly hasten the acceptance of the Protestant religion in Wales, the 1563 Parliament authorized the translation of the Bible into Welsh.

The Welsh Bible of 1588 (along with the Welsh Book of Common Prayer of 1567) ensured that the only official and public use to which Welsh might be put was religious: its civil status, taken away by the Act of Union, was restored by the 1588 Bible, but transferred to a spiritual plane. It is an old cliché of historians and *littérateurs* that the translation is also the foundation stone of modern Welsh literature, providing an elegant, standard literary form for a language which might otherwise have declined into a series of mutually unintelligible dialects. But more importantly for our purpose, it established Welsh, in the words of Gwenallt, 'as one of the dialects of the revelation of God'. In the pages of divine revelation, the link between the Welsh language and religion was now inseparably forged. Old Testament ideas of cultic purity and the idea of national territory as a variety of sacred place throw light on the identity now attributed to the Welsh language, the most obvious vestige of national separateness. In the course of time, the association of language and religion gave Welsh something of the odour of sanctity, making it a symbol and a tabernacle of a separate national-religious identity. Moreover, remembering Eliade's claim that *being* is only truly predicated of those who are in close contact with sacred places, Heidegger's dictum that 'language is the house of Being' takes on a particularly Welsh flavour.

Developments in religious history in the centuries following the Act of Union and the Elizabethan settlement compounded this process of sacralizing the Welsh language. We will leave a consideration of the seventeenth-century developments in religious and national Welsh history to Charles Edwards and Chapter 4 below. Most historians mark the eighteenth century as a turning-point in Welsh history, marking the slow and lingering death of the final vestiges of an old independent, Catholic Wales, and the birth of a new one, Protestant and dependent on England, but which was still dimly aware of its historical past. This new Wales was born through the efforts of antiquarians who sought to revive a noble Welsh past – and who invented for later generations' benefit what they could not discover.[3] Most notably, the arrival of Nonconformism, which gained ground quickly and dramatically through the series of Methodist revivals, transformed the national and religious self-image of the Welsh.[4] Geraint Jenkins notes that

> there grew up among the middle strata of Welsh society . . . a certain consciousness that the nation possessed values which should not be lost and that there was a need to create and invent spiritual and cultural institutions that would enable them to supply the . . . needs of their fellow countrymen.[5]

In all of these developments, cultural and religious values were seen to fit snugly together. The revival of Welsh national identity became identified with evangelical religion, most especially Nonconformism, which, if it was conscious of the Welsh national past, was itself perceived as being a break with that past, and as the creating of a new, vibrant and essentially Protestant Wales. The tendency of this new religious consciousness was to accentuate consciously the intellectual and national distinctiveness of the Welsh. The Marxist historian Gwyn Alf Williams notes that 'the character of national consciousness was always vague and partial. The consciousness of national identity became a defensive mechanism, a siege mentality.'[6] For Israel, according to Jonathan Z. Smith, the experience of being besieged led to the concept of national territory as a sanctuary, a pattern in which holy place is a corollary of defensiveness. Yi-Fu Tuan notes that separation and sacredness tend to cause each other. Isaiah Berlin's observation that the exaggeration of a nation's real or imaginary virtues is the response to being scorned or patronized may also be relevant here. It is not difficult to see the psychological and political mechanisms by which national identity can also become imbued with holiness, and that holiness become a source of pride.

By 1885, three-quarters of the population of Wales were members of Nonconformist churches, the majority of which used Welsh as their sole language of worship. Nonconformism became the religious and cultural norm: 'Being Welsh was within a hairsbreadth of meaning the same as being a Christian. It was difficult to describe national Welsh characteristics without referring to Christianity.'[7] As we will presently see, the same pattern of admixture of religious and national identities is found in Gildas in the sixth century, at the time when the concept of 'Wales' was just beginning. It is noteworthy that the first known occurrence in

Welsh of the name 'Cymry' (the Welsh) is in a possibly seventh-century poem in which the word 'Christ' also appears for the first time. Despite its many innovations, Welsh Nonconformity was clearly tapping into very ancient ways of thinking and feeling.

The mid-nineteenth-century Nonconformist apogee created its own series of myths, propagating the image of Wales as an essentially rural, law-abiding, teetotal and generally highly moral people. This is *Gwlad y Menyg Gwynion*, the Land of the White Gloves, presented to magistrates when no cases were brought before them. This is also the Land of Song, where God was praised in chapel through hymns and arias. And as we have seen, it is these shaping myths, the icons of a nation, rather than more complex realities, which have the power to move people. In this nineteenth-century vision, Wales is considered primarily as a socio-religious unity, in the Wales-as-Church paradigm:

> We are, through God's mercy, morally and religiously superior to our neighbours, if not also in general knowledge.

> [The Welsh] are one of the most scripturally enlightened, loyal and religious nations on the face of the earth.[8]

These two quotations illustrate a certain abiding ambiguity towards the English, to whom Wales owed political, but not religious loyalty: the link between *British* nationality and religious identity clearly was at odds with the Welsh experience. The dualism expressed itself in the separate arenas in which the two languages were used: English as the language of commerce and the worldly prosperous, and Welsh as the language of the uninstructed, if holy. In the late eighteenth century, the revivalist minister Howell Harris had beseeched the inhabitants of Pembrokeshire 'not to be taken in by the pride of the English and their language and forget their own tongue. I told them that God was a Welshman, and could speak Welsh, and that he had told many people, in Welsh, "Your sins are forgiven".'[9]

The truth that God communicates to all in their own language is here transferred from a theological into something approaching a literalist register, in a bathetic effort to bring together spiritual and material realities: the Wales-Israel dynamic includes a tendency towards literalist understandings, in which material realities are subsumed into a spiritual sphere to the extent that facts become limitlessly malleable. Thus, in similar vein, we find delightfully, on the lips of the Reverend William Roberts, an Independent minister, expression of linguistic-spiritual apartheid in 1876: 'When the world is spoken of on the Sabbath, then let care be taken that one speaks of it in English, lest our ancient Welsh tongue be sullied by such a usage.'[10]

Welsh was also the language of religious orthodoxy, a linguistic sanctuary from alien ideas. Four years previously Gwilym Hiraethog, another Independent minister, thundered against cultural and religious infidelity:

> Nothing would be more pleasing to Satan than to find you, the men-servants, asleep . . . and looking at Wales, without doubt he would like to see our ancient tongue fall into disuse soon, in the hope that its evangelical religion would also fall into disuse with it; and this is indeed what has happened to a large extent, in those parts of our country where [Welsh has fallen into disuse]. There is no Englishman in England, nor any traitor to the language in Wales who would like to see this happen as much as Satan.[11]

It was the growing awareness of a separate religious identity which led to the first modern calls for a separate political identity, centred around the political-religious issue of the disestablishment in Wales of the Church of England. Yet, paradoxically, at the very time that the demand for political recognition of the distinct religious identity of the Welsh nation was gaining strength, a sea change was taking place:

> Between 1890 and 1911 . . . the majority of the population ceased to speak Welsh. As a result of losing their language, people lost the connection with their own past. And this was not only a matter of losing connection with the religious past. It meant also losing a sense of national identity. For those who knew Welsh, religious services and Sunday school and concerts and publications were a link between them and their national and Christian past. The Christian churches were increasingly forced to bear the responsibility for safeguarding the national tradition and culture . . . Complicity with the state of affairs which considered Welsh a holy language, the language of poets, writers and prophets, and English the language of all else was a fatal path for the churches.[12]

During the twentieth century, the decline of the Welsh language has gone hand-in-hand with the decline of sociological

Christianity, most notably of Welsh-speaking Nonconformism. Welsh has yielded to English as the language of daily life in most areas of the country, becoming in many places a language restricted in its use to worship, education, public administration or culture. This is the ecclesial and linguistic background against which most of the writers studied in this chapter formulate their ideas on the relationship between Christianity and national identity.

This century has also seen the development of a Welsh separatist political party, Plaid Cymru, founded explicitly on Christian humanist principles. Modern political nationalism from its very beginnings until the 1970s was happy to continue to identify Welsh nationality with Christianity: 'Anyone who has met the Welsh nationalist movement knows what a curious blend it is of co-operative socialism and Christianity, internationalism and pacifism.'[13] Most of the Welsh writers I consider below were in origin, if not in practice, Nonconformists; several were ordained ministers. Most of them are at least sympathizers if not active members of the nationalist party. They are also all Welsh-speakers, a fact which deeply affects the content of their writings: while not all Welsh-speakers are nationalists, nor vice versa, the sentiments these writers express are far more typical of the rurally raised Welsh-speaking intelligentsia of west and north Wales origin. The population of the industrialized valleys of south Wales, generally English-speaking, is less self-identified as exclusively Welsh (rather than British, or Welsh *and* British), and is more socialist in tradition and sympathies, whereas many of the inhabitants of the coastal strips of north and south Wales and the border areas are effectively English in culture and affiliation. The writers I consider are also representative of an older generation, most of them writing in the period 1930–70. Many, if not all, Christian Welsh nationalists of the first two-thirds of this century also employed acritical definitions of what exactly constitutes 'Welshness', and their images of Wales were often derivative of those Victorian icons we have met above.[14] They thus represent only one strand in twentieth-century Welsh spirituality, but the most articulate and prolific strand, and one which has consciously sought to foment and perpetuate a distinct Welsh spiritual and national identity.

The complex links between being Welsh-speaking, being Christian, having a sense of national identity and owning political nationalism continue to change. Within the last thirty or so years, 'for the first time since the sixth or seventh century when the Welsh could have said to have come into existence as a separate people, being a Christian is not, for the majority of them, an essential part of being Welsh'.[15] In a sense, then, the strand of Welsh spirituality which this chapter examines is itself, like the language in which it is written, disappearing. I would like to argue, however, that even in the anglicized and de-Christianized late twentieth century, its unconscious echoes still resonate deep within ideas of Welsh nationality, and that they still have much to say to a wider audience.

Twentieth-century Welsh writers on nationality and nationalism

It is not entirely surprising that the subject of nationality and nationalism has received most attention in countries such as Wales and those smaller nations of Europe where an awareness of the fragility of distinctive national identity is acute. The sense of sacredness of a place is often most heightened when the integrity of that place is threatened from outside. The threat may also come from within, in the shape of possible dilution through cultural colonialism. In Wales, awareness of the perennial potential dilution of Welshness – whether through large-scale English settlement or the loss of the Welsh language – has historically acted as a spur to create a greater consciousness of that separateness. Nor, given what we have learnt of the distinctively religious tinge to Welsh nationalism, is it surprising that Welsh theologians and spiritual writers – rather than, say, politicians or philosophers – have devoted so much energy to these issues. Despite the modern secularization of Welsh identity, old attitudes persist, sometimes disguised in humanist or secularized clothes. The agnostic writer Ned Thomas describes Welsh consciousness as a 'protest against inhumanness', and Welsh literature as 'holding up a picture of a humane and civilized society'. Thomas echoes ancient Welsh-Israelite beliefs and a *pars pro toto* nationalism as he asserts that

the language of religious experience with its metaphors of depth, of uncovering the true man, has adapted itself readily to the analysis of

Welshness. And in the end it is perhaps not merely an analogy. To assert the value of a human community and the continuity of one's thought with those of one's ancestors, versus the self-interested logic of administrators and profit maximizers, *is* a kind of spiritual assertion.[16]

An older generation of writers did not fight shy of explicitly identifying Christian values, if not Christianity itself, with nationalism. The presence of Emrys ap Iwan (1851–1906), one of the founding-fathers of modern Welsh political nationalism, stands behind all of the writers discussed in this chapter. In resounding cadences, ap Iwan's sermon 'The Old and New Teachings', eloquently preaches Christian nationalism or nationalist Christianity:

> Remember that God who made men also ordained nations; to destroy a nation is only one grade less of a disaster than to destroy the whole of mankind, and to destroy the language of a nation one grade less of a disaster than to destroy the nation itself . . . It pleased God to reveal that he made people as nations . . . Remember that you are people of the same blood as the English and the Boers and the Kaffirs and the Chinese. Be therefore ready to render them all the rights that you would wish for yourselves. Remember also that you are a nation, through God's ordinance. Do therefore all you can to maintain the nation as a nation, by maintaining its language, and all other valuable things that may pertain to it. If you are not faithful to your country and your language and your nation, how can you expect to be faithful to God and humanity? Do not be ashamed of those things which distinguish you from other nations; and if you wish to imitate the nation next to you, imitate her in those things in which she excels, but not in her pride, her arrogance, her boastfulness, her love of war, her frivolity, her narrowness of thought and her lack of sympathy with other nations.[17]

Ap Iwan contrasts two nationalisms: that of the English, based on irreligious values, and that of the Welsh, which should be based on duty and responsibility. Here *pars pro toto* nationalism is blended with the colours of the Wales-Israel paradigm. A notable moral aspect of ap Iwan's nationalist passion is his anger at the political sin of those Welsh who neglect their national identity:

> Now the major amount of this nation's idolatry runs through two channels – the worship of money and the worship of the English!

Instead of squandering their hearts amongst many gods as they did previously, the Welsh have now concentrated all their lust on two calves – the golden calf and the English calf.[18]

Such prophetic disdain, directed at compatriots, is a familiar part of nationalist rhetoric. Here, the nineteenth-century nationalist writer reiterates a theme which appears as early as the sixteenth century, where we find both Protestant and Catholic apologists criticizing their compatriots' lack of national and linguistic pride. Jeremiad appears frequently in Welsh writing and its stylistic and ideological roots are scriptural. Ap Iwan's sermon contains themes which are still constant in twentieth-century Welsh spirituality, and whose roots stretch back many centuries: the association between religion, nationality and morality; the idea that nations are part of God's ordinance; cultural nationalism or patriotism; and the anti-model of intimate association between political subservience, materialism and degenerate morality. Biblical imagery applied to Wales is a constituent part of the Wales-Israel paradigm, in which use of language is more than mere metaphor, but seeks to express a theological truth. We should also note the biblical metaphors applied equally and inseparably to England and to the love of wealth. The obverse face of the association of Welshness and virtue is the tradition, equally long-lived, of associating England with negative values, along the lines of the polarized universe of sacred and profane proposed by Eliade.

Ap Iwan's strictures are developed and given more solid theological basis in the writings on nationalism of J. E. Daniel (1902–62), Nonconformist minister and professor of theology. Plaid Cymru, the Welsh nationalist party, had been founded in 1923 by Saunders Lewis[19] and others. Daniel joined the party in 1928 and, rather than devising his own nationalist policy, he built on Lewis's philosophy. For Lewis, the basis of civilization was his concept of tradition, by which the riches of the past were handed down from generation to generation, without a break in succession.[20] But in his specifically theological justification of nationalism, Daniel differed significantly from Lewis. He did not wish to stress the central role of the Church in maintaining the cultural, political and religious unity of Europe, nor did he blame Luther for destroying that unity. Nor was Daniel willing to base his theology, as had Lewis, on a Thomist understanding of natural law. Within his own tradition Daniel found repugnant the Calvinist theology of election. Rejecting the Catholic understanding of tradition, secular nationalism, and any sense of divine predestination (whether of individuals or nation), Daniel brought together the biblical rhetoric of Emrys ap Iwan and the theology of revelation of Barth to create a nationalism based on the Word – a nationalism considerably more accessible for most Welsh people than Lewis's conservative, would-be aristocratic stance.

Gwaed y Teulu (The Blood of the Family) is Daniel's most famous sermon.[21] Like Emrys ap Iwan's classical homily, 'The New and Old Teachings', *Gwaed y Teulu* takes as its text Acts 17: 26 ('and he made of one blood all nations of men to dwell on all the face of the earth, and determined the times before appointed, and the bounds of their habitation'). Daniel teaches that, since God has the first and most important claim on a person's loyalty, it is impossible to divinize the nation – an accusation frequently brought against nationalism by its derogators. Inheriting a nationalism of rights deriving ultimately from German Romanticism, Daniel asserts

> There are plenty of superficial thinkers ready to argue that since the rights of the nation are limited then it has no rights at all, and that since to make an idol of it is a sin against God, then its very existence is also a sin, that since it may not be worshipped then neither may it be loved.[22]

Since whole societies, as well as individuals, are divine creation, the nation – as a social, divinely ordained reality – has a place within his plan. As God exists as the society of Father, Son and Holy Spirit, so humankind, created in his image and likeness, has been created in the image of the Trinity, for the Bible tells us that 'it is not good for man to be alone'. Like other Welsh writers, Daniel sees the nation as an analogue of the family, both being divinely ordained.[23]

> It is as if the Creator himself recognizes that man is not complete in his imagehood until he has been placed in a community. One of the kinds of community, according the Apostle, in which God intended man to be placed is the nation . . . Like the family of which it is an extension, it is part of the divinely ordained frame of the life of man.[24]

Daniel bases his doctrine of nationalism on his theological anthropology, a biblically based humanism which concedes transcendent importance to the social placement of human beings. This is the theological expression of a Christian nationalism incompatible with a narrow individualism, and one which demands a consciousness of the importance of social and geographical environment for the development of the human person. In the terms I have essayed in Chapter 1, the vision is of a society in which there is a healthy and essential relationship between the individual and the social, the sacred and the secular.

Daniel's clear emphasis on the spiritual importance of the social and national dimensions is entirely typical of the Welsh nationalist tradition of spirituality. Compare, for instance, the insight of Gwynfor Evans, successor to Saunders Lewis as president of Plaid Cymru, the first Plaid Cymru Member of Parliament and a President of the Union of Welsh Independents:

> Each human being is a social creature; he is affected by his society, and his society is conditioned by its history. The character of his society and his roots in it are all-important to every person. Each individual's character is decided by the nature of the community or communities to which he belongs.[25]

Daniel is at pains to distinguish different forms of nationalism. The place of religion within Christian nationalism is as a moral force, calling us to remember that the nation is part of the order of creation and thus to resist the temptation of turning it into an idol, as in Pannenberg's 'civil religion':

> We must show the place of the nation in a Christian system, and show the limits of its rights. The unity of humanity depends on the fact that we are all in the image of God, but that unity is deeper than the differences of race, nation and culture which may exist between them. Since God created the nations, the Christian has no right to wish to see the nation wiped out.[26]

A triple emphasis on Acts 17: 24 summarizes and recapitulates the authentic Christian attitude towards nations:

> '*He* made every nation of one blood. That puts an end to any Christian attempt to set the nation in place of God . . . He made every

nation from *one* blood. That puts an end to any idea of *Herrenvolk* or 'lesser breeds without the law'. Here, once and for all, is the unity of mankind. The unity of mankind is not so evident to Aristotle, nor Nietzsche or Hegel. For the Christian it is a revealed truth. He made *every* nation of one blood. It is not God's will that humanity should be uniform and unvaried.[27]

The search for unity-within-diversity is a constant topic amongst Welsh writers. Babel, Daniel says, is the story of the attempt of man to reach God through a politically based, imperialistic uniformity, mistaken as being identical with unity. The diversity of tongues – and therefore of the nations who are defined by their use of particular languages – is divine gift rather than punishment. Daniel's vision of the unity of the nations is the 'eternal Pentecost' – 'perfect harmony in mutual understanding and singing together'.

Daniel's insights are repeated by many other writers on religion, nationality and language in Wales. The then Archbishop of Wales, G. O. Williams, notes the tension between the unity of humankind and the purpose of God in creation where 'of necessity every man belongs to a particular family and people'.[28] Like Daniel, he differentiates between different forms of nationalism: Christian social justice demands the decrying of the aggressive nationalisms of those countries with developed economies, along with any nationalism based on discrimination, hostility or imperialism. Nationalism reveals itself in Welsh writers to be a complex force, capable of both moral and immoral variants.

In the writings of Gwynfor Evans, Daniel's ideas are repeated and developed. As is the case in the work of many Welsh writers, Gwynfor distinguishes carefully between different forms of nationalism. The inherent nationalism which lies at the root of imperialism may well be invisible to those whom it benefits. The status quo of imperialism is threatened by the rise of other, defensive nationalisms. It is these which imperialism seeks to conflate with extremism, terrorism, racism, or exclusivism, in an attempt to maintain power and divert attention away from its own political sins:

The fact is that the character of nationalism varies from country to country, and that there are two different kinds of nationalism

competing for the commitment of the Welsh people, namely Welsh
nationalism and the nationalism of the British political parties,
(nationalisms which are) respectively pacifistic, moderate and non-
violent, anti-militaristic and anti-imperialist, and that of nations of
great military power, militaristic and imperialistic . . . The campaign
for freedom and justice for Wales is part of the campaign for world
peace which is so important for humanity, and it is all part of the
campaign for the Kingdom of God. The Welsh Christian's place is in
the pacifist movement.[29]

Behind Gwynfor's sincere rhetoric it also is possible to glimpse
distant ancestors: Herder's idea of *Volksgeist*,[30] the Welsh-Israelite
bipolar association of Britain (for which read England) with imperialism and a lower grade of civilization and moral achievement, the conflation of the interests of Wales with those of God.
Such a continuance of ancient ideas in new forms is entirely
characteristic of the conservative nature of Welsh spirituality. But
Gwynfor Evans is also entirely typical of the spirituality of
twentieth-century Welsh Christian humanism in that for him,
nationalism is a force which has significance *ad extra*. Evans's
emphasis on a nationality and nationalism based on Christian
duty and responsibility (which complements Pannenberg's notion
of election) is a contemporization of the historical Welsh instinct
that the nation has some particular role to play in divinely guided
history, an instinct in which national distinctiveness equals
universal spiritual distinction: 'When the tradition of a nation
incorporates the values of Christianity, creating a way of life
which is more civilized and humane, then it may have world-wide
significance even though it be as small as ancient Israel and
Athens.'[31]

Despite its many anti-English *boutades*, the thrust of modern
Welsh nationalism is generally universalist and pacifist in its
reference, based on a *pars pro toto* understanding of national
identity considered as a moral responsibility rather than as a
right. It is a nationalism which is anything but imperialist. Yet the
bipolar, besieged model of holiness as separation, inherited from
Old Testament theology, nevertheless lends itself also to a secular
reactive nationalism, based on national grievances, and on the
rights of a nation. Both patterns, the Abrahamic-vocational
model (for the sake of the nations) and the strategic-hamlet

model coexist in Welsh nationalism, and both are ultimately religiously derived. A generalized perception that the political state of Great Britain (for which read England) has ingrained imperialistic and militaristic tendencies and that much of Welsh nationalism has a pacifist nature has continued ancient patterns.

Many Welsh writers do not distinguish clearly between a sense of nationality and nationalism as a political creed. This fact reflects the audience whom they are addressing (well-educated, middle-class, and nationalist in their cultural, if not political sympathies) and voices an assumption that the stream of national consciousness must inevitably, for all right-thinking Welsh people, issue into the wider river of political nationalism. The Baptist Dewi Watkin Powell's article on election and the Welsh nation[32] is entirely typical in this respect. His theological justification for the existence of the nation and nationalism is a series of syllogisms: since the God of the Old Testament created the nation of Israel, then

> it would be entirely inconsonant with the changeless nature of God suddenly to desist from expressing himself in and through nations . . . If the nation of Israel was and is God's creation, it follows that every nation is his creation and that he has created it, as he created Israel, for his own purpose.[33]

In the survival of the Welsh language and the Welsh sense of national identity, Powell sees God's hand at work; history as divine providence guides each nation as surely as it does each person:

> In [the] divine pattern, our nation has a purpose which we do not fully know and which we can perceive only as through a glass darkly. But we are part of the divinely ordained natural law. It is hard to explain the existence and the continuation of the Welsh nation outside the terms of Providence.[34]

Since the nation is part of the order of creation, then loyalty to the nation, in the form of defending its continued existence, is part of a universally binding moral law. Thus Powell sees that *any* Christian missionary work in Wales must include a call to Welshness: 'For many Christians, promoting Welshness has never been part of good works, but now there is a call to consider

Welshness as a field of activity which is no less worthy than feeding the hungry or defending the weak.'[35] By 'promoting Welshness', Dewi Watkin Powell means mainly giving money and time to Welsh-language activities. Following the logic and convictions of his argument and beginning from the nature of God, we arrive inexorably, via 'promoting Welshness', at political nationalism:

> If we accept that the Welsh nation has been ordained and created by God, it follows that it has an innate moral duty to take political responsibility for its life and for the prosperity of its people. This is a vocation, a call for Christians in Wales to concentrate our political energies on securing freedom and success for the Welsh nation on the basis of Christian morality.[36]

For Powell, the specific political form by which all Christians *must* be loyal to their divine calling is by espousing a covenantally informed, Christian nationalism:

> The theology of national identity is essential to the fullness of faith. With the covenant, nationalism which is submissive to the sovereignty of God has a saving power which purifies and brings together and restores to man the dignity and the society which he had lost.[37]

Dewi Watkin Powell represents the amateur theologian, and yet his work is important as an example of the underlying thought-patterns of much nationalist writing. A more theologically nuanced and less strident proposal of Christian nationalism has been put forward in numerous articles and sermons by the theologian R. Tudur Jones. His starting-point, as for all of the writers we are considering, is human nature as portrayed in divine revelation:

> Man's life is service to God first of all, and service to man as a consequence of this. By emphasizing the fundamental significance of man's personal relationship to God, we exclude all those concepts of modern life which make of man a mere product of his historical, national, social or economic circumstances.[38]

Writing within a classical Protestant position in which all action is sacred if carried out for God's glory, Jones delineates very carefully the place of the nation in the divine scheme of things. 'God', he argues, 'did not create nations. God created man and man formed nation. That is why it is misleading to talk of nations as one of the orders of creation.'[39] The theological problem facing Jones is that of the location of holiness, since his non-sacramental theology does not allow for any mediated or derived holiness. Making no distinction between the divine and the sacred, worship and veneration, Jones asserts that to insert the nation into the order of creation is to run the risk of divinizing it and of adopting the political manifestation of this divinization in the form of imperialism, thus creating a con-catenation of sinful reaction and counter-reaction. He warns that

> Modern nationalism has often been prone to precisely this kind of blasphemy. It has proved extremely easy to connect nationhood with religious feelings and to invest national symbols with a numinous overtone . . . The nation provides many people with an object of cultic reverence in place of a traditional faith that has lost its hold over them. The nation can very easily become an absolute. The nation that is oppressed by the overbearing imperialism of another faces an alluring temptation to assert the divinity of its own nationhood.[40]

Jones's anthropological vision is that humanity is primarily engaged in the creation of culture, defined as the activity by which man and woman co-operate with God. In that it has to do with obedience to God's mandate, culture may be seen to be an essentially religious activity, in which the sacred and the secular are united. The idea of culture respects fundamental and essential human liberty, and the existential search for meaning and purpose in life is met by and expressed in culture, which provides the medium for us to express faith in concrete form. It is to the order of culture thus understood, rather than to creation, that the nation belongs.

> A Christian nation is both the work of man and the work of God. Nations too are subject to God's beneficent law. In that sense, nations have a relationship of a fundamental kind with God's work as creator. To make nationhood one of the ordinances of creation is to run the very serious risk of elevating national history into salvation history . . . That is not Christianity. It is paganism. A nation is a cultural construct . . . a matter of cultural commitment.[41]

For Jones, as a cultural construct, the nation falls within the covenant by which all human activity and all forms of community are governed by God's natural law. Thus 'the nation is a religious community, which is to say that it exists to serve God. This is implied in the statement that the nation, like other forms of human community, is rooted in God's covenant with man.'[42] The function of the nation, as part of human cultural activity, is to express the meaning latent in God's manifold creation. Each nation, each society of societies, reaches out to and enriches the life of the whole of humankind. For Jones, since the service Christian citizens owe a nation is discharged within the bonds of God's covenant with humankind, it is possible for the practice of specific national consciousness to be a religious duty, one of the ways of serving and worshipping him. Though expressing nationality may take a political form, it is essentially one of the works of charity: 'By insisting that the political objective is not independence but freedom, Welsh nationalists have consistently sought to express their conviction that the nation is no absolute and that it owes a service to God by serving humanity at large.'[43]

In line with Emrys ap Iwan, for R. Tudur Jones the language struggle is part of a twofold, cultural-religious effort: to respect the inheritance of the past and to serve God by enhancing human freedom. Essential to Christian notions of freedom is a sense of responsibility, involving commitment, which must issue in political form:

> And the best of all ways to foster the sprit of responsibility is to proclaim in time and out of time, the Lordship of Christ, and what that means for us . . . We are responsible to God for this nation. It is time for us to demand for the nation the chief medium which God has ordained for it to bear its responsibilities, namely a government chosen by the people of Wales and answerable to them. Self-government for Wales is not a convenient policy. It is rather the next step in Wales' growth towards maturity before the King of Kings.[44]

Within the specific context of Wales, Jones holds that since the historical language of the Welsh nation is the storehouse of cultural memory and the guarantee of national identity – both for those who speak it and those who do not – the preservation and fostering of the Welsh language is intimately bound up with the freedom of the ordinary Welsh citizen. This *pars pro toto* sentiment, which gives the Welsh language a universalizing remit and Welsh-speakers, by virtue of their language, a moral responsibility towards non-Welsh-speakers, is based on inchoate assumptions about the nature of Welsh nationality and language itself, assumptions whose ultimate source is the Wales-Israel tradition.

Jones's subtle dialectic is not always easily followed, and part of the difficulty arises in establishing the relationship between the sacred and the secular. It is true that his theology, unlike the scholastic separation of the spheres of nature and grace, works within the classical Protestant distinction between common grace and particular grace. An argument whose starting-point is Christian anthropology issues almost inexorably into the nationalist movement, and if not a theological then at least a pragmatic argument for national self-determination based on Christian ideas of freedom. Although Jones carefully makes clear that the nation belongs not to creation but, as a form of culture, to the order of covenant, and although he sees that duty towards the nation is to be done in the light of the covenant, there is a sense in which his is a foregone conclusion, namely that self-government is for *all* Christians, whatever their nationality, the morally binding option. As such, it is the incarnation, the concrete historical, political manifestation of religious conviction.

His theological sophistication sets Jones rather apart from most other Welsh writers on nationalism. Yet, at the same time, he stands firmly in the nationalist, Christian humanist tradition of Emrys ap Iwan and J. E. Daniel: the instinctive weight of that Welsh tradition guides him almost inevitably home to familiar territory. I would argue that, whatever the officially espoused, academic and Christian theologies of most Welsh writers, the work of most of them – and just as importantly, most nineteenth- and twentieth-century preachers and hymnists – is fired rather by their national-religious instincts, within a universe which tends to separate itself out into a duality of sacred and secular, a model derived from Old Testament models of holiness, and whose deepest anthropological roots are in those ancient Near Eastern cosmologies out of which Eliade formulated his models. Out of that mind-set a number of common themes have emerged in the works of the writers we have studied: the importance of the religious element in Welsh national identity; the interplay between religion, language and nationality; the importance attributed to the social aspect of nationality in the constitution of the Christian person; and political nationalism as an almost inevitable Christian duty.

Many writers on these themes recognize the interdependence of these elements: in D. R. Thomas's essay on national identity and religion, the experience of Israel in which 'nationality and faith are *mixed together*'[45] is used as a paradigm for all such relations; J. Gwynfor Jones[46] talks of a 'close *interrelation* of religion, language and nationality'; for G. O. Williams[47] 'in Wales . . . the lives of the people and the Christian faith have been closely *entwined* together'. None of these writers makes an attempt to define either 'nation' or 'nationality', but it is clear that, given their common humanistic base, they all talk essentially of the nation mainly in its social rather than in its territorial aspect. The relation of the social and religious value of Welshness to the geographical reality of the place of Wales is not widely discussed in their theological notions of national identity, in an effort to avoid all suspicion of the deviation which would identify *place* with race – 'blood and land' political policies. There also exists a theological difficulty in Protestant discussion of specific place, in the shape of the preference of Protestant understandings for a sense of homogenous holiness in both place and time. We are left with the question of the significance of *place* within twentieth-century Welsh spirituality and its relations with national consciousness and indeed Welsh nationalism. How, theologically speaking, can we justify or make sense of such assertions as these by Ned Thomas?

> One should not underestimate what it means to live in a country where fields and rivers and hills conserve old and human feelings . . .

> A thought in Welsh has innumerable and untraceable connections with the thought of past centuries, with the scenery even.

> Even the landscape takes on a different quality if you are one who remembers. The scenery is then never separate from the history of the place, from the feeling for the lives that have been lived here. Always the outlines of the scenery are deep in the Welsh consciousness.[48]

Such assertions may tell us much about the nature of place in Wales: that it acts, for those who have by their social and cultural background access to the fullness of its meaning, as a mnemonic of identity. I have already suggested that a sort of theological poetics – in which we pay attention to the descriptive images that are used – can be an important element in a *theological* understanding of the lived experience (the spirituality) of place. But it would be wise to be wary of falling into a *purely* aesthetic stance. There is still a need for a more philosophical and objective understanding of what it means to belong to a place, of those hard-to-grasp connections between a people and their country, in order to avoid potentially fascist emotional stances which place all such experiences at a level of exclusivist, ethnic consciousness. In the work of the philosopher John Robert Jones and his concept of *cydymdreiddiad tir ac iaith* – the interpenetration of land and language – a new hermeneutical key is provided for such a process of description and comprehension.

J. R. Jones and *cydymdreiddiad*

Many thinkers of the Western traditions of the second half of the twentieth century have been explicitly concerned with the search for meaning, in a world in which the pattern and flow of human existence has seemed to turn into universal chaos. The massive totalitarian regimes of imperialism, fascism and communism may be seen as attempts to create strongholds against such meaninglessness, yet each of them engendered further examples of inhumanity. After Passchendaele and Auschwitz and Stalinism, how can human life be said to have any ultimate meaning at all? Jung's work shows a life-long concern with the failure of meaning in individual adult lives; the work of existentialist writers and psychologists such as Viktor Frankel all centres on this issue. Some of the writers on place whom we met in Chapter 2 evidence a concern with meaning – a concern ultimately deriving from Descartes's conversion of the object of philosophy from experience to language. Inevitably, theologians too have made meaning a central category in their anthropology: it was from the theologian Tillich that J. R. Jones derived his notion of the 'crisis of meaninglessness'.

Now in the late twentieth century, with the demise of large-scale, final-solution political systems, with the resurrection of secular nationalisms and the drive towards decentralization, and in a postmodern world which denies the possibility of an answer to the question of meaning, the issue has turned into one of *belonging*: where and to whom do I belong? How exactly do I belong? Clearly, for the Welsh writers we have now met, a strong sense of one's national identity, of being a member of a nation, is one of those dimensions of life which give us life in all its fullness, offering at least a partial response to the quest for meaning. J. R. Jones provides us with a deeper understanding of the mechanisms and the spiritual import of belonging to a people and to a place, showing that the question of meaning and of belonging are responses to the same existential search.

For J. R. Jones, human existence is set within the two frames of time and space. The tendency of the self to transcend itself means, however, that humans constantly live in danger of finding themselves lost in a meaningless world, in a vacuum of identity. The self-transcending being then has an innate need to 'come home', to become rooted, by finding location in space which symbolically and physically counters potential or actual meaninglessness:

> The need for roots is to be understood above all as a need for an earthly place, or a foothold. And since the human being is spirit as well as body, this means that nothing less than a whole, located society will supply the need for a home and neighbourhood to him. The need for roots becomes a need for a neighbourhood, community and a country. It is impossible to overemphasize the territorial aspect . . . According to Tillich: being means having space, or more exactly, providing space for oneself.[49]

Such a space – or 'place', in the terms of the previous chapter – is the land of one's people:

> Humankind needs a 'familiar place' in the vacuum and infinity of space – and the widest space that a man may stand on and feel at the same time that he is an organic part of it is the land of his own People. There are a thousand secret ways in which he is tied to it . . . Indeed, the weaving together of the life of man and his familiar place is a bond almost too deep for words.[50]

The human person, an incarnate reality in place, has another, temporal need, that of continuity in time, in order to conquer the threat of meaninglessness which the passing of time inexorably includes:

> [Man] must become part of a track within a time wider in scope than the span of his own lifetime and of his family lineage, that is he must

be aware of standing in a flow of time, in a track which spans the ages.[51]

But can individual lives, family descendants and the chronicles of history of the neighbourhoods in which we live provide a sufficient anchorhold to withstand the flow of time? J. R. Jones believes that the nation alone can meet the need for being rooted in time:

> Superficially, a nation is a part of space, yet it has a temporal, historical dimension as well, the dimension of the past. And what makes of them a nation, placing a people in a framework of national identity, is their awareness of that age-old temporal dimension.[52]

A nation may be thought of as an intersection of time with place, a here-and-now which provides humanity with meaningful footholds, in space (by means of its land) and in time (by means of a sense of national identity). In his essay on Simone Weil's '*L'Enracinement*', J. R. Jones develops the French writer's idea that the significance of the nation is similar to that of food, a source of sustenance of life. In this way Jones seeks to dethrone the idea that the nation exists as an absolute. In contradistinction to all forms of totalitarianism, the nation exists for the benefit of the person, not vice versa. In a passage which stands as a corrective to some strident and acritical forms of Welsh patriotism, he states

> Christian nationalists have difficulties in deciding whether the nation or the individual soul stands higher in the value of things. What weighs the balance towards the nation is the belief – which seems for some reason to be felt to be implicated in nationalism – that the nation has some purpose or mission in history. This belief has produced a sort of fundamental pollution in many nationalists. Their moral stance has been weakened, so that we will never get from them any clear response to the lie that the end of all nationalism is Hitler. The truth is that a nation has no purpose or end in history. What could that purpose be? Two nations, says Weil, namely the Romans and the Jews, have left us with the false idea that the collective is an embodiment of unconditional worth. This is idolatry. The misfortune is to suppose that a nation has no purpose unless it can be shown to have purpose 'within History'. If it has no purpose then it is worthless. But each nation does have a purpose – that of being food for a specific number of souls, that people which happens to live in its territory now and

over the generations. And this instantly restores the ultimate value to the only thing to which Christianity allows us to attribute ultimate value on this earth, namely the individual soul. And it enables us to derive the value of the nation directly from the value appertaining to the human soul. The nation has a derivative value, the value which belongs to a medium.[53]

Clearly, since it is not based on an idea of sacredness as separation, nor on a duty-based sense of national electedness, but on natural law, Jones's philosophy does not square easily with the Wales-Israel tradition. Likewise, in stressing that the individual person has the highest and the most sacred value, Jones stands out against most of his compatriots, who subscribe to the Welsh-Israelite tendency to undervalue the individual in favour of the nation. For J. R. Jones, the value of the nation can be no more and no less than the value it has for persons. Since each individual is a single separate existence of the world, each person having the value of the whole world, in a certain sense, then the wholeness of the world is within each one of us, as a micro-*kosmos* or sacred space. What, he asks, can be the role of nationality for each individual person?

> The world is presented to the experience of man . . . there within his own experience, not in its global universality, but rather through the medium of the circles or microcosms which are instilled in him by natural forms of distinctiveness – the distinctiveness of place and origin and neighbourhood, as the cradle or background to these national distinctivenesses. The fundamental value of the nation as microcosm lies not in that it is a part of the world in the sense of being a part of the face of the earth, but rather in its being a whole summary or crystallization of the world, in one people.[54]

In the same way as every individual person is a unique, created vision of the whole world, so is every nation a world in itself:

> A nation, tied together by its language, its land, its traditions and its history forms a world, an incomparable microcosm which, if you lose it through violence or through letting it die, cannot be restored by anything on earth. Only once does God create a nation.[55]

It is this quality of specificity – both personal and national – which . provides a bulwark against the tendency of modern industrialized society, and of all totalitarian and imperialistic states, to make of the human person a base unit, instrument-alizing and dehumanizing him or her. The significance of distinct national identities is that they stand as symbols and guarantees of the sacred inviolability of the human person: the sacredness of the nation lies in its value for the sacredness of human life and in its significance for the sustenance of the human soul. The nation is created, 'not of course by man, but by Time'[56] and by God: 'Men did not form the variety of people in the world. They are creation. God, ultimately formed them.'[57]

The total *œuvre* of J. R. Jones offers varying definitions of nationhood and of its characteristics, but the cornerstone concept is that of the interpenetration of land and language:

> Substances interpenetrate when one runs as it were totally through the other; when one goes as it were into the other, without merging, but rather creating an interior relationship which does not come about when substances are merely joined together. It is thus a metaphor from the world of the relationships of objects in space.[58]

The interpenetration of land and language functions to set time, place and cultural inheritance in inseparable relationship with one another:

> A people has two constitutive links – one is exterior, namely the territory which has been lived in across the centuries; and an interior link, namely their language – not so much as a function or technique of communication, but rather as a tradition, an inheritance which is enriched by the passing of the centuries, language in the sense that all the past cultural history of a people is enshrined in its language. Language and land work together to form a people in interpene-tration.[59]

He quotes Fichte to confirm his standpoint: 'Those who speak the same language are bound together by a thousand ties, by nature itself, long before human invention and art. They understand each other – as a community which communicates – and are by their very nature, therefore, an inseparable cosmos.'[60]

The concept of interpenetration is central to Jones's nationalist philosophy. In using the term, he does not mean that the speaking of Welsh in Wales has physically or quasi-physically altered that place: his notion of place makes no room for any neo-pagan *genius patriae.* In line with the understandings of phenomenologists, Jones is not teaching that a place can have some innate, intrinsic quality either of Welshness or holiness. Rather interpenetration is a matter of consciousness, of human relations – individual, social and national – with the land. Ever the philosopher, with the skill of making nice distinctions at his fingertips, Jones teaches that

> It is important . . . not to mislocate this interpenetration. Subjectively, the interpenetration of land and language takes place in the souls of people, and objectively in human society. It does not happen within nature as some magical transformation in the composition of the land. This would be a senseless idea. *It is in us that Wales is one.*[61] . . . In this marriage, we are a People as it were taking hold of our land, and weaving it into our lives through the medium of our language. The language of a people interpenetrates their territory as the daily language of a people on their land. As far as Wales is concerned, the interpenetration is that life has been lived through the medium of Welsh in these territories for generations.[62]

In the specific interpenetration of the Welsh language with the land of Wales lies the distinctiveness of the Welsh sense of national identity. Any threat to that marriage of land and language besmirches that distinctiveness and brings us nearer to the destruction of the Welsh national community, a unique piece of God's creation.

The historical experiences of the twentieth century caused Jones to be pessimistic about the survival of the Welsh language: internationally, the totalitarian systems of communism, fascism and anglophone cultural imperialism tended to level out or obliterate differences between nations and places, differences essential for full human development. The Welsh language continued to decline, and along with it, the number of those places where land and language still interpenetrated, where daily life was still lived out through the medium of the Welsh language, decreased, thinning out the warp and weft of national identity. Despite his earlier misgivings over modelling national identity on the Israelite model, at the end of his political essay 'Gwaedd yng Nghymru' J. R. Jones offers us for imitation the example of Israel, a small and powerless nation who in the face of disasters worse by far than those undergone by Wales had nevertheless managed to re-establish its foothold:

Is it not . . . significant that they should have sought that foothold in a return to a rich new interpenetration between their own ancient land, and their own ancient language – that they, from out of their scattering and reduction all over the globe, should come back to the land of Canaan and seek to restore that land to its original interpenetration with the Hebrew language?[63]

Jones writes as a Welshman, fully inserted in the traditions of Welsh literature for which the Bible is a mine of images, and in which Israel suggests or implies Wales. Consequently, we find Jones ending a number of his political essays with ample citations from the Bible, particularly from Jeremiah. Most notable is the account (Jer. 32) of Jeremiah's buying of the field in Anathoth, 'in the face of bleak prospects and portents of the end – that they may survive. For houses and field and vineyards will again be occupied in this land.'[64]

In many ways, Jones stands apart from most other Welsh writers of his generation. His language and thoughts clearly express the fact that he is a professional philosopher rather than a theologian; his version of Christianity made him the subject of accusations of unorthodoxy, of being more of a humanist than a 'biblical Christian' – accusations which betray their authors' separatist understandings of the relationship between nature and grace. Yet the potent and inchoate emotion which such biblical quotations evoke, in which it is shimmeringly ambiguous whether it is Wales or Israel to which he refers, means that Jones too finds a place, even if *sui generis,* within the Welsh-Israelite tradition.

Interpenetration – a theological consideration

The philosophical notion of interpenetration bears close resemblance to some very fundamental theological concepts, an unsurprising fact, given that the ultimate source of J. R. Jones's idea is Fichte. Ned Thomas's study of Waldo Williams[65] notes how German Romanticism, deriving from the collision of the Enlightenment with Pietism, tended to transfer theological patterns to secular subjects, and quotes Abrams's *Natural Supernaturalism* to the effect that

[Romantic writers] undertook . . . to save traditional concepts, schemes and values which had been based on the relation of the

Creator to his creature and creation, but to reformulate them within the prevailing two-term system of subject and object . . . the human mind and its transactions with nature.[66]

Deriving from a theological concept based on the idea of relationality, interpenetration is an appropriate term to express the intimate connections between such religious and social realities as national identity, place and spirituality.

In his evaluation of J. R. Jones's nationalist writings, R. Tudur Jones praises the concept of interpenetration. His wish to extend it as a general category, beyond questions of language and land, shows the potential application of the concept (and illustrates incidentally the continuing influence of the Romantic mind-set on Welsh theology and political theory):

A nation is a community which spans all aspects of created reality. It is not limited to language, land and state. Linguistic and aesthetic features interpenetrate in the same way . . . When there is not harmonious and just interpenetration between economics, land, and the aesthetic aspect of life, our valleys and mountains are raped, turning paradise into hell . . . A nation also has a religious aspect. At least, a nation like Wales, which was born from the womb of the Christian faith. Let us remember that 'environment of the ages'; it would not to do ignore the transcendent reference of its existence. *'The dust of all the saints of the ages and the martyrs lies in your embrace.'*[67] The religious aspect . . . interpenetrates the other aspects of the life of the nation . . . The Welsh language also has a spiritual aspect in that it has been consecrated over so many centuries to symbolize the Christian truth in so many and varied manners. And our land also has a spiritual aspect. *'Wales is a vineyard given unto my care.'*[68] A state does not interpenetrate with land and language alone. It interpenetrates in varying ways with all aspects of a people's life – economically, culturally, ethically, aesthetically, legally, historically and religiously.[69]

Within a strict theology of revelation or within the canons of a restricted systematic theology, such passionate and globalizing assertions as these, and the more impassioned but theologically more naïve contributions of some nationalist rhetoric, are difficult to justify. Nevertheless, in that they articulate common convictions they have their own value, belonging to a category of theology which gives due credence to human experience – in our case experience of the intimate links between Welsh religiosity, language and nationality – and to the images which are used to describe that experience, taking seriously Hobsbawm's insight that image, rather than reality, shapes and expresses human experience. J. R. Jones states that 'the weaving together of the life of man and his familiar place is a bond almost too deep for words. At least it cannot be broken down into abstracted elements, but belongs rather to the language of poetry.'[70]

Mention of poetry serves to remind us that in Wales poets have often been regarded as privileged custodians of memory and of national identity. The above quotation from R. Tudur Jones contains two citations from poems, and is a good example of an imagistic, poetical theology in which place and nation are understood as symbols and channels of human experience of the sacred. But is there any other way, apart from a poetic one, in which we might describe for example the manner in which place and community and each individual human being 'belong' to each other?

For J. R. Jones, place and nation are complex, multi-layered phenomena, each involving relationships: of place with time, time with place, and each individual with the transgenerational community of which he or she is a member. The great virtue of Jones's concept of interpenetration is that it enables us to explain *how* such different categories come together, allowing for both unity and diversity. The integration of Chalcedonian concepts permits us to describe a relationship in which there is unity, but no merging, and in which the boundaries between metaphysical spheres are respected. Thus all the material, historical, spiritual and psychological dimensions of place and of nation, can be allowed their own autonomies without confusion of linguistic registers, or a false transference of ontic realities from one plane to another.

The application of perichoresis as a further element in this Chalcedonian-informed interpenetration allows us to view the connections between such planes as the individual and the social, the sacred and the profane, and the symbolical and the historical, as a series of processes. In this creative tension between opposites, the Chalcedonian concepts function as checks against imbalances. Different tendencies or preferences, such as the paradigms I have outlined in Chapter 1, likewise act as correctives to each other's potential partialities, an emphasis on salvation, for example correcting any over-insistence on creation, and vice versa. J. R. Jones's original idea of interpenetration of land and language then reveals itself not only as an ontological description of a relationship, but also as an ongoing, intra-historical quest for equilibrium within and between concepts. In Christian terminology, the relationship between people and place reveals itself to be not only a matter of faith (with its constellation of emphases on divine presence, the static, the aesthetic, the contemplative, and human rights) but also a task (stressing morality, the dynamic and the temporal, divine action and human responsibility). Interpenetration in its fullest sense engages both these aspects, allowing for those creative realms of tension and paradox which are an essential part of a healthy spirituality.

This Chalcedonian, Trinitarian interpenetration clearly lends itself to the understanding of sacred place under the aegis of incarnation. It illuminates the manner in which place may be thought of as an icon or a sacrament, in which two realities – material and spiritual – are similarly bound together, without forcing us into the simplistic conclusion that they are identical to each other. Interpenetration also solves the theological problem which underlies many of the writings of Welsh writers concerning the exact religious status of the nation, namely whether it belongs to the order of creation or salvation, nature or grace. The nation may be perceived as a spiritual, religious, or even sacred reality, without running the risk of divinizing it through attributing intrinsic holiness to it, since its holiness is derivative, rather than essential. The same mechanism may apply equally to place, permitting theologically cogent description – and the legitimate and appropriate veneration – of holy places.

The theology of the icon and sacrament are likewise relational, since both involve human encounter with the world of the transcendent. Derivatively, place is a category dependent on human encounter with a geographical location. J. R. Jones clarifies the different levels of relationship implicated in interpenetration: subjective, individual involvement, and objective, social level involvement. A modern search for a sense of place, often tinged with individual, existential concerns, shows itself to be a different animal from the social sense of place more typical of pre-industrial, rural societies. Insofar as Christianity is both an individual and an ecclesial concern, and as the relationship of individuals to the universal community of believers may also be described as interpenetrative, then a Christian spirituality of place will need to be aware of and maintain both individual and social elements in equilibrium with one another.

Similarly, for a spirituality of nationality and a theology of nationalism, interpenetration offers us the virtue of clarity. Although the nation cannot be held to be a reality which is *inherently* religious in the sense of unconditional divine presence, the insights of such theologians as Pannenberg, J. E. Daniel and Simone Weil to the effect that healthy national identity involves a religious component may be honoured: interpenetration allows us to attribute appropriate spiritual and psychological value, and moral rights and responsibilities to the nation, but without sacralizing it, or falling into the sort of national idolatry which critics of nationalism so ardently abhor, or writing it off as a totally secular reality. In both place and national identity, then, the ideal and the task is to maintain the boundaries between the sacred and the secular, in a way which respects their autonomous spheres but which places them in healthy, inseparable and dynamic connection with each other.

Conclusion

One of the twin aims of this chapter has been to give to the general reader some idea of the particular interest and thrust of much of Welsh Christian writing on nationalism during the middle years of this century. The second aim has been the ongoing one of the extrapolation of elements which may be part of a wider spirituality of nationality, and its relationship to a sense of place. Certain patterns have emerged as common to all writers: the close association between religion, nationality and language in Wales; the strong emphasis on the social constituent of human nature and Christian life; the conviction of the psychological and spiritual significance of a sense of nationality in human life; and political nationalism as an almost inevitable manifestation of love of country. Although a theology of place generally shows less explicit development, Welsh considerations of national identity show an underlying relationship with land: both the social and geographical aspects of nationality are inseparably part of each other.

The writers considered here show other common features, which we should note, since these help to give the general reader some of the particular landscape of Welsh spirituality. Content and ideas apart, even in translation many of these writers share evident stylistic features, notably an enthusiastic rhetorical style which lends itself as easily to political as to religious subjects, the membrane between the two often being permeable. The political nationalism which they all propose is informed by Christian and humanist values, in a *pars pro toto* model which considers Welsh identity as a task or moral responsibility. The roots of this instinct are religious, and its paradigm is biblical Israel. The Welsh-Israelite tradition is, I believe, the most resonant bourdon in Welsh history, both spiritual and political. Certainly it is heard time and time again – in hymnology, in poetry, in political writings, in sermons and in place-names – and its semi-conscious, instinctive echoes are to be heard in many places even today. The next chapter of this book investigates its origins, its many ramifications, its contemporary manifestations and its practical implications.

4

Extra Cambriam nulla salus:
nation as Church and Church as nation[1]

For Old Testament Israel, the question of land is inseparably bound up with questions of religious and national identity. The elucidation of a specifically Christian theology of national identity is more problematic. The connections between spirituality and national identity have played themselves out in Wales over the last century or so in a number of typical paradigms. All the Welsh writers encountered so far write within a discursive, intellectual register: such writing has been an important part of the Welsh literary tradition, from at least the sixteenth century onwards. But in looking for an intellectually sufficient theology of place and nation, I have suggested the possibility of a theological poetics, one which pays attention to the images used to describe the human experience of place and sense of national identity. If we are to do justice to the spiritual traditions of place and nationality, then we must also look to literary traditions as a source of theological reflection – an approach particularly necessary in Wales, given the great cultural, political and religious contribution of literature to such issues.

Both the Wales-Israel spiritual tradition and its derivation, the image of Wales-as-Church, appeared in the writings of Welsh theologians studied in the previous chapter. The identifying of Welsh with Israelite experience led to a close association of national and religious identities which might be described under the category of interpenetration. However, application of the four Chalcedonian adverbs reveals that the complex association of these realities does not fit into such a neat scheme. The identification has sometimes been held to be closer than that of interpenetration: the frequent commingling and confusion between secular and spiritual notions of Wales could be described as a practical heresy against the first of the Chalcedonian adverbs. More such heresy frequently occurs in the pietistic and spiritualizing tendencies of the Wales-Israel tradition, in which national identity is transmuted into an eschatological reality.

The Welsh instinct that the land and people of Wales have a religious referent has a deeply rooted history. The spread of religions and the development of group identity often involve a process of both continuity and rupture: it is a familiar concept that early Christianity – and indeed later Christianity – in the Celtic-speaking areas of Western Europe shows some distinctive features which may derive from pre-Christian Celtic cultures. Of possible relevance, therefore, to the study of Christian sense of place in Wales is the fact that

> the Celts were a very religious people. This variety and complexity is due largely to the essential animism upon which Celtic religion is based. Everything in the natural world was numinous, containing its own spirit. Thus . . . the gods were everywhere . . . The topographical nature of some divine spirits is shown by the occurrence of a god whose name ties him to a particular sacred place. Of the more than 400 Celtic god-names known from inscriptions, 300 are recorded only once. Places of worship were often not built shrines, but *loci consecrati* or natural sacred places.[2]

The Celtic gods of territory were often of topographical origin: woods, rivers, mountains, springs. However, it is worth noting that these are *specific* places of holiness, each with their own numinous presence. The Christianization of such individual places was facilitated by the Christian cult of the saints: many Christian wells, for example, are of pre-Christian origin, a phenomenon which shows the anthropological roots of the Catholic-local traditions of Welsh spirituality. Such a sense of locative holiness is connected to the religious psychology in which the whole territory of a tribe is considered as sacred place: as we have seen, national territory tends inexorably to assume a mantle of separateness and holiness.

Celtic sacral kingship offers another possible source of later developments in Wales. In pre-Celtic Ireland, for instance,

> the king was fundamentally bound up with the fortunes and prosperity of the land. If the king's character was good, Ireland would flourish . . . The ritual marriage took place between the king and the land. The concept of sacral kinship was intimately associated with

sacred places, and in particular sacred trees which were . . . perhaps also representative of the land itself.[3]

Writing on the putative connections between pre-Christian Celtic religion and medieval Celtic literature Miranda Green warns us that

> References to religion and mythology in later Celtic literature cannot safely be used to illuminate a subject which is essentially pre-Christian and a part of pre-historic Europe. The message of this medieval Celtic literary material, then, is 'examine with interest but use with extreme caution any possible direct link with the later first millennium BC and the early centuries AD'.[4]

However seductive the temptation to discover direct connections between pre-Christian Celtic-speaking cultures and Christian Wales, it is worth remembering that the close association of the political, the territorial and the religious is by no means unique to early Celtic societies, but rather informs many cultures, including Old Testament Israel. Be they Celtic or biblical in derivation, political and territorial considerations are central aspects of certain strands of Welsh spirituality, from its earliest beginnings.

Gildas

Some of the major foundations of Welsh spirituality lie at a point when the Welsh nation did not yet exist. Some time around the year 540, indignant at what he saw as the moral decadence of the political leaders and churchmen of Britain, the British monk Gildas composed an open letter, addressed both to them and to the whole of his nation. Denouncing their religious laxity, Gildas hoped to turn his countrymen away from the political and social disasters which – in the shape of further Saxon invasions – he saw looming on the horizon, as a punishment from God.

The particular style of biblical hermeneutics which Gildas employs in *De Excidio Britanniae* views national history through the prism of Israelite history, and is, I believe, a constitutive element in the Wales-Israel spiritual tradition. The biblically informed association of religious and political histories sounded a note which has resonated down through the centuries, function-ing as a central theme in the development of the national myth of the Welsh as a nation fundamentally religious in constitution, with the consequent understanding of Welshness as a moral state. I use the word 'myth' in both its technical and pejorative senses.

We may think of the Wales-Israel tradition as a metaphorical river. Gildas's idea of the intimate association of the Britons and Christianity goes underground for several centuries, yet remains sometimes audible. With the Reformation, it surfaces again in Richard Davies's important Introduction to the Welsh New Testament, but most explicitly in Charles Edwards's *Y Ffydd Ddi-Ffuant* (The Unfeignèd Faith), appearing again in the nineteenth century in hymnody and sermons, before issuing finally in one of the most famous passages of twentieth-century Welsh poetry, the 'Vineyard' speech in Saunders Lewis's *Buchedd Garmon*. This long current survives and adapts itself to different purposes, so that even at the end of the twentieth century Gildas's thought still echoes and flows.

It is generally thought that Gildas wrote his *De Excidio Britanniae* at the monastery-school established by his teacher St Illtud, in what is today Llanilltud Fawr on the banks of the Severn Estuary. Born around AD 495, Gildas lived at a time when Roman rule in Britain was still remembered, but no longer through first-hand experience. Hanning[5] notes that: '*Romania* was more of a memory and less of a political heritage there than anywhere else in Europe.' In the years following the departure of the Roman troops in 440, the island of Britain had been beset by invasions, its partially romanized culture threatened by northern Picts, Irish and especially the massive wave of Germanic tribes who were gradually settling territories. *De Excidio* is an attempt to make theological sense of national loss, and in his vision, Gildas brings together in a striking synthesis the inherited memory of that Roman presence, a biblical vision of divine providence at work in the events of the world, and the notion of the British as a nation-church.

The population of Britain was heterogeneous – partly roman-ized, partly romanophile and partly insular Celtic – but the romanized *cives* of the settlements considered themselves to be Romans. From the generation preceding Gildas onwards, a large portion of the place which was once Britannia was gradually lost, sending many people into effective or psychological exile. We should remember here Jonathan Z. Smith's observation that a sense of place is often felt most strongly when that place is under threat, has been lost, or when one is in exile. The history of the Romano-Celtic Christians – and of their cultural descendants, the Welsh – is that of a people whose land has been under constant threat of invasion and whose existence has always been parlous. Smith's reasoning contributes to explain why Gildas – and later Welsh spirituality – has such a strong sense of place and national identity, in a situation which positively invites nostalgic looking back to a glorious and disappeared past. The common concept of a 'golden age' is the specific ground out of which later Arthurian myths arise, and the root of the concept of the 'national redeemer'.[6] The sense of internal exile, of dismay at the disappearance of his world, is at the root of Gildas's anger, an indignation which became part of the cultural inheritance of the Britons and the Welsh. Isaiah Berlin's understanding of nationalism as 'a response to collective humiliation' may well serve to illuminate the psychological sources of Gildas's patriotism.

De Excidio is marked by not a few influences: the Bible, first and foremost, which Gildas quotes extensively. Gildas also inherits the sense of history and biblical interpretation of such early Christian writers as Eusebius, Orosius, Rufinus and Salvian, ideas which lie at the root of his ideas of national identity. In view of the influence of Gildas on later Welsh spirituality, we can usefully expend some time on exploring this vision of history.[7]

In the early medieval period, the movements of history were often read as parts of a larger design – usually the design of God in history. The Hebrews had thought of history as a dynamic process in which past and present fitted in a long arc through which God guided the nation, and for the Christians of the first centuries, history was predominantly understood as being what was revealed in the Hebrew scriptures. In the historiographical style inherited by the early Christians, history is neither background nor description, but a medium of divine revelation. An extensive use of typology as a hermeneutic and a basic thought-pattern meant that developments in time applied to the relationship between the Old and New Testaments. But in this view of history it was also logical that the prophecies of ancient Israel should be fulfilled in the events of the earthly life of the new Israel, the Church.

With the gradual spread of Christianity throughout the empire, Christian thinkers were led to consider the relationship between

Church and state. Interpreting post-biblical church history according to norms which in the Bible govern Israel's unique relationship to God, and in a belief in the divinely providential development of time, Eusebius understood the Roman empire as necessarily having a place in God's scheme of things. The Church, punished for its sins by state persecution and rewarded for its reformation by state acceptance and concomitant flourishing, continues in the pattern of divine providence. Just as the patriarchs of ancient Israel had been, in their way, proto-Christians *avant la lettre,* so Constantine was a new Moses, patriarch, representative and embodiment of a people now fully dedicated to God's service and calling. In Constantine, history reaches a new and definitive apogee. Gildas follows Eusebius in the use of biblically flavoured language and an elaborate use of typology in his biblical interpretation.

Augustine's theology of history, expounded in *The City of God,* in many ways filleted Eusebius' political theory.[8] Yet Hanning notes that 'in the medieval Church, Eusebian freedom triumphed over Augustinian control in the writing of history'.[9] Paulus Orosius, although a pupil of Augustine, constructed a history of Rome, modelled on biblical Israel, but with Roman events as its central concern. Hanning contends that Orosius' work is 'un-Augustinian', since in it 'city and empire become monuments to God's ordering of history . . . The ironclad logic that "all power and all government come from God" cannot be confined, as Augustine would have it, to the history of Israel.'[10] Applying typological exegesis to important events in Roman history, Orosius taught that Israel has been succeeded by Rome which provides universal evidence of the peace it brings. For Gildas, too, *Pax Romana* and *Pax Christi* coincide.

De Excidio is structured in two main parts: a block of denunci-ations of five British kings, accused of a number of serious moral improprieties, and a more extensive and vituperative series of imprecations and denunciations of clerics for their moral and pastoral laxity. Prior to these sections Gildas paints a highly selective picture of the history of the Roman period in Britain. With the defeat of the first attacks of the Picts and Scots, the victory gained was merely a military one, for 'the enemy retreated from the people, but the people did not retreat from their sins'.[11] An earlier period of sinful calm had been followed by an even worse national disaster: the arrival of the Saxons. The implication is that God has an equally crushing punishment for the sinful men of Gildas's own generation, unless they mend their ways.

Certain features of Gildas's work are most important for a proper consideration of later Welsh spirituality. First and foremost is Gildas's biblicism. For him, the Old Testament is 'a mirror reflecting our own life',[12] and the New reflects this with an even more sparkling clarity. Regarding his biblical interpretation, Gildas informs his readers: 'I should certainly like, so far as my feeble talents allow, to interpret in the historical and moral sense, all these testimonies from the holy scriptures that I have so far inserted.'[13] On Paul's Letter to the Romans, he writes: 'This may appear to be addressed to the heathen; but observe how readily it may be applied to the priests and peoples of this age.'[14]

Employing a historically orientated biblical hermeneutic, Gildas sees the events of his world as the current working through of the Old Testament prophecies:

> The word of the prophet Isaiah was fulfilled here also: 'And God has called to wailing and baldness and girding with sackcloth . . .': And they convened a council to decide the best and soundest way to counter the brutal and repeated invasions and plunderings by the people I have mentioned.[15]

Gildas employs in his typology a number of different methods: sometimes British historical events are seen as direct fulfilment of Old Testament prophecies. Most frequently, he is more allusive, suggesting by means of simile and metaphor that current events and situations are 'like' or 'comparable to' biblical parallels: 'Lechery . . . grew with vigorous growth, so that to that time were fitly applied the words "There are actually reports of such fornication as is not known even among the Gentiles".'[16] Equally pervasive is a more subtle use of biblical parallels or nuances which may not be tied down to any one verse. For Gildas, the Bible is not only a source of morality, but a way of thinking and a quarry of images. In this universe, spiritual and material realities are intimately interwoven, and so the defeated Britons 'wander' (as in the Book of Exodus and parable of the lost sheep) in military defeat, under the scourge of a plague (Exodus again). The Britons wallow in the same moral turpitude which the prophets denounced in Israel. Although Gildas warns that 'you will have to understand all this in the spiritual sense, as a warning that your souls may wither because of such as pestilential famine for the word of God',[17] the weight of the evidence is that Gildas understands and uses biblical prophecy in a more historical, literal sense. Gildas's understanding of ecclesiality is applied to the people of Britain. In both nation and Church there is an intimate and inseparable relationship between the individual members (particularly the individuals who exercise responsibility) and the whole of the body. As in the case of Israel the sins of the leaders of the Britons are visited upon the people.

In his denunciations of the rulers and priests of Britain Gildas hurls scripture with a prophet's zeal. Vortipor, *tyrannus* of the Demetiae tribe, is 'like' Mannaseh son of Hezekiah, bad son of a good king, thus receiving from Gildas the sort of scolding that Mannaseh suffered from the prophets of his time. Long quotations from Jeremiah and Amos invite those British kings who have ears to hear to listen and to apply the biblical prophets' fulminations to their own lives, for the sake of the very survival of their kingdoms. Biblical resonances apart, we might here see a shade of the Celtic sacral kings, and their relationship with their lands: the Christian British kings, like their Celtic and Israelite forebears, carry responsibility for their nations' welfare, and it is national responsibility – rather than national rights – which claims Gildas's interest.

The British priests are charged in their turn with not living up to biblical models of holiness.

> Which of [the priests of Britain] was inspired with a wonderful zeal for God, and rose energetically like the priest Phineas to punish fornication with no delay, healing the emotion of lust with the medicine of penitence so that an anger should not blaze against the people, so that this might be counted to him as justice for ever?[18]

A concordance of Gildas's scriptural quotations reveals that he is most fond of the prophets, in their most accusatory voice, suggesting that he sees his own role as a prophetic one. Gildas's British prophetism fulfils the role of Old Testament prophecy: proclaiming God's hand at work in current human history, denouncing the chasm which lies between the actual and the ideal, wielding the threat of intrahistorical divine punishment if there is no repentance, and assuring that divine blessing is the reward for repentance. Like the Old Testament prophets, Gildas thus straddles the worlds of the secular and the divine, a man denouncing his own fellow-countrymen, both at one and at odds with them, in an admixture of patriotism and scorn. To readers familiar with Emrys ap Iwan and others, Gildas's prophetic posture, the admixture of sacred and secular, and the application of biblically derived dynamics and images to national history all begin to take on a familiarly Welsh tinge.

In the Old Testament, 'Israel' describes a place and a people both of which derive their meaning from each other. Brueggemann interprets the land of Israel as a proto-sacrament, in which historical and symbolic meanings are united. For Gildas, soaked as he is in the Old Testament, the Isle of Britain along with its Christian romanized inhabitants, is likewise imbued with historical memories and religious symbolism. As in Israel, 'Britannia' is both the people and the land they have been given. Through biblically inspired poetical images, the theologically orientated history and geography of Romano-Celtic Christian Britain are intimately woven together; terms such as 'wilderness' and 'house', redolent with spiritual associations, are used to describe geographical realities, and vice versa. Classical references abound in Gildas's work: the Island of Britain is first presented as a Virgilian *locus amoenus:* 'Like a chosen bride arrayed in a variety of jewellery, the isle is decorated with wide plains and agreeably set hills . . . To water it, the island has clear fountains, and clear rivers, guaranteeing sweet sleep for those who lie on their banks.'[19] But grace builds on nature: having presented a cultural image of the island, in scriptural parallels, similes and metaphors, Gildas gives his readers the image of Britain as a holy land, a new land of Israel for a new people of God.[20] A Christian dawn lights up the darkness of the land:

> To an island numb with chill ice and more removed, as in a remote nook of the world, from the visible sun, Christ made a present of his rays (that is his precepts), Christ the true sun which shows its dazzling brilliance to the entire earth, not from the temporal firmament merely, but from the highest citadel of heaven that goes beyond all time.[21]

The theological image of Israel as vineyard is applied by Gildas to Britain, in a description which is both symbolic and historical:

The vineyard that had once been good had degenerated into sourness, so that . . . there are rarely to be seen grape-cluster or corn-ear behind the backs of the vintagers and the reapers.[22]

This was the warning to the wicked king of Israel – companion-in-arms to these kings of ours – by whose collusion in a plot of his wife's the innocent Naboth was eliminated for the sake of his ancestral vineyard.[23]

Given Gildas's ample use of Old Testament texts to refer to Britain, much of what Brueggemann and Davies have to say concerning the significance of land in the Old Testament applies analogically to Gildas's understanding of the land of Britain. Mention of the vineyard brings to mind Brueggemann's discussion of the incident of Naboth's vineyard as an illustration of two opposing attitudes towards land – that of land as inalienable, divinely given inheritance, versus that of land as commodity, or in the terms I have sketched out in Chapter 2, of land as place versus land as space. In the understanding of Old Testament, land is both gift and challenge, involving human responsibilities, both grace and works. Britain is not only God's vineyard. Other biblical images, too, by implication and transference, contribute to the notion of Britain as Holy Land. A typological mentality sees reality as one, inter-related warp and weft in which small realities are part of a larger whole, in space and time. In later Judaism, Jerusalem or the temple came to sum up and symbolize the whole land of Israel, so that in biblical dialect, mention of the temple could mean the whole land of Israel and/or the temple building. Gildas expands this typological fabric to include Britain. Through biblical image and typological thinking, we are allowed to see Britain also as vineyard, sanctuary, and temple, place of God's saving presence and action in history:

There was fulfilled for us also what the prophet said in his lament: 'they have burned with fire your sanctuary on the ground, they have polluted the dwelling place of your name.' And again: 'God, the heathen have come into your inheritance; they have desecrated your holy temple.'[24]

Genesis sees creation as the establishment of order – a *kosmos* – out of chaos. A strong strand in all strata of the New Testament sees the Christ-event as a new creation. The typological tradition is present in the New Testament itself, in which Christ's baptism is presented as antetype of the creation of the world and the creation of the nation of Israel in its passing through the waters of the Red Sea and Jordan. Thus we have here an initial creation of Britannia through the ordering and civilizing presence of the Roman empire. In his description of the providential working through of history, Gildas presents a vision of civilization and order brought initially by the Romans:

> The Roman kings were able to impose peace . . . the keen edge of flame, holding its unbending course westwards, could not be restrained or extinguished by the blue torrent of the ocean. Across the strait . . . and meeting no resistance, it brought the laws of obedience to the island.[25]

Just as the early Church suffered its persecution before the arrival of its saviour in the person of Constantine, so the Christian British nation suffered its own due martyrdom, the blood of the martyrs again consecrating by contact the soil, the lamps of their deaths lighting up the northern darkness. The empire also gives Britain its own *alter Christus* in the person of the martyr Alban, and his miraculous crossing of the Thames: 'a route resembling the untrodden way made dry for the Israelites . . . accompanied by a thousand men, he crossed dry-shod, while the river eddies stayed themselves on either side like precipitous mountains'.[26] The evocations of the Red Sea and the crossing of the Jordan work typologically to baptize the Island of Britain, making the island a place in which civilization is not only Roman but also Christian. Eusebius's Byzantine solidarity of nation and Church finds a place in the far west of Europe.

Yet peace and security for Britain, as for Israel, is perennially fragile. The sea, Old Testament symbol of chaos and evil, surrounds the land of Britain, quondam place of civilization: the sacred lies encircled and besieged by the profane. Britain's geographical insularity and the distinctive beauty of its land are the symbols and causes of its holiness, but separation and beauty are also the causes of continual threats both to its sanctity and its political integrity.

Nowhere is Gildas's scheme of sacred and profane more clear than in his treatment of the peoples who are the actors of this drama. For him, the people of Britain at their best are *cives Romani*, guardians of Christian civilization. Yet they are also, like the Israelites, capable of being 'ungratefully rebelling, stiff-necked and haughty, now against God, now against their own country-men, sometimes against kings from abroad'.[27]

Eliade notes that those who do not belong to a sacred place, who live in a sphere which is not connected to the *axis mundi* and which is therefore not a place in the fullest sense of the word, are considered as not fully partaking of being. Thus we should not be surprised to find the Saxons described by Gildas as 'hated by man and God . . . like wolves into the fold'.[28] Description of the enemies of Britain as animals is entirely typical of Gildas: for him, they are 'beasts', 'serpents', 'dogs', 'devils', or 'swine'. As heathen barbarians from outside the Roman empire and Christian world, they are unregenerate by their lack of baptism, and consequently sub-human beings who do not belong to any world of meaning. Gildas's patriotism and his xenophobia – especially his anglophobia – is essentially theological in its justification. The scheme of values is simple and expressed in a binomial opposition: Anglo-Saxon = pagan = barbarian and damned, whilst Briton = Roman = Christian and saved. Missionary zeal is not a part of Gildas's Christianity: his concern is that bad Christians should accept their moral responsibilites for maintaining the ontological and political separation between the sacred and the profane. It is a scheme which, in Welsh spirituality and politics, has echoed consciously and subconsciously down through the centuries.

Gildas's theologically based scheme of things, rooted in an Old Testament understanding of sanctity as separation, and informed by his sense of history as providence, leads him famously to identify the people of Britain as *praesens Israel*. We should note that this is not just a simile, in which x is said to be *like* y. The metaphor, where x *is* y, identifies or joins the two realities, functioning in a way similar to interpenetration. Gildas's description is more than a literary device: in a typological sense the Christian Britons *are* the inheritors of the Old Testament promise. However, a very important shift is at work here: in patristic tradition, it is the Church which is the new Israel. Gildas, however, conflates *ecclesia* and *patria* so that we end up with the nation of the Britons considered as Church. Here is the root of the Wales-Israel and the Wales-as-Church paradigms.

Yet within this nation-church, there is an even further separating out of holiness. Gildas's book had little political effect, but within a generation a social change of great cultural impact had begun to take place:

> His readers did not reform society, but opted out. In the previous twenty years, monasticism had attracted large numbers of followers in Mediterranean lands. Welsh monasticism had aroused little response until then, but within ten years it had become a mass movement in South Wales, Ireland and Gaul.[29]

In a nation whose spiritual and political leaders are hopelessly corrupt, the mantle of maintaining civilization and with it national identity has fallen onto the shoulders of a remnant: the monastic core within the new Israel. Here we have the beginnings of the spiritualization and eschatologization of British and Welsh society: in the face of political disasters, national identity is transferred to and held to be perpetuated at a religious level. This survival tactic for the perpetuation of national identity carries within it the poisonous seed of the idea that the nation can *only* survive in a future, disembodied sphere, with the result that, in Pannenberg's terms, the nation is excluded from the covenant. And as we have seen, *quod non assumptum, non salvatum.*

Gildas illustrates a tension which characterizes all Christian attitudes to temporal things. On the one hand, fidelity to Gospel values and to the call to universal evangelizing demands a commitment to matters of this world. On the other hand, the transcendent dimension of human life reminds us that 'our true home is in heaven'.[30] Despite all his patriotic romanophilia and his concept of Holy Britain, Gildas's final chapter points to a citizenship in a kingdom which is not of this earth:

> May the Almighty God of all consolation and pity preserve the very few good shepherds from all harm, and conquering the common enemy make them citizens of the heavenly city of Jerusalem, that is, of the congregation of all the saints: the Father, the Son and the Holy Spirit, to whom be all honour and glory for ever and ever, Amen.[31]

The fact that Gildas's call to moral regeneration preceded a massive and widespread rush to monastic life in Britain provides us with an indication of his notion of spirituality. Although it is ostensibly the *whole* Christian people of Britain, inheritors of Roman tradition, who must take on the twofold spiritual and political mantle, the responsibility for maintaining the world as a habitable place of meaning against the forces of chaos now falls essentially to the monks, who are engaged in spiritual, but not political, militancy. The ideal of the monastery as a reformed version of society, a paradise set in and against surrounding chaos is found in Cassian – when the secular city becomes a moral and political wilderness, the desert of the monastery becomes the city of God. Thus *praesens Israel* becomes Britain, and the monastery *praesens Britannia* in a retreat into essentialist spiritual purity. Curiously, then, instead of the nation as a sort of church, we end up with the Church, or rather the monastery, considered as a sort of nation. This pattern, begun in late Antiquity, survives in twentieth-century Wales, in the cultural responsibility felt by many Welsh-speaking Christians in particular to keep alive a distinctive national identity, a *Wallia Pura*.

Gildas's ecclesialization and monasticization of early British national identity may be seen as one, local, conclusion of the working through of a Eusebian-Orosian understanding of history. The understanding of history-as-providence had also brought about in its train the sacralizing of the land of romanized and Christian Britannia as *praesens Israel*. Monasticism was not to be the last manifestation of this pattern. Given the cultural and political role of the monasteries in later Welsh history, Gildas proves to be a remarkably far-seeing prophet. Over the following millennium the monasteries developed into repositories of indigenous and classical learning. After the Norman conquest, they also became at times centres of Welsh patriotism and aspirations to independence. Only with the dissolution of the monasteries under Henry VIII would this particularly rich synthesis of culture, nationality and religion come to an end. But the instinct that nationality was inseparably bound up with Christianity was channelled in new directions, almost a thousand years after Gildas, by Welsh Protestants.

From Gildas to the Reformation

I have talked of the Wales-Israel current as a stream which lives some of its life underground. In the centuries following Gildas, the consciousness of a Welsh identity grew gradually, sharpened by the gradual loss of lands to Saxon invaders, and the separation from the Brythonic-speaking cultures of the north and the south-west of the island of Britain. To use the term 'national' of this period is to run severe risk of anachronism, and it would be as well to distinguish between a sense of ethnicity (*ethnos*) and a sense of nationality (*natio*), the former being a sense of membership of a specific group of people (and sometimes a place and a language as well), and the latter being a comparatively modern idea. Medieval Latin *lingua*, and the Welsh word *iaith* (= language) could refer to a group of people who spoke the same language. *Cenedl*, the modern Welsh word equivalent to 'nation', is best translated in the medieval period as 'extended family' or 'kin-group'. Current concepts of national identity are not easily exported to the situation of a thousand or more years ago.

Gildas stands at the fountain-head of a stream which seems to plunge underground almost as soon as it appears, for the following thousand years of British and Welsh literature carry only faint echoes of his *praesens Israel*. While it is true that there is much spiritual and indeed patriotic literature, interest in the whole nation of Wales yields to local considerations. There exist poems which are patriotic in tone, either elegies or praise poems for the kingly or aristocratic patrons of the professional court poets. Welsh poets of the Middle Ages are aware that they belong to a separate *ethnos*, defined increasingly, as its grip on its territory is gradually loosened by conquest, by its use of a particular language.[32] The poets are also aware that their poetic use of that language is a divinely inspired, priest-like craft.

There are other signs of the continuance of the Welsh instinct that religion and nationality are intimately associated.[33] The Norman invasion of Wales gradually brought to an end what remained of distinctively Celtic ecclesial practices and imposed a different form of episcopal authority and state control. It was in the face of this that the Latin *Life of St David* was composed by Rhigyfarch at the end of the eleventh century, appealing to the traditions of the past for religious justification to maintain independence for the see from Canterbury. The Christian cult of the saints had found a home amongst former pagans accustomed to their own local gods. Many of the early Welsh saints are identifiable by one or two place-names only, and in the centuries which follow Gildas the cult of the saints was often connected to specific, local places – often with political connections with particular noble courts. Such specificity of place and cult fits easily into the sort of phenomenological understanding of holy place – place as a distillation of being, meaning or identity – which we explored at the beginning of this book. In the Catholic centuries which separate Gildas and the Protestant Reformation, there is sparse prima-facie evidence for a spirituality of nationality or of national place. What does exist, in the world of folklore and cult is a rich Catholic-local Welsh spirituality – one which incarnates, in specific places and communities, a wider national sense of place and a distinctive nationality.

Of the typologies of Welsh sense of place I defined, it is probably the Wales-Israel model, explored in this chapter, which has been the dominant tradition from the Reformation onwards. Here, the dominant sensibility is a sense of religious nationality, from which derives a religious sense of a national land. What I refer to as Catholic-local spirituality often expresses itself in the centuries between Gildas and the Reformation in poetry of place. From the earliest period onwards, Welsh poetry has evoked, praised and mourned the loss of particular places. Undoubtedly a theology and – in the wider sense of the word – a spirituality underlie this whole body of work, yet this poetry of place is not often as obviously religious or specifically theological in the sense that the Wales-Israel tradition is. Only with the influence of German Romanticism (which affected both poetry and political thought in Wales) does landscape poetry begin again to express the numinous, and perhaps only in the works of Gwenallt and Waldo does great *theologically* inspired poetry of place reappear in Welsh literature, after centuries of silence. What is important to note, however, is its contemporary continuation: sense of place, constellated around particular Welsh locations, continues as a living *literary* theme and tradition, well into the beginning of the third millennium, the direct linear ancestor of the earliest poetry of place and the Catholic-local thematic strand.

If the literary tradition of a sense of local place in Wales, whether implicitly or explicitly religious, is easily identified, the same cannot be said either for a sense of national place or of national awareness. The historical development of national identity in Wales is a disputed academic and practical question, which lies well beyond the limits of this study. Some background in this, however, is essential if we are to understand the development of the Welsh-Israelite theme: we have already seen how the dramatic changes brought about by the Act of Union, and the consequent arrival of Protestantism affected the nature of Welsh national identity. Welsh humanist Reformers, both Protestant and Catholic, argued for the soul of Wales. Both sides also sought to maintain its language, status and cultural identity. In the seventeenth century, Wales produced a spiritual writer who penned one of the most influential of books in Welsh history.

Charles Edwards

Charles Edwards (1628–91?) is described in histories of Welsh literature as *littérateur*, editor, publisher and priest, but perhaps 'national Jeremiah' would be a more accurate all-round description. Misfortune seems to have been a keynote of his professional and personal life: caught up in the stormy period at the end of the Commonwealth, he found himself on the losing Puritan side and was ejected from his college at Oxford. Only after a recantation was he able to graduate. Even then the sincerity of his oath of loyalty to Charles II was doubted. His secure and profitable living in Wales was taken from him in obscure circumstances; after an armed robbery on his household, he himself was imprisoned; his marriage ended in separation; and late in Edwards's life, he seems to have been ejected from yet another living.

To meet with one of these events might be considered a misfortune; to undergo such a lengthy catalogue of personal disasters suggests psychological disorder. The vicissitudes of his life help to explain the dark tone and tensions of Edwards's only work of real import, *Y Ffydd Ddi-Ffuant* (The Unfeignèd Faith). As a Puritan, Edwards considers himself and the Protestant nation to which he belongs as elect and saved. Yet Edwards's own bitter experiences, the constant infidelity of the Welsh to the divine calling and the historical punishments they have undergone, suggest a darker, more complex reality, and a providence more ambivalent in its intentions.

The book is divided into three main sections: (1) the history of the Christian faith 'from the beginnings of the world' until the implantation and spread of the Protestant religion in Britain, (2) the history of the faith amongst the Welsh, and (3) a more 'spiritual' section on the virtues of the faith. *Y Ffydd Ddi-Ffuant* is

Edwards's attempt to justify the ways of God to man, in God's dealings with the nation and the individual soul. The theological tenet which serves to unite the three sections is the belief that God acts in exactly the same way in dealing with individuals as with larger social groups, such as church or nation: punishing sin and rewarding virtue. History is the result of divine intervention, and thus all history is essentially spiritual history, a reminder of the judgement included as an essential element in the divine covenant. The individual may thus profit spiritually from the lessons of human, ecclesiastical and national history.

It is difficult to overstate the influence of *Y Ffydd Ddi-Ffuant*. The Welsh scholar Derec Llwyd Morgan notes: 'Many Welsh people are still happy to echo unconsciously the patriotic claims and the historical and philosophical-political statements which are the basis and material of this work.'[34] Its piety is of great national significance:

> The treatment of the salvation of Wales in *Y Ffydd Ddi-Ffuant* is very short, but its song has echoed remarkably long and loud in our literature, and has been expressed in varieties of literature patterned on the Bible, in historical interpretation of prophecies and in lamentation.[35]

Edwards's work is a seventeenth-century *summa* of history seen as the dealings of God with humanity. In the section on Welsh history, 'Charles Edwards has defined an important piece of the Welsh imagination and psychology . . . joining the theology of election with the old claim of our nation on the whole of the British Isles.'[36] In the same way that Gildas's vision synthesizes the memory of the Roman presence, the biblical vision of providence and the notion of the British nation as a quasi-church, Edwards's themes bubble together in a rich cauldron: it is precisely his association of the claims of the Welsh nation to spiritual distinction with its political claim on a 'lost' territory that makes of him such a powerful writer.[37] In both authors, divine revelation is regarded as working not only within, but through history, the world of politics being thus connected inseparably with the world of the soul. Yet although this meeting could be defined as interpenetration, in the case of Edwards, a voracious spiritual appetite often digests any social or political implications of his argument. In the work of Edwards, as in Gildas, Wales is found guilty of a number of Chalcedonian heresies: at times variously confusing national and religious identities, attributing chronological or ontological primacy to one or other, fragmenting aspects of the spheres of the spiritual and the secular, or divorcing them one from another.

The central concern of both the Protestant Reformation and the Catholic Counter-Reformation had been to find the answer to the question 'Where is the Church founded by Jesus Christ?' Both sides made opposing truth-claims, often drawing on the same material. On the Protestant side, in a desire to be able to connect newly created state churches with ancient and unsullied Christian roots, a Europe-wide interest developed in the history of the true faith. In England and Wales, this interest was intensified by the Civil War, as people sought to make sense of religious strife. In his *Book of Martyrs*, John Foxe created something of an English national myth, making of the faith gradually legislated into existence by Henry VIII and his successors something indigenous, culturally appropriate, and garnishing it with an ancient pedigree. In Foxe's philosophy, it is the English who are the chosen people of this world, raised up through the centuries to bring the light of the reformed faith to a benighted and enslaved world – a myth with its roots in Bede, and among whose many fruits was the development of the British (*sic*) empire.

Although the first edition of *Y Ffydd Ddi-Ffuant* accepted Foxe's anglophile premises and conclusion, the 1671 version of the book was witness to a highly significant change in attitude. The 'Letter to the Welsh' of Richard Davies, originally the preface to the 1567 Welsh New Testament, was reprinted in the 1671 revision of Edwards's book. Davies's epistle is a brilliant reworking of Welsh history. Making use of the inchoate religious instinct that what could be shown to be most ancient and indigenous was also most likely to be genuine, and evoking ancient memories of the Welsh claim of sovereignty over the whole of the Isle of Britain, Davies posited that Anglicanism, far from being an alien 'faith of the Saxons' as it was being perceived by Catholics in Wales, was nothing more than a restoration of the ancient national church of the British-Welsh. The old Britons had held to the word of God, a stance which brought them privilege and pre-eminence. Moreover, theirs was a true Christianity:

There was a great difference between the Christianity of the Britons and the false Christianity which Augustine of Canterbury gave the Saxons. The Britons kept their Christianity pure and immaculate, without admixture of human imaginings. Augustine's Christianity veered rather from the matchless purity of the Gospel, and was mixed in with much superficiality, human opinions and vain ceremonies, which did not accord with the nature of the kingdom of Christ.[38]

Moreover, Davies made a number of claims for the Welsh or the ancient British nation itself, pointing out not only its spiritual distinctiveness, but its claims to pre-eminence:

The qualities and virtues were more widespread amongst the Britons in the past than in any other surrounding nation, [especially] their unsullied faith, their pure Christianity and their valuable fruitful religion. Since Sabellius tells us that the Isle of Britain accepted the Christian faith first, of all these islands; since in the twenty-first year after the ascension of Christ, the venerable Joseph of Arimathea, the disciple of Christ came here along with other disciples. This was no small excellency.[39]

It was these historical notions that Edwards espoused, assuming a prophetic mantle and chastizing the whole of his nation for their tardiness in reforming their ways and for their indifference towards the Protestant faith. In Gildas, Edwards found a typology which served his purposes well, a theory of history which was congenial, and an admixture of religion and patriotism which reflected his own desire to restore, through *sola fides*, Wales's ancient dignity. As Welsh, they had inherited the ancient rights and privileges of the Britons. As Christians, the Israel of the spirit, they were the arena in which God would fulfil the promises made to the ancient Israel according to the flesh. Taking Gildas as his model and inspiration, Edwards included and adapted in one of his chapters a large section of the *De Excidio*. But ever the enthusiast, he pushed Gildas's images and metaphors to an extreme: rather than typologically seeing the experiences of the Israelite and Welsh nations as being part of the same divine dispensation, Edwards literally identified Wales with Israel.

Gildas's prophetic stance likewise informs Edwards's understanding and use of national history. From the heights of the ages, Charles Edwards seeks to see the Welsh nation in perspective, claiming for the Welsh pre-eminently among *all* the nations, by virtue of their ancient, Christian identity, the federal or national covenant which God had originally made with the Israelites of the Old Testament. Following the dynamic of his largely Old Testament inspiration, Edwards's viewpoint is deuteronomic: looking at history, the memory of the nation, he seeks to find the meaning of the present and a way to a future. According to Derec Llwyd Morgan,

> His treatment of the mythical Israelitism of Wales is the richest account of that subject we have. But for Charles Edwards, myth did not exist. This is the truth for him, his reality, namely living as the new Israel under God's unfailing governance. An awareness of the covenantal relationship of Wales with God through His Son gave special intensity to the cares and joys of Edwards' daily life.[40]

It is largely through the power of his literary battery that Edwards conveys the theological arguments of his vision of the Welsh-as-Israel. Theological considerations apart, the quality of Edwards's splendid – and splenetic – rhetoric alone guarantees him a place in the pantheon of Welsh literature. A summary familiarity, even in translation, with the images of the Welsh history section of *Y Ffydd Ddi-Ffuant*, will greatly enrich our understanding of this strand of Welsh national-religious identity.

The first thing that will strike the reader of Edwards's work is the extensive use of biblical quotations (marked out in the original and facsimile editions by the use of an italic typeface): they are woven into a seamless robe where the God of the Bible and Edwards finish each other's sentences.[41] Such a style in itself is neither original nor surprising, for the New Testament and the patristic writings evidence a similar use of scripture, in which biblical allusions, quotations, parallels and similes abound. This use of the Bible is in itself a theological statement and a view of history, a literary analogue of the belief that the behaviour of God is constant throughout heaven and earth and time, and thus that divinely inspired words spoken in the past can describe and include the current realities of all readers. There is, however, I believe, one important difference in the case of Edwards, namely that he is writing and quoting the Bible in the vernacular, Wales's distinctive mark of identity. In Edwards's theology, God speaks Welsh. With this stylistic device, through the almost macaronic interweaving of his own Welsh prose and the Bible, Edwards is linguistically inserting Wales into the history of salvation. The prophecies of the Old Testament are fulfilled in the Church, in the life of the individual Christian – and also in the history of the Welsh nation. For example, of the state of Wales following the guerrilla war under Owain Glyndŵr against the English invaders, Edwards writes:

> the oppressive captivity of our nation continued through the reign of five English kings, long enough to bring upon [Wales] real poverty and ignorance and to make wretched or to extinguish completely the generosity, skilfulness, art, faith and good manners which were found there formerly. In this state it found cause to lament before God as Zion afflicted: *We have transgressed and have rebelled. Thou hast not pardoned. Thou hast covered us with anger, and persecuted us. Thou hast slain, thou hast not pitied. Thou hast made us as the offscouring and refuse in the midst of the people. The crown is fallen from our head; woe unto us, that we have sinned!* Since in her the threat of God was fulfilled quite directly – *because thou served not the Lord thy God with joyfulness, and with gladness of heart, for the abundance of all things; therefore shalt thou serve thine enemies which the Lord shall send against thee, in hunger, and in thirst and in nakedness, and in want of all things; and he put a yoke of iron upon thy neck.* [42]

Notions of captivity are applied to describe political, territorial subjugation by the Romans, the Saxons, the Normans, and the English generally, at least up to the time of the Reformation. But 'captivity' also describes spiritual impurity, in the form of Catholicism. Since from Rome nothing good can come, Edwards omits Gildas's cultural romanophilia, substituting for it Richard Davies's version of history, in which the British (for which read Welsh) received the purity of the faith directly from an apostolic, non-Roman source, well before the English. In this deuteronomic vision, chronological primacy is the guarantee of purity. Liberation of the Welsh from Romish superstition is part of the divine plan, a plan initially foreshadowed in the return of the Israelites from their Babylonian captivity. Welsh Protestantism is a return to that original holiness in which God had destined the Britons to be separated out, illustrated in the geography of the place in which God has set them. As in Brueggemann's Israel, for Edwards, the symbolic and historical meanings of land coincide:

As Tertullian shows: *those places which belong to the Britons which cannot be reached by the Romans have given themselves over to Christ* . . . And Origen: *The strength of the Lord is with those people in Britain who have been set apart from our world, and with all in this universe who believe in his name.* [43]

In his chapter summarizing Gildas, Edwards repeats the assertion that 'we' are *praesens Israel,* the 'we' now being the Welsh. One more layer is added to the palimpsest of history: the same patterns of divine and human behaviour recur, in an *éternel retour.* But just as grace abounds and rebounds in history so also, according to this typological vision, does sin. In Edwards's rehearsing of Gildas's accusations against the immoral clerics of *his* time, we see the same cyclic pattern of doom and immorality: the lukewarm Welsh priests of Edwards's time are seen through the prism of the simoniac British priests of Gildas's time, and they are all accused with the language in which Old Testament prophets attack the sinful priests of that time:

The Holy Joel, accusing the neglectful priests, and over the loss of his people for their sins, said, *Awake ye drunkards and weep, and howl ye drinkers of wine; because of the new wine; for it is cut off from your mouth.* To you belongs the word of the Lord in Amos: . . . *Behold the days come, says the Lord, that I will send a famine in the land, not a famine of bread, nor a thirst for water, but of hearing the words of the Lord. And they shall wander from sea to sea, and from the north to the east, they shall run to and fro to seek the word of the Lord, and shall not find it.* [44]

Significantly, a note printed at this point in the margin of *Y Ffydd Ddi-Ffuant* advises the reader that 'This was wholly fulfilled in Wales'. In Edwards's description of the cycles of time, there flows a certain dark undercurrent: despite their many opportunities, the Welsh have not learnt the lessons of history, and sin always returns to sully national eminence. Judging by the evidence of Welsh national history, grace and sin in this cosmic struggle are not equal partners – the balance almost always tips in favour of sin. In the work of Edwards, there lies an apocalyptic despair that the Welsh can ever achieve national salvation within the world of time. The fruits of national election can only be enjoyed outside this temporal and vicious circle – in a kingdom which is not of this world.

As is the case with Gildas, Edwards's biblical allusions are often subtle. He employs simile widely, with the continual implication that there is some special affinity between the Welsh and the Israelites. But of all the attempts at identifying Wales with Israel, none is more curious than Edwards's attempts at proving that the Welsh language – as we have noted, the main and incontrovertible emblem of Welsh distinctiveness – is a sister-language to Hebrew. Ancientness in itself is a virtue for Edwards. In the scheme of things which Edwards proposes, the ancient Christian roots of the British and their close link with the people of Palestine are sources of national pride. In seeking to find traces of Hebrew in Welsh, Edwards seeks to set Welsh prehistory – and Welsh national identity – in an even closer relationship with the sphere of the sacred, since Hebrew is language *par excellence*, the tongue spoken both in Eden and in heaven, a linguistic alpha and omega. He addresses the Welsh reader at the beginning of his work:

I found that there is much Welsh in the Hebrew Bible, and I supposed that I should not conceal that fact from my country, nor hide the candle under a vessel which was lit in my hand from above, without the help of man. And since we have something still of the language of the Prophets, let us endeavour also to be owners of their graces also, and to act according to their words.[45]

Although the idea that the Welsh language was somehow 'closer' to Hebrew than English was not original to Edwards, he gave full expression to an instinct which had been suggested in muffled tones over the previous century or so. Wales's claim is not unique. The search for the ur-language of humankind is an ancient endeavour, and one which frequently carries overtones of ethnocentrism: at roughly the same time as Edwards was writing his book, the Swede Andreas Kempe claimed that in Eden God spoke in Swedish, Adam and Eve responded in Danish, while the serpent expressed himself in French![46]

The 1677 revision concludes with a section almost entirely devoted to Welsh and Hebrew philology. Included in this is a sub-section which consists of three tables: (1) biblical verses in the Welsh translation; (2) a phonetic transliteration of the Hebrew originals; and (3) a Welsh sentence, phonetically similar to the

Hebrew, and which, according to Edwards's mind at least, encapsulates some of its meaning:[47]

1. *Bryssia i'm cynnorthwyo* (Ps. 20:19, 'Make haste to help me')
2. *Legeserithi cussah*
3. *Lle cyssurit fi chwsa* ('Sweat where you would solace me')

Logically and philologically, it is deliciously eccentric nonsense. Theologically and politically, it is highly significant nonsense, none the less. Edwards's linguistic fantasy is part of his attempt to strengthen the grafting of Welsh national identity on to the trunk of Israel. Although his work gives primacy to the world of the spirit, it is also true that Edwards's book evidences a desire to *unite* religious and national identities, to bring the worlds of spirit and of flesh together in a closer relationship, as divine election demands.

In Edwards's linguistic endeavour, it is hard not to see a compensatory and reactive nationalism at work. Edwards's attitude towards the English is conflicted: it is through the English that the 'unfeignèd faith' has been restored to Wales, but at the same time national pride is injured by the current material realities of Welsh life. Edwards's own life experiences of frequent injuries to his pride may also be relevant in this conflicted psychology. Whereas Gildas's concern had been to ensure the religious purity of his people, in a situation where a Christian Isle of Britain was surrounded by a hostile sea, Edwards finds himself in a different political situation, and seeks to confirm the divine election of the Welsh as spiritual distinction rather than distinctiveness. Such pre-eminence is translated to where it really counts: heaven, where God speaks, if not Welsh, then the language closest to it, namely Hebrew. And certainly not English. But the linguistic connections between the Welsh and the Israelites hint at an even closer relationship: 'Doubtless our Nation has dwelt in this isle for many years, and it is likely that it came originally from the countries of the east, for there is so much agreement between our tongue and the tongues of these parts.'[48]

Thus not only are the Welsh *praesens* Israel. They carry in their veins as well as on their lips something of ancient Israel:

Some suppose that we are the offspring of Cam, and some of the remnant of the Gentiles who escaped from the land of Canaan

towards the West from the avenging destruction that came over them
in the time of Joshua. If this be true (since the story is not without
foundation) then let us be gracious, and the blessing of Christ will
wash away the curse of Noah.[49]

In such statements as these we see the curious results of the
transmutation across the centuries of the notion of Israel in the
spirit. In his search for spiritual authenticity for his nation,
Edwards seeks to make the Welsh aware not only of their spiritual
but also their material and ethnic origins. The slightly strange
logic of this stance has theological roots: for Eusebius the patriarchs of the Old Testament were 'really' Christians *avant la lettre*.
For Edwards, then, the surest guarantee of the purity of Welsh
evangelical faith is an intimate relationship with that fore-
shadowing of the Church, the nation of Israel.

Edwards's theology falls into the trap of confusing linguistic
registers, literalizing what were originally conceived of as metaphors, and thus transferring the typological vision of the church
as Israel according to the spirit to a national-cultural and even a
genetic plane. As a result, the divine nature of the covenant runs
the risk of losing the element of judgement, and theological
election ends up being perilously close to racial superiority.
Edwards's desire that the Welsh nation should be an Israel
according to the spirit tends towards subsuming one plane
entirely into another. Instead of healthy interpenetration of spiritual and material realities, there is substitution, and a potentially
rather dangerous muddle.

To be fair to Edwards, notwithstanding his eccentricities and
patriotic particularity, and the potential confusions and dangers
of his piety, we should remember that it is always looking to the
salvation of the soul of the Welsh, as a pedagogy urging moral,
covenantally governed behaviour, that he seeks to identify the
Israelitism of the Welsh and to remind them of it. The mind of
Edwards is set on the welfare of his nation, from the very
beginning to the very end:

Let us honour the privileges and the gentility of our forefathers, that is
their evangelical faith, and their strength of godliness. And for this, my
dear fellow-countrymen, *I gave all diligence to write to you of the common
salvation, and exhort you that ye should earnestly contest for the faith which*

was once delivered unto the saints, yes, amongst the Britons. Paul loved
Timothy calling him *to embrace The Unfeignèd Faith that was in him . . .*
May the Welshman become beloved by God in the same way.[50]

The very stylistic pattern of such paragraphs as this is biblical
in its inspiration and form, and thus serves further to associate
Wales and Israel. God's will be done, in Wales as it is in Israel:
obedience to God will bring about prosperity. But how will this
come about other than through the hearing of the Word? How
will the Welsh hear if the Word is not preached to them?
Edwards's patriotic pride in the glories of the Welsh past does not
blind him to the present neediness of his country.

> Then one could ask, *by whom shall* Wales *arise, for she is small? But the
> Lord remembered us in our low state, for his mercy endureth for ever;* and he
> worked his redemption like that of Israel in the time of Ahasuerus, and
> Esther through marriage, making *her enemies dear to her, and her
> persecutors, a delight to her.*[51]

The marriage is of course between England and Wales. He points out
to the Welsh that 'those who were once as ravening wolves have
become our shepherds'.[52] In the curious mentality of Charles
Edwards – and possibly in the minds of the many Welsh preachers,
divines and hymnists influenced by him over the centuries – political
subjugation is a small price to pay for pure faith and eternal salvation.

Edwards's Welsh Israelitism is used to justify both Welsh
national spiritual distinction and the political and cultural
assimilation of the descendants of the Britons into the descendants of the Saxons. Wales, for Edwards, is essentially a spiritual
⁻ather than a temporal reality. The Israel which is Wales is no
longer threatened by the invasions of the Assyrian-English.
Paternally – or paternalistically – the former enemies of the Welsh
now wield political power over them for their own spiritual good.
Now that the sheepfold has been enlarged to contain both sheep
and shepherds, the true wolves come from outside in the shape of
the spiritual pollution whose source is Rome.

The Orosian-Eusebian vision sees all temporal power as
coming from God. Many centuries later, in a small town in rural
Wales, we find Charles Edwards expressing the same tradition of
theological historiography:

And so I say to the Welshman who has been set free, according to the charge which Christ gave to the sick man who was healed – *Behold thou art made whole; sin no more, lest a worse thing come unto thee.* The will of God is revealed in this age.[53]

The deuteronomic vision looks fundamentally toward securing the existence of a future: in the eyes of Edwards, the workings of God have ensured that the past glories of the ancient Britons will have continuation in their descendants, but henceforth on a superior, spiritual plane rather than on an inferior material one. In Edwards's spiritualizing vision, there are more than distant echoes of Plato and Origen:

> This is Charles Edwards' explanation of the history of Wales, the small nation which never succeeds in gaining earthly self-rule but which nevertheless receives divine favour. Wales is the present day Israel, a powerless historical nation which adopted the warrant of glory to come.[54]

As long as Wales keeps to the terms of the covenant, the survival of the Welsh nation is secure – in English, Protestant hands. Charles Edwards's vision of the ideal Welsh nation is reserved for some future existence. Whether this is material or spiritual glory or both is not made clear. Gildas suggests that it is in the life of the monastery, a remnant within the remnant, that the true Israel will survive, materially as well as spiritually. Edwards's ambiguity might allow us the opinion that he could be dreaming of a future, intra-historical realization of the national dream. But the degree of prophetic gloom that his book expresses, along with Edwards's religious and political anglophilia and his spiritualizing apocalyptic tendencies, all point to a Wales whose national vocation is to be fully realized outside time and place. Considerable ambiguity lies in the nature of Welsh spiritual excellence: is this a *pars pro toto* understanding of national election? Or is Edwards constantly looking over Offa's Dyke, eyeing greener pastures and responding to the parlous state of the Welsh nation through what Isaiah Berlin defines as 'pathological exaggeration of one's real or imaginary virtues and resentment'? At the end of Edwards's great national address to his fellow-countrymen, all the verbs express an uncertain future:

Let us be gracious . . . And the nations surrounding us will know *that
we are not the border of wickedness, nor the people against whom the Lord
hath indignation for ever. But they who see us shall acknowledge us, that we
are the seed which the Lord hath blessed. And let us consider one another to
provoke not unto hate and evil doings, but unto love and good works. For
righteousness exalteth a nation; but sin is a reproach to any people.*[55]

Whether such a national vision is to take place in the body or
out of it, in this world or in the *eschaton,* is probably in the end a
question irrelevant to Edwards. He is sure that, if the Welsh obey
a God who has done great things for their nation in the past,
there will be a place of some sort in the future for the Welsh to do
great things for Christ, and vice versa. Godliness is the 'onlie
begetter' of any sort of national survival and eminence.

The vineyard

The deuteronomic perspective, prophetic postures, the use of
biblical typology applied to Wales, and the Wales-Israel paradigm
in Welsh spirituality have all long outlived Charles Edwards. But
the history of themes of both place and national identity in Welsh
spirituality is that of the underground river. Neither the material
place of Wales nor the spiritual meaning of nationality – and
certainly not the holy places of the country – were among the
concerns of early Welsh Methodism, whose piety tended strongly
towards the personal and the eschatological, though it did also
include an awareness of the need for national renewal. We would
look in vain for manifestations of these themes in, say the hymns
of Pantycelyn or Ann Griffiths. Yet by the mid-Victorian period,
the current of religious nationalism had begun to rise to the
surface again, with the beginnings of a secular national consciousness, fuelled by influences from German Romanticists such
as Herder. We cannot spend time exploring the many rich
Victorian recreations of the myth of Welsh holiness, other than to
pause to note the survival of biblical typology: in the pedestrian
poetry of the nineteenth century, paradise is sometimes described
as antetype of the Welsh Sabbath, a relationship which substitutes
a temporal for a locative notion. The image of the land of Wales-
as-paradise began to gain particular currency with the 'discovery'
of the Welsh landscape by English painters in the second half of
the eighteenth century.[56] The Romantic understanding of the

land of Wales was fostered by such poets as Islwyn (William Thomas, 1832–78), and is present in the image of Wales carefully promoted and nurtured by the educationalist, writer and cultural entrepreneur O. M. Edwards, who handed such ideas on to generations of Welsh schoolchildren.

We must press on, however, to 1936. In the interval between two trials for his part in the first modern political protest in Wales, Saunders Lewis[57] was commissioned by the BBC to write a radio play on the age of the saints. Lewis's *Buchedd Garmon* is a remoulding of the visit of St Germanus of Auxerre to Britain – an event referred to by both Gildas and Charles Edwards – in which the bishop organized resistance against the Pelagian heresy. The play is set precisely during that period when Romano-British civilization – and along with it, orthodox Christianity – was under threat.

In the centuries which lay between Charles Edwards and Saunders Lewis, Wales had been transformed from a rural, largely monoglot society to an industrial economy where, in the words of J. R. Jones, the number of those footholds where land and the Welsh language interpenetrated had seriously declined. From the turn of the century, a secularist Welsh mentality had begun to develop: the roots of Welsh socialism were initially religious and Welsh-speaking, but by the 1930s, church-going was already on the decline, and the internationalist mentality and the values of the British state both considered the Welsh language as an irrelevant anachronism and an impediment to material progress. The uncertain survival of the Welsh nation and the parlous moral state of the whole European civilization as it geared itself up for war are reflected in Lewis's play. The offence for which he was tried was the symbolic gesture of burning down a Bombing School of the British (*sic*) Royal Air Force, built despite many protests on a site of great cultural and religious significance for the Welsh.

In the familiar union of national and ethical consciousness, Lewis's action had been a moral call-to-arms, as much a prophetic gesture as a political protest. Lewis's belief that the basis of civilization is tradition is deuteronomical in its foundation: in the cultural glories handed on to us from the past we find the meaning of the present and make a future possible. Thus the preservation of the memory of the past is essential to national survival. Lewis's vision of Welsh tradition, most signally of the literary tradition, is that of one unbroken chain – with something in it of apostolic succession. Writing on the links between a domestic poet of the 1770s and the first great epic poetry in Welsh, composed around the time of Gildas's death, Lewis comments:

> There is I think something essential in the development of Welsh poesy. We call it the literary tradition of Wales. It means you cannot pluck a flower of song off a headland of Dyfed in the late eighteenth century without stirring a great northern star of the sixth century. And all the intermediaries are involved.[58]

That Lewis applies his notion of literary tradition also to the spiritual tradition of Wales is evidenced by the high point of *Buchedd Garmon*, in which Ambrosius eloquently expresses the *pietas*[59] due towards one's country, and invites the bishop to join in the military battle against the Pelagian Saxons:

> God's Prince
> A certain man planted a vineyard on a fertile hill
> Dug it and planted it with the noblest vines
> Enclosed it and raised a tower in the middle and gave it to his son
>   as an inheritance
> To maintain his name from generation to generation.
> But a herd of swine rushed in on the vineyard
> Smashing its enclosure, to trample on the vines and devour them.
> Is it not right for the son to stand in the breach
> And summon his friends to him,
> So that the breach may be closed and his inheritance saved?
> Germanus, Germanus,
> Wales, my country, is a vineyard given into my care,
> To be handed down to my children and my children's children
> As an eternal inheritance
> And see the swine rushing upon her to despoil her.
> I too now, call upon my friends, lay and clerical,
> Join me at the gap, stand with me in the breach,
> So that we may retain for the ages to come the beauty that has been.
> And this my Lord, is the vineyard of your beloved:
> the clearing full of faith, from Mary's church to Mary's church.[60]

Any reader of Gildas and Charles Edwards will immediately recognize the register of Lewis's language: Wales is addressed with the imagery of Israel. An exegesis of this speech alone would provide us with many scriptural resonances and parallels with and allusions to Gildas and Edwards. But there is also a sense in which Lewis has moved the tradition on somewhat, for here 'Wales' is fully as much a *place* as a society. Lewis's Catholic sense of sacramentality leads him to give full weight to the physical reality of Wales as a value in itself: as in Gildas, the land of Wales is imagistically described by Lewis as a sanctuary. This speech is probably one of the most eloquent evocations of Wales as *place* in the whole of the Welsh literary tradition. But let us note carefully the implications of Lewis's typology. In patristic literature, Naboth's vineyard is seen as *typos* of the *Church*. Here, however, it is the nation and the land of the nation, which is the God-given inheritance. Lewis's conception of Wales as inheritance is usefully illuminated by Brueggemann's comments on inheritance as a land ethic. On the concept of Wales as vineyard and as a 'clearing full of faith', we should remember Jonathan Z. Smith's idea of place in Israel as a 'strategic hamlet', a place of meaning and shelter surrounded by potential hostilities. Eliade's division of sacred and profane is also relevant here. In the image of Wales as vineyard, Lewis is stressing the need for boundaries, proposing a strict separation of Wales. It is both an ontological recognition of the fact of inherent national distinctiveness, and a call to take up the responsibility of making that distinctiveness incarnate, at both spiritual and political levels. Here, as in Old Testament Israel, material, social and spiritual significances of place meet together: it is the land of Old Britain (for which Lewis's listeners were invited to read contemporary Wales) which is holy, of religious import for its significance in the life of the individual and of the nation. Here Lewis's evocation of the place of Wales approaches the understanding of J. R. Jones and Simone Weil concerning the nation in Chapter 3: both land and nation are macrocosms and prime media of the cultural and religious senses which are the only source of human meaningfulness. The whole national territory of Wales is worthy of defence – just as was the site at Penyberth in Llŷn, a microcosm of Wales symbolically defended by Lewis.

Lewis is not proposing here an other-worldly pietistic Welshness in the line of Edwards. Rather, it is precisely because of the perennial call to an *incarnate* holiness – to be followers of the incarnate Lord – that the nation is now called to take direct political action. All political action however, if it is to be valid, is to be undertaken in the light of the tradition of God-oriented, moral and civilized living. Lewis's writings are the latest layer of a palimpsest: the struggle of Naboth against Jezebel, of the Britons against the Saxons, of culture against ignorance, salvation against damnation, Welsh pacifism against English imperialism, are all part of the same pattern, in which the whole is visible through the various strata. Just as each part of the Welsh literary tradition evokes the whole, so the internal, moral landscape and the battles in the field of cultural and religious endeavour are the same, though the names in the story may change. A constituent part of Lewis's vision of Welsh traditions is that of the poet, who acts not only as prophet, but also as priest. Through the power of the poetic imagination, the processes of history are identified, distilling and transcending time, and providing a sense of place and national identity.

Ambrosius Aurelianus's speech has subsequently assumed its own independent existence, having been adopted by two generations of Welsh nationalists as their poetic credo. Its theological complexity and its moral aspect have often been undervalued, with the resultant tendency somewhat to sacralize the land of Wales, depriving it of any more than a summary transcendent reference. This is to neglect the element of human responsibility incumbent on the receiving of divine gift, making Wales into faith without works. As we have seen, to live on the land without a sense of divine transcendence and judgement can lead to two opposed consequences: (1) worship of the land itself, and its social analogue of worship of the nation which lives there, and (2) an ignorance, wilful or otherwise, of the social implications of land – the aestheticist-individualist tendency, and its close relations, colonialism and imperialism. To attribute essential and unconditional holiness either to Wales or to its people would be repellent to Lewis's Christian sense of nationalism. Equally as significant in Lewis's vision are three lines which Germanus speaks prior to the 'Vineyard' speech, often excluded when the Vineyard speech is quoted out of context:

For on us has fallen the day for defending,
the day of the twofold defending,
The day for building Christianity, and maintaining the frontier.[61]

The two aspects of building Christianity and maintaining the frontiers of national separateness meet and intermingle throughout the history of Welsh spirituality and indeed Welsh literature, and have their deepest sources in the Old Testament and the theology of late Antiquity. In his essay on the influence of the Bible on Welsh literature, Derec Llwyd Morgan concludes that

> Our literature has been essentially Christian, and our spiritual consciousness and our literary imagination have been largely dependent on one another. Even now, our literary imagination is still soaked in religion, even unconsciously, in its patterns of seeing and speaking . . . Since the strength of the relentless imagination which the Welsh people and the Welsh language have suckled from the Bible is so exceptionally powerful, it is doubtful whether there can be in Welsh, ever, a purely secular imagination.[62]

And, in the light of what we have seen in this chapter, I would argue that the same holds true for the whole of historical Welsh national consciousness.

Conclusion

Our long journey has taken us from sixth-century *Britannia*, via the British Wales of the Restoration, to twentieth-century Wales. This pattern is in itself witness to the extraordinary sense of continuity of Welsh tradition. Historically, it is possible to find the sources of Saunders Lewis's 'Vineyard' speech, written in 1936, in ancient Near Eastern ideas of the sacred and the profane; in the Old Testament; in the typological method of Eusebius; in Orosius and also in Augustine, and even in Origen; in the political understandings of the relationship between church and state in the Christian empire of Constantine and his successors; in Gildas, whom Lewis consciously and artfully evokes, and especially in the work of Charles Edwards. What we have seen in this chapter is the persistence of an idea or an image through the centuries: it is this which makes tradition.

I have used the metaphor of a river to describe this tradition, but perhaps a better suggestion is a musical analogy. We might think of a theme which is worked and re-worked in different ways to respond to differing needs – the growing Christian church under the late Roman empire, the perilous situation of a distant colony of that empire, the spiritual and moral state of the descendants of the citizens of that colony in the seventeenth century. The melody is still heard in pre-war Europe, and continues in a modern politicization as a popular Welsh air up to and including the end of the second millennium AD.

Uniting all these periods in time is the image of divine election, the covenant between God and a people. But this union of times also has the effect of associating together the people and places which it involves. The result of all this is that in some, theologically oriented sense, twentieth-century Wales *is* at the same time both itself and also Israel, the first expression of God's creation of nations. Given the influence of the Bible on Welsh literature, it can be argued that the essential, imaginative geography of Wales is at least that of a holy land, if not the Holy Land itself. For J. R. Jones, interpenetration describes the relationship between the land of Wales and its language. The language also incorporates its biblically inspired literary imagination into this relationship:

> This totalizing Biblical influence has been very great in our literature. In the modern period, it is religious literature from root to branch, and it is not surprising that its main readers should see themselves as a spiritual Israel living in Bethlehem and Carmel, whether in Carmarthenshire or in Caernarfonshire . . . If those who had undergone a religious revival saw themselves as a spiritual Israel, others, before and after the Methodist revival of the eighteenth century, sought to identify Wales and Israel in a more comparative, or even essential way.[63]

The internal workings of much of the literary and political traditions of Wales have been patterned, unconsciously and consciously, on its religious tradition. In the experience of many nations, the membrane between political and religious experience is always at least semi-permeable, and images and metaphors are transposed from one plane to another, with curious, and sometimes tragic and violent results. In Wales, this river has issued sometimes into strange seas – notably the linguistic and even racial suggestions of Charles Edwards. At its worst, Welsh Israelitism runs the risk of ending up as Cambrian Zionism, a secular and exclusivist nationalism which identifies place *tout court* with nation and justifies political action with a summary reference to God.

Although a strong thread links Gildas with Saunders Lewis, Welsh understandings of national and religious identity inevitably evolved fundamentally over the millennia, particularly with the subsuming of Wales into England and the birth of 'Great Britain', and the gradual spread of Protestantism and especially Nonconformist spiritualities. Political union tended, it is true, as we have seen in the case of Charles Edwards, to transfer Welsh national identity to a religious register. But with the rise of Nonconformism and the concomitant plurality of denominational allegiances, what began to bind the Welsh nation together was an increasing consciousness of their common national identity, made manifest especially in language. However, the lack of concrete political, secular manifestations of such national identity tended to maintain the quasi-religious national identities of the Wales-Israel and Wales-as-Church paradigms. And, it might be argued, spiritualizing attitudes such as these might well have colluded in the perpetuation of the political status quo.

When we look at the Welsh spiritual tradition concerning place, an opposite dynamic seems to be at work, particularly with the gradual rise of an explicit political nationalism over the last century and a half. Under the influence of German Romantic transcendentalism, writers of the last century and of this have sometimes erred towards the other extreme, tending to attribute intrinsic holiness to the land of Wales, making it into an end in itself, where according to Islwyn, 'mae'r oll yn gysegredig'[64] (all is sacred) – a theologically problematical assertion.

Old Testament notions of the sacred as separation from the profane have often informed Welsh spirituality and understandings of both place and national identity. Yet a *pars pro toto* understanding, of holiness as engagement with and for the sake of the world, is similarly part of Welsh traditions. I would wish to argue that a healthy relationship between the spheres of the secular and the religious, and a balanced sense of national identity are greatly assisted by a strong, incarnate sense of Church. Similarly, an experience of a generalized holiness of place is intellectually illuminated by the concept of sacramentality. A theologically cogent explanation of the potential holiness of place can be found in the actual sacraments of the Church, in which there takes place *par excellence* an interpenetration of the material with the spiritual – without any commingling or change or division or separation.

It might be thought surprising that the category of sacramentality might be found in a discussion of the Welsh spiritual tradition, as influenced as it has been over the past few centuries by Nonconformist Protestantism. Yet I believe that a sacramental understanding both of place and of nation is another of the currents flowing through the Welsh spiritual tradition, variously under and above ground. The following chapters of this book introduce us to the writings of Gwenallt and Waldo Williams, in which these streams rise to the surface again. As we will see, from the treasure chest of their literary, spiritual and political traditions, these two very different householders take out things old and new: sacraments and sacramentality, Church and nation, the people and place of Wales, all humanity and all places.

5

A kingdom of priests: Gwenallt

The Welsh literary tradition contains many different literary genres, and a corresponding number of possible roles for the poet. The *bardd gwlad* (the local poet) is often one who has received his craft by tradition rather than academic instruction, who has his pulse on the instincts of the society from which he comes and of which is he is a part. Lending his words and craft to celebrate those things and events which are important to them, the image-making of the *bardd gwlad* helps to maintain a community's sense of social identity, and its sense of unbroken tradition. In twentieth-century Wales, in questions of national identity, of Wales considered as place, and of individual places within Wales, David James Jones (1899–1968), known in Wales by his bardic *nom de plume* Gwenallt, is the most eminent of national poets, his own poetic role being that of *bardd gwlad* not so much to localities, as to the whole of the nation. T. S. Eliot noted that Yeats was one of those few people whose personal history is part of the history of their own time, and who are so much a part of the consciousness of an age that it cannot be understood without them.[1] A similar historical significance may also justly be attributed to Gwenallt, since his poetry expresses many of the most representative concerns of Welsh-speaking Christians of the earlier part of the twentieth century. Gwenallt's work expressed and developed a particular image of national identity and a sense of Wales which continues to affect national spirituality and politics.

To characterize Gwenallt only as *bardd gwlad* does not do him justice, for there is in his work much that is informed by academic study of literature and theology. Moreover, Gwenallt's poetical discussion of place and nation includes insights which are applicable to a wider commonwealth than Wales. Within the Welsh spiritual tradition, Gwenallt's most distinctive note is his wide-ranging sense of sacramentality and his interest in the Church. To questions of both nation and place Gwenallt's sacramental spirituality has much to offer.

The poet

In the same way that the history of twentieth-century Welsh spirituality cannot be understood without Gwenallt, Gwenallt himself cannot be properly appreciated without some notion of the background from which he emerged. Brought up in the Glamorgan industrial village of Alltwen, Gwenallt had intimate, first-hand knowledge of the life and landscape of the industrial Wales of the southern valleys, a face of Wales often ignored by rurally focused Welsh writers or despised as an anglicized aberration: the idealized Wales of O. M. Edwards, for example, with its cultured peasantry, is fundamentally rural. Many of Gwenallt's poems deal specifically with his particular industrial social background, revealing it, too, to be 'place' just as fully as areas of natural beauty. Through his family connections, Gwenallt had frequent and close contact with that other, rural Wales – the life, landscape and deep religious and cultural traditions of Carmarthenshire, where time-honoured patterns of life and death which respected the dignity of the human person were still in existence at the beginning of the twentieth century. Gwenallt's poetry constantly plays out in tension between two images of Wales – a besmirched, demoralized Wales of industrial Glamorgan, and rural Carmarthenshire, a *Wallia Pura* of cultural purity and of perennially deep spiritual values. In both areas historical and symbolic values of land and society coincide.

In the rich cultural and political atmosphere of the industrial valleys, the young Gwenallt had come under the influence of the atheist Rationalist movement. Political convictions, tinged with the pacifism of certain strands of Calvinistic Methodism, along with a burgeoning nationalist sensibility, led him to register as a conscientious objector during the First World War. This stance led to his imprisonment, an experience which left deep scars upon him, but which was, in the words of Saunders Lewis, 'the crucible in which the poet was born'. Another crucible, of molten metal, had been responsible for his father's early death in a cruel industrial accident, an incident which only served to deepen

Gwenallt's hatred for the dehumanizing tendencies of industrial capitalism. Although many of his poems celebrate the dignity and the humanity of the workers of industrial society shining through the humiliation of their working and living conditions, God for Gwenallt is essentially a God of the countryside.[2]

At Aberystwyth, Gwenallt studied Welsh and English literature, becoming exposed to a wide range of literary influences, notably Pascal and the French Symbolists. Importantly, he was a member of the second generation of poets whose conscious awareness of the whole of the Welsh poetical tradition came through academic study. Although through his rural and industrial roots Gwenallt had been brought into contact with the remnants of the riches of the popular bardic tradition of poetry, he shares an academic background with such writers as J. E. Daniel and J. R. Jones. Yet despite the richness of his imagery and his evident scholarship, there remains in Gwenallt's poetry an earthy and easy rustic tone.

A journey to Connemara in the 1920s to study Irish opened Gwenallt's eyes to the significance of national tradition, something which he had found missing in Marxism.[3] Embracing political nationalism, Gwenallt also turned back to Calvinistic Methodism, now recognizing in it those spiritual and cultural values which had previously been obscured for him by its pietism and its unwillingness to apply the principles of Christianity to the national dilemma and to the social concerns of the workers of the south Wales valleys. This cultural and religious rediscovery is the background to his first volume of poetry, *Ysgubau'r Awen* (Sheaves of the Muse) of 1939.

His return to Calvinistic Methodism was not the last stage of Gwenallt's spiritual and intellectual pilgrimage. Exposure to Romantic poetry convinced him of the value of symbol and image. During the middle period of his life, Gwenallt turned for spiritual succour to the Anglican Church in Wales: *Eples* (Leaven) of 1951 and *Gwreiddiau* (Roots) of 1959 are both witnesses to a strong interest in the liturgy of the church. It is in the poems of this period in particular that Gwenallt displays a notable sense of sacramentalism. At this time also he read widely in Catholic theology, but his repugnance at the alien ethos of the Catholic Church in Wales, Catholic teaching on birth control, along with a Catholic tendency to abstract truth into dogmatic formulas all kept him away from the embrace of Rome. The similarly uncomfortable English atmosphere of the Church in Wales and its refusal to espouse pacifism finally caused him in the last years of his life to abandon Anglicanism and to return to the society of the Calvinistic Methodists. Gwenallt's spiritual and national vision is a synthesis of the different insights with which the different stations of his religious and intellectual pilgrimage provided him. Bobi Jones notes that in Gwenallt's work we find a particular combination of sacramental worship, Methodist emphasis on religious experience, and Calvinist thought,[4] all of which are applied to his ideas on Wales and Christianity.

In a final period of failing health and waning creative powers, Gwenallt continued to write: *Y Coed* (The Trees) of 1969 is a posthumous volume of poetry, much of it written as a result of a pilgrimage to Israel. For the most part, the writings of this last book, especially those which deal with Israel, are discursive reflections, almost prose; and we are left with a tranquil Gwenallt in old age, a prophet whose fierce image-making power has almost burned out, and yet whose commitment to his ideals remains.

The poems

In the thirty or so years since his death, a number of Gwenallt's most political poems have continued to be read, memorized and recited in Wales. But as with Saunders Lewis's 'Vineyard' speech, the specifically Christian element in Gwenallt's work has often been ignored or toned down, its demagogic tendencies felt to be old-fashioned, and incompatible with modern, secular Welsh nationalist philosophy. The biblical prophetic stance which inspired Gildas and Charles Edwards continues in Gwenallt's work, a prophetism as political as it is religious. The anger which powers the most vituperative of his nationalist invective is also directed at the hypocrisy and moral degeneration of contemporary Wales.

Gwenallt's poems are as challenging as they are inspiring, and their author has been described variously as the greatest of Welsh nationalist poets, the greatest of national Jeremiahs, a sacramentalist, a writer with a Catholic viewpoint, a radical and a conservative. To make a selection of the work of any poet is automatically to interpret, a process which runs the risk of setting up a David James Jones of history against a Gwenallt of faith, making a Gwenallt in one's own image, or looking for resolution of tensions where there is none to be found. Most critics would agree that Gwenallt is essentially a poet of Christian Welsh nationalism, and as such he is placed firmly in that deuteronomic mode of Welsh literary tradition, in which appellation to the light of a glorious past serves to illuminate the decay of the present, seeking to awake both guilt at neglect and remedial action to correct the lack of personal and social responsibility. For Gwenallt, as for Charles Edwards, the past is of itself a value, a type of holy place. The contrast is between a civilized and domesticated past, a *kosmos*, in which life was according to God's commandment, and a present which is moral wilderness. The existential difference is often spatially presented, in a pattern of 'now is x where once was y':

> The earth was once so near
> As near as a neighbour, and it spoke the dialects of Welsh . . .
> In the inaccessible fastness of the mountains,
> We built a lodging place for angels between two worlds.
> The earth has been turned into a giant laboratory . . .
> No longer does it speak the homely tongue of man.
> Pylons now where angels were,
> And concrete damming up the stream.[5]

If for the classical deuteronomic vision, time is an agent of divine revelation, for Gwenallt time acts inexorably to bring decay. The theme of loss of place and identity is most notably expressed in 'Rhydcymerau'. The dramatic divergence of worlds, past and present, the social and religious values of lost neighbourhood of his ancestors' lands – compulsorily purchased by the British Government for afforestation – and those of the political system and values which justify legalized acquisition of land, engenders great prophetic anger in Gwenallt. At heart are two attitudes towards land – land as place, carrier of meaning and belonging, and land as space,[6] in which land is a mere commodity – and these attitudes are also existential and religious creeds. In biblical terms, this is the struggle of Naboth versus Jezebel. Indeed, Gwenallt's longest published poem, 'Jezebel ac Elias', directly identifies Jezebel with all forms of imperialism and dehumanization. Belden Lane's dictum that 'sacred place can be tread upon without being entered. Its recognition is existentially, not ontologically discerned' applies to all places threatened by such processes. For Gwenallt, as for the Western Apache, place is intimately connected with states of awareness and social identity: against essentialist understandings which claim that places inevitably evoke similar reactions in all, Gwenallt insists that the identity of the observer is a key element in a sense of place. Different observers will interpret localities differently, and act according to their perception. Thus, in 'Rhydcymerau', an idealized, rural Welsh past has yielded to an anglicized, decadent present. Both occupy the same position on the map, yet they are not the same place:

> And by this time, there's nothing there but trees,
> Impertinent roots suck dry the old soil:
> Trees where neighbourhood once was,
> And a forest that once was farmland.
> Where was verse-writing and scripture is the South's
> bastardized English.
> The fox barks where once cried lambs and children,
> And there in the dark midst,
> Is the den of the English minotaur;
> And on the trees, as if on crosses,
> The bones of poets, deacons, ministers and teachers of Sunday
> School
> Bleach in the sun,
> And the rain washes them, and the winds lick them dry.[7]

Place and past come together in a way which is more than merely symbolic: the place which was Rhydcymerau has been physically and morally replaced by the faceless rows of trees, in an anti-place. Both the cultural past and the landscape in which it was enshrined have vanished for ever.

The polarization of values is strong and evident, allowing for no compromise or dialogue between them: the anglicized, materialistic, dehumanized and deracinated present, is weighed in the balance and found wanting against the past, associated with a good, rural way of living, with Welshness, with cultural and religious activity and with ancestral belonging to place. At this point we might remember Eliade's strict separation of the two spheres of the sacred and the profane, a polarization which is present in the Old Testament understanding of holiness as that which is separated out. Precisely the same understanding of holiness as separation is found in the works of Gildas and Saunders Lewis, along with the same existential need to preserve boundaries between the worlds of the sacred and the profane, and a concatenation of binomial political and cultural oppositions. Eliade's concept that being only properly belongs to those who live in contact with the *axis mundi* applies to Gwenallt's Carmarthenshire, a location in which the sacred sphere of the past can still irrupt, via the poet-priest's image-making, into the present consciousness of his readers.

But it would be reductive to present Gwenallt merely as a lamenter of inevitable decay. His prophetic stance, it is true, suggests pessimism and bitterness. But as in the case of the biblical prophets, denunciation of the present in the light of the past functions to provide the possibility of a future, and this biblically inspired dynamic informs the whole of Gwenallt's work. By telling the truth of the present, Gwenallt hopes to set his nation free in the future. Exactly how this will happen Gwenallt does not explain: he is more Jeremiah than Nehemiah and, unlike Saunders Lewis, is no politician with a concrete policy.

Biblical influence in Gwenallt's work goes far deeper than prophetic stance alone. The chapel-going, hymn-singing culture in which Gwenallt was brought up was as equally permeated by the language and imagery of the Bible as was Gildas's world. Throughout the whole of his life, he was an avid amateur student of theology. We should not be surprised to find therefore many consciously sought biblical references and resonances in Gwenallt's work. He does not shrink from a propagandist's application of biblical images to present political realities. The modern crisis of Wales is seen in biblical terms, familiar biblical terminology used emotively, morality being the common ground between religious and political concerns. In 1963, the Welsh valley of Cwm Celyn with its scattered Welsh-speaking communities was, despite widespread political protest within Wales, compulsorily purchased to provide a new reservoir for Liverpool. Gwenallt added his voice to the general indignation.

> The Goliath of money arose in Liverpool
> To shame and despoil the people.

> Come, David, with your stone from the river,
> And God behind your sling,
> To keep the hymns of Capel Celyn
> . . . from the murderous water's of the devil's dam.
> Capel Celyn will not have an empty graveyard,
> Nor will home and crops and song and harp
> Be buried under the dam of the uncircumcised giant.[8]

Expressing variously anger for his nation, and at it, Gwenallt places biblical and national characters shoulder to shoulder, in a combination of scriptural and secular references. Modern Wales is 'a remnant' who

> Like Isaac . . . will draw up the clay from the pits,
> The clay put there to choke the Philistines, the rich dairy
> farmers,
> The establishment men, the tail-waggers and the traitors
> of every kind;
> And we will dig in the mountains for the running
> fountains,
> The fountain of Moses and the Maccabees, the fountain
> of Glyndŵr and Emrys ap Iwan,
> And the fountains which issue from the grace and salvation
> of God.[9]

Imagistic transparency between Wales and Old Testament Israel places Gwenallt here in the Wales-Israel spiritual paradigm. Recalling Hosea's and Ezekiel's denunciations of Israel's political and religious infidelity in terms of prostitution, Gwenallt's Wales is a similar figure, whom 'we swore at and whipped,/Calling you a pain, a bitch and a whore'.[10] The nation is more than merely the sum of the individuals who currently compose it: it has a temporal existence which spans the generations. In a series of poems each called 'Cymru' (Wales), the nation is addressed as a person:

> You, the filthy street prostitute with the servile voice[11]

> Your old freedom is a sword in our hand.[12]

> Your saints are an excellent company[13]

> Forgive us if we have been too heavy-handed with you.[14]

Out of these poems, a portrait of Welsh national identity emerges. Like Israel, Wales is capable of great infidelity to God and to her own identity, and both infidelities involve and are expressed in each other. In line with all the Welsh writers which this book studies, Gwenallt holds that only fidelity to Christian values can safeguard the political survival of the Welsh nation. In 'Ar Gyfeiliorn' (Lost), he calls upon the Virgin Mary to guide 'our stubborn ship to one of God's harbours',[15] – applying the ecclesiological *typos* of Peter's barque to the nation of Wales, in an image which evokes Wales as Church.

The interests of the Wales-Israel paradigm tend towards claiming spiritual pre-eminence for the Welsh nation, a stance which does not consider the universal, anthropological role of nationality. If Gwenallt subscribes in some of his poems to this instinct, his insights on the importance of all nations witness to an interest in the wider, theological issues of national identity. He places on the lips of St David his conviction that the nations are part of divine creation. The nation, as part of God's ordinance, is a constituent part of this vision of the world considered as *liber naturae,* revelation of and participation in divine goodness. To God alone corresponds the right to create or destroy a nation: political subservience of one nation to another and gradual cultural dissolution of national identity are viewed under the prism of morality, as sinful acts of idolatry against

> . . . God's natural law.
> The person, the family, the nation and the society of nations,
> And the Cross which prevents us from turning any of them into
>   a god.
> He said it was God who made our nation
> For his own purpose,
> And were it to disappear, creation would be blemished.
> Anger showed on his brow
> As he whipped us for licking the backside of the English
>   Leviathan,
> Letting ourselves be turned, in his Christian country into
>   Pavlov's dogs.[16]

If the nation is divinely ordained, then it follows that the language which is a constituent part of national identity is in some way a response to the same mandate. The religious-political concern applies especially to the fate of the Welsh language, signal mark of national identity. In the case of Welsh, the translation of the Bible into Welsh has graced the language, making of it a vehicle of transmission of the Good News, 'giving it dignity and highest honour, making it one of the dialects of God's Revelation':[17] the irruption of the sphere of the sacred has made Welsh into a holy place. Visiting the church of the Pater Noster on the Mount of Olives, Gwenallt gives thanks for finding there the Lord's Prayer written in Welsh, among eighty-four languages:

> Welsh in the Church on the Mount of Olives,
> The greatest privilege she ever received.
> Thanks be to God for Welsh,
> One of the most Christian languages of Europe,
> One of the dialects of the Trinity.
> Its vocabulary is the Nativity;
> Its constructions are Calvary;
> Its grammar is the grammar of the Empty Grave;
> Its phonology is Hosanna.[18]

That the Welsh language, as language of religion, has been consecrated by contact with the Scriptures is an insight which is hardly original to Gwenallt, given the link between religion, language and nationality in Wales. His assertions evidence the abiding ambiguity in the Welsh tradition concerning the relation between sacredness and Welshness, centred around the issue of election and notions of holiness, national distinctiveness or national distinction. Does 'Welsh is the language of heaven' assert that nationality has a religious referent? Or does it imply a spiritually superior, elect status for the Welsh nation? At its heart is the theological problem of the distinction between holiness and divinity. The fact that nationality has a religious referent, or that a place is regarded as a holy place, demands clarification of our understandings of holiness and how it is located in intramundane realities.

Two biblically informed dynamics are at work in Gwenallt's notion of national sanctity: the Wales-Israel tradition, with its preference for divine transcendence, for questions of time and for the nation, and a more Catholic notion, with a preference for immanence and place. The Wales-Israel tradition operates largely through a deuteronomic vision of time interpreted as history, as an arena in which the past has a meaning and pattern which may be discerned and used to interpret the present. It is to the past that Gwenallt constantly returns for inspiration, in an effort to guide his people. In a television broadcast for St David's Day in 1953, Gwenallt stirringly preached, in an outflow of patriotic-Christian rhetoric, that

> Wales is a Christian inheritance. In her lie the dust of St David and the early saints, the dust of monks and the abbots of the Middle Ages . . . of Ann Griffiths and Pantycelyn and Emrys ap Iwan. Our duty is to hand down to our children the inheritance which we have been given, a heritage of preaching the Gospel of the Son of God, of praying and taking action, and of making Wales a society based on Christian moral principles.[19]

The deuteronomic vision fundamental to the Wales-Israel tradition stresses responsibility: the possibility of a future depends on the moral action, in our own here-and-now, of individuals who have inherited the traditions of the past. Gwenallt shares the anthropological conviction that individual human identity is fully realized only when a person is inserted in a network of family, neighbourhood and nation – a process which may be described as interpenetration of the spheres of individual and society. This relation is neither abstract nor static but rather one which is intra-historical and dynamic, allowing for the possibility of sin as a result of freedom of choice in human action. Gwenallt's anthropology, in its awareness of the dimensions of sin is of an Augustinian intensity: the nation, considered corporately as a moral person, is affected by sin, just as much as its individual members.

> The soul is so bare, the naked unclean-ness.
> The primitive mire is in our poor material
> The slime of the monster in our marrow and our blood.[20]

This essentially pessimistic version places its centre of interest largely in human action. But Gwenallt's poems also express a second, more faith-filled dynamic at work: one which gives the nation assurance of the indwelling of God and of salvation already achieved, if only inchoately. This is the concept of salvation achieved obscurely, a vision of hope with its centre of interest in divine presence. Here, as in the Catholic-local, and the Wales-as-Church strands of Welsh spirituality, the emphasis is on divine immanence, rather than on human or divine action. Even in the primeval forest of sin, grace abounds:

> We discover through the branches a piece of Heaven
> Where the saints sing anthems of grace and faith,
> The Magnificat of his salvation;
> Like wolves we lift up our muzzles
> Howling for the Blood which redeemed us.[21]

As in Israel, so for Wales there can be reconciliation to God and to its own truest nature, a resurrection which is both spiritual and political. The nation is not beyond redemption:

> We see you, Wales, with the dull eyes of faith
> Once flourishing in your beautiful virginity,
> The candle of kings, the star of a free people.
> . . . Have mercy on her, most merciful Father,
> Give us strength to raise her up, then we will robe
> Her body in the robe of all her glory.[22]

Such bridal imagery applied to Wales evokes the whole Old Testament constellation of Israel's relationship with God, involving prophetic denunciation and consolation, and expressed in the figures of the bride of the Song of Songs, the bride of Psalm 44 and the pregnant virgin of Isaiah. Similarly present in this typological imagery are New Testament female figures, from the Samaritan woman, the woman caught in adultery, Mary of Magdala and Mary of Bethany to the Church of the Book of Revelation, as Bride of Christ itself. The rich panoply of ecclesial imagery is applied to the Welsh nation, Gwenallt vesting Wales in chasuble and stole, out of considerations which are essentially religious but which have political repercussions.

In his application of New Testament imagery to Wales, Gwenallt differs significantly from the mainstream of Welsh spiritual writers. Here, Wales appears as Church. Whereas the Wales-Israel tradition raises problems concerning the exclusivity of national election, the Wales-as-Church offers us keys to a specifically Christian spirituality of national identity and one of more universal import, based as it is on a more inclusive model.

In identifying Wales with the Church, in a way rather different from Gildas, Gwenallt is inserting the nation also within the order of Christian redemption, grace building on nature. For Gwenallt, Jesus' specific nationality is part of the essential humanity of the Incarnation, an insight similar to that of Duns Scotus who understood history as being part of the Incarnation. God chose to become part of history, a limit like gender, language, and culture. The logic of the classical christological argument that what was not taken up into the Incarnation is not saved offers two possibilities: either nationality has a religious remit or it is an exclusively secular reality. But to exclude Jesus' national identity from the Incarnation effectively sins against the third of the Chalcedonian adverbs. That God took flesh in a specific place and at a specific time argues moreover that the specificities of time, place and national identity are a necessary part of all spirituality deriving from the Incarnation. Thus, for Gwenallt, if each individual Christian life is to be truly incarnational, then it must also be aware of and engaged with the specific place, time and nationality in which it finds itself, a process which involves insertion in culture and history. Owning a nationality, and taking appropriate responsibility for one's nation, is for Gwenallt part of what it is to be authentically Christian.

Insofar as the Church – at least in Catholic theology – mediates and is mediated by its sacraments, it is itself a sacramental reality, one in which the world of time partakes of eternity, and the physical world is joined with the world of the spirit. Moreover, as mediator of grace, the Church has a remit to the world around it, to which it is inseparably connected, but with which it is not identical. A sense of the sacred based on a radical separation and a national identity which derives from this model do not do justice to the New Testament sacramental idea of holiness, in that they tend to leave unanswered the relationship between the sacred and the parts of the secular world where the sacred has not irrupted. In biblical terms, we are left with the task of elucidating the relationship between Yahweh and the Gentiles, and the nature of time which is not included in salvation history. A Christian sense of the sacred realities of the world is better described as a universally engaged relationship, in which holiness, centred essentially in the person of Jesus Christ and ministered *par excellence* through the sacraments of the Church, is found in various forms and intensities also in the world outside the formal limits of the Church. Showing a sacramental, Catholic sense that the whole matter of creation – which includes Wales – has been transfigured by the Incarnation and the paschal mystery, Gwenallt's theology offers us a Wales which is holy not by virtue of any unconditional spiritual pre-eminence, but as a sign of the potential holiness of all nations and places:

> And the Holy Spirit nested
> Dove-like in your branches.
>
> Poets heard in Wind and breeze
> His cry of sacrifice, His gasp of pain,
> And in the middle of your forests
> The Tree of the Cross was seen.
>
> His resurrection was your springtide
> Your summer was His green salvation,
> And in the winter of your mountains
> He raised tabernacles of grace.[23]

This is a deuteronomic vision which is encouraging, rather than critical, a reminder of blessings received. Although all the verbs are in the past tense, there is a sense in which this tender vision of a Wales transformed and penetrated by the Incarnation offers a vision of hope for the present.

The Wales-as-Church model of spirituality suggested by Gwenallt's imagery is congenial to inchoate notions of sacramentality of the nation, which may be found in earlier Welsh writers. For J. R. Jones the function of the nation is that of being the medium of meaning and identity – values which are essentially spiritual, but which are incarnate in a specific group of people in a specific place. They exist in tension with the spiritualizing tendency of the Wales-Israel paradigm to consider the Kingdom – and along with it, the Welsh nation – a purely eschatological reality. Bobi Jones eloquently summarizes what he refers to as Gwenallt's 'sacramental nationalism':

In the same way as God becomes incarnate in a human body, in the same way as he expresses the Godhead in creation, in the same way as the Holy Spirit works in individual souls, thus also in Wales, in a specific place . . . a specific expression of God at work crystallized . . . Through that closeness, the wide world is reached, and indeed the cosmos. The character of Wales has been transformed by the One who is beyond all time and place but he has done this within place and time. The picture we get is one of a country where the gospel has been a penetrating presence and God has shown how he can touch personally the earth here. It is as if God has reminded his creation that it is his locality. In this way, the nation like many other nations, is similar to a sacrament – an object in which God embodies himself.[24]

The sacrament, like the symbol, embodies a profound ambiguity and polyvalence, uniting both divine and human actions, amongst which we must include the political. Avoiding the spiritualizing tendencies of the Wales-Israel tradition, Gwenallt's earthy, sacramental spirituality gives full attention to the material world. This helps to explain his appeal for non-Christian thinkers such as the Marxist Ned Thomas, who describes his own gradual espousal of nationalism:

In my mind was a doubt about the compatibility of socialism and nationalism. I do not mean nationalism in a strictly political sense, but as pride in traditional forms of Welsh life. The religious and puritanical element was a particular obstacle . . . Gwenallt is our national poet of the century not because he celebrates Wales but because he expresses the passions and tensions at work here, without leaving anything out. I am more sure of his greatness, because his eventual, religious synthesis is not my own . . .We come to something in Gwenallt – and in Wales – that both socialists and Christians can find hopeful. In reverting to Christianity, Gwenallt did not give up the fight for a better secular order . . . Gwenallt does not separate into religious and political periods and very often the two elements are there in the same poem . . . His religion and his rebelliousness fit a Welsh pattern which run together back into the Welsh past.[25]

As an expression of divine transcendence, the sacrament also contains within itself something of eternity, being therefore a sign and a medium of triumph over the entropic tendencies of time. As we have seen, J. R. Jones conceives of the nation as being a collective in which the individual, facing the enormities of eternity, may find a place of shelter, identity and meaningful existence. The deuteronomic traditions we have seen at work from Gildas to Saunders Lewis illustrate that the present and the past can be bridged and time transcended via an awareness of national, religious history. The identifying of providence at work in history means that time, rather than being the agent of chaos, reveals itself as the medium and arena of divine action, providing security and direction. And since wherever God has trod becomes consecrated by contact, then all time becomes, at least potentially, holy time. Throughout the works of Gwenallt, these ideas are repeated in a rich synthesis, with an emphasis on the contemporary sacramental significance for the individual of the history of the nation to which he or she is bound: 'The religious past of Wales is not an illusion or a ghost, nor are its religious traditions dreams. That past is a substance and a truth and a living spirit.'[26]

In discussing the nation as 'sacrament', I use the term with considerable trepidation, and in an applied sense only, fearful of the danger of a sort of 'pan-sacramentalism' which runs the risk of denying the specificity of the sacraments of the Church, and of dissolving the autonomous value of creation. The potential error here is that of 'commingling', the first of our Chalcedonian nouns, of blurring the boundaries between the divine and the natural to the extent that we end up with a *tertium quid* which does not honour the value of the material or the natural or the human. Clearly, if a strong sense of the religious import of national identity and a sense of holy place can both be important humanizing influences, they also have a shadow side, in disequilibria of understanding and the actions which derive from these. The potential dangers of the Wales-Israel tradition include imputing unconditional holiness or predestined spiritual preeminence to the Welsh nation, a stance which approaches the nation-worship that critics of nationalism fear. Brueggemann alerts us to the idolatrous or imperialistic dangers of imputing any unconditional transcendence to place, for fear of a similar idolatry. Does the Wales-as-Church tradition offer any guarantee against such theoretical and practical deviations from the ideal?

Although it is true that Gwenallt often rigs out the nation in the vestments of the Church, there is another understanding of the relationship between sacred and the secular to be found in his work. If for J. R. Jones awareness of national identity answered the existential 'crisis of meaninglessness' of the twentieth century, for Gwenallt, especially in his poems of the middle period, it is the Church, which provides a stronghold of order and meaning amid the potential chaos of time and place, and the specific cultural difficulties of this age. Gildas's understanding of the Church and the monastery as *praesens Britannia* is not so far away from Gwenallt's understanding:

> When the stars oppress our flesh
> And the terror of our ancientness is in the skies,
> She raises up a fortress where our poor spirit
> May flee to her, at night, and bend its head.
> And there we lay by Your feet
> The burden of our sinful smallness,
> The humble fragility of flesh and blood,
> And the fear of your strange creation.[27]

As a historical reality, the Church provides a place of shelter and meaning within time. In the calendar, Gwenallt sees God doubly at work within time, divinely given grace building on divinely given nature:

> But it is spring which is coming, yes, two springs to the world,
> From the depths on the third morning:
> The lily comes, the primrose and the daffodil
> Following the Redeemer, from the Egypt of the soil.[28]

Reflecting on the liturgy of the Orthodox Church in Cyprus and the struggles for Cypriot independence, Gwenallt understands the political life of a nation – itself part of the God-given natural order – as being taken up into the paschal mystery. Gwenallt understands that in the liturgical, sacramental actions of the Church eternity is made present and the spiritual made concrete. Here, three different orders of time are united together in a dynamic synthesis: the cyclic time of natural seasons, time as the platform of God's salvific actions through Christ and in the liturgy, and political history. Divine ordinance is the element common to all, to the effect that all time – including the history of a nation – is perceived as the sphere in which God lives and moves. Once again, the Eusebian-Orosian vision of history-as-providence asserts itself in modern Welsh spirituality:

> From the light behind the altar every candle is lit,
> And taken to light up again the candles on every hearth,
> re-lighting street, square, vineyard and graveyard
> . . . They will dance, leap and feast
> When another dawn rises on their island;
> The dawn of the birth of the nation
> A dawn red with their blood,
> Blessed by the Bishops of the Church.
> Two dawns,
> The dawn of grace and the dawn of the nation.
> Blessed are they.[29]

Jonathan Z. Smith holds that the liturgical cycle of the Church itself functions as a temporizing of what was originally a locative system. In the development of the liturgy in Jerusalem,

> two different temporal systems were fused – an ahistorical system of salvation (Lord's Day, Pascha and Pentecost) and a historical system of commemoration, memorialization and recollection. Temporality guaranteed replicability. Liturgies tied to particular places in Jerusalem could be expropriated and exported. The sense of time, the story, have allowed a supercession of place.[30]

Another understanding of liturgical action, however, would see it as the expression, within certain times and places, of the potential holiness inherent in all places. The function of liturgical sacramentality therefore is to be a sign of the *potential* sacredness of all places and times. One of the particular emphases of Eastern Christian theology is that, in the Incarnation and the Resurrection, all matter is transfused with spirit, and thus all intra-mundane history and all place become inexorably transformed by their connection with eternity. Insofar as the Incarnation is the model of interpenetration, the sacramental liturgy of the Church, understood as the continuation in all times and all places of the Incarnation, expresses and channels this interpenetration:

> There is no boundary between two worlds in the Church;
> The Church militant on earth is one
> With the Church victorious in Heaven
> And the saints are in both churches, which are one.

The saints, our oldest ancestors,
Built Wales on the foundations of
The Cradle, The Cross and the empty grave.[31]

In line with much of patristic theology, for Gwenallt it is the
specificity and solidity of the Incarnation, extended into the
matter of the sacraments, and beyond and through them, which
makes *all* matter and places, especially the most ordinary,
potentially holy:

> He was imprisoned by His flesh and his Jewish bones
> Within the limits of his country,
> And he gave them as living boards to be hammered on,
> And they were raised from the tomb, despite the guarding,
> By his Father, as a catholic body.
>
> And now Cardiff is as near as Calvary
> Bangor every inch as close as Bethlehem.
> The storms are calmed in Cardigan Bay
> And on every street the madmen may be healed
> As they touch the hem of his garment.
>
> He did not hide his Gospel in Judaea's clouds
> Beyond human tongue and eye,
> But gives the life that will last for ever
> In a sip of wine and a piece of bread,
> The gift of the Spirit in drops of water.[32]

Gwenallt's interest in the liturgy of the Church is a distinctive
contribution to Welsh spirituality, and enriches an appreciation of
the sacramental nature of national identity. An understanding of
the sacraments of the Church, in their relation with the surrounding world, as the source and the distillation of a more generalized
holiness, allows us to set the spheres of sacred and secular, in an
interpenetrative, perichoretic relationship. Applying the notion of
liturgical sacramentality to national identity, nationality is revealed
as divine gift and human action in response to this. Among the
practical advantages of a close – but differentiated – relationship
between ·Church and national identity is that it circumvents the
dangers of turning national identity into a surrogate religion, or
religious allegiance into a merely social identity. Put simply, a

strong, sacramental understanding of Church and a strong sense of material, embodied national identity help to maintain necessary boundaries, and by clarifying the relationship between political and religious spheres, strengthen a sense both of national identity and of Church.

The concept of sacramental liturgy also illuminates and refines a spirituality of place. Since liturgical spaces are sacred place *par excellence*, fitting into several of the phenomenological typologies indicated in the first chapter of this book, then what Gwenallt implies through his poems invoking the liturgies of the Church also has import for a spirituality of place. In the worship of the Church, this world intersects with the transcendent world, and the present with the past.

> There was only a wall between the Saviour in the Chapel
> And the Creator of the world outside it.[33]

In that the Church is a unity of spiritual and earthly realities, its materiality is the very wherewithal by which the transcendent is glimpsed. Functioning in the same way as icons in Eastern Christian traditions, the Church acts as a window on to the eternal:

> On All Souls' Eve
> The veil between two worlds is so thin
> That a series of faces is seen on it, one after the other . . .
> Amongst them, two faces are particularly clear;
> Two faces, two industrial women from the South
> Two faces who now are shining and grace-filled
> Praising their Sustainer in heaven,
> Who held them firm in the widowing fire
> And in the dust and flow which broke their breadstaff.[34]

If, as I have suggested, the Church's sacraments are the maximum, intense expression of a generalized sacramentality of the created world, then in Gwenallt's works we can posit a similar relationship: between the liminality of the Church considered as sacred place and a more generalized, potential openness to the transcendent, which is shared in by all places, beautiful and commonplace, Carmarthenshire and Glamorgan. Among these, Gwenallt considers the holy places of rural Wales:

I walked to the early world crossing the Pembrokeshire border.
In a sheltered corner by the sea,
between the rocks and the prehistoric layers,
I saw the saints setting out in their boats for Ireland or Gaul.
The silence of St David's has been purified and hallowed
    through the centuries,
So that airplane, train and car are a blasphemy there.
And let us bless God for the privilege of having his Gospel in
    Wales
Stunningly new, anciently old.[35]

Places outside Wales may also serve to reflect something of this. Oberammergau, like Carmarthenshire, is a place of a traditional, rural way of living. This way of life is a model or ideal which we are called upon to perpetuate or to make present and real in the specific circumstances of our lives. But significantly, Oberammergau is the place where the Passion is staged, the Easter mystery represented, as in a sacrament:

Its land had no industrial resources,
For the ass-eared Mammon to raise up
And establish the banks' modern civilization
On coal tips, scrap heaps and hovels.
Forests and family farms were there,
And rural crafts, centuries' tradition behind them,
That tradition rendered supple to meet all needs.[36]

Amongst the virtues of sacramentality is that of permitting the possibility of apprehension of the transcendent with and through human physical senses. Gwenallt's starting-point is the goodness of the world, a tenet which complements the assertion of J. E. Daniel that, although God has forbidden us to worship the nation, this does not mean that we may not love it. In his well-known sonnet, 'Cnawd ac Ysbryd' (Flesh and Spirit), Gwenallt teaches that

God has not forbidden us to love the world
Nor to love mankind and all its works,
To love them with all our naked senses
Every sight and colour, all words and voices:
Our blood will be rounded out when we see the traces
Of His skilful fingers in the roundness of creation.[37]

Such a relationship of love means that the eternal and transcendent has the possibility of becoming familiar and intimate by means of the physical. The perception of holiness reveals itself to be closely dependent on the ability of the perceiver to recognize it. The perpetual potential closeness of the transcendent, discoverable in even the most unlikely of places, is at the root of Gwenallt's image-making, in which he undertakes a prophetic role of identifying divine presence in the apparently secular world. Belden Lane holds that sacred space is ordinary space ritually made holy: through their Sunday prayers and worship, the coal miners of Alltwen are raised up as in an elevator in a mine-shaft from the depths of their daily lives to the fresh air of heaven, their liturgy being a participation in the worship of the angels. Just as ordinary time becomes sacred through the practice of praise, the places where praise occurs become holy: the homes of the workers are the meeting-place of the divine and the human, at once both fully secular and fully sacred, in a Welsh manifestation of St Gregory of Nyssa's dictum that 'all places represent Jerusalem':

> Their children and their friends were miracles;
> The home was Christianity and culture;
> The human family, civilization.
> . . . That home in Nazareth
> Was a home like our homes here.
> A worker's home, so the Word tells us.
> Thank God that the Messiah was a workman
> That a craftsman died on the Cross
> That Mary was a workman's mother.[38]

Despite Gwenallt's predilection for the rural and the antique, he understands that industrial and domestic homeliness can become the locus of sanctity even in the midst of dehumanized industrial society:

> I saw David travelling from country to country like a gypsy of God
> The Gospel and the Altar in his caravan;
> . . . On the steelworks platform he put on the visor and the blue
>   shirt
> Showing the Christian being rendered pure
> like metal in the furnace.

He brought the Church to our homes,
Put the Sacred Vessels on the kitchen table
And got bread from the pantry and rough wine from the cellar.[39]

Together with praise, social intercourse renders material reality translucent to the world of the divine, rendering what might be experienced as space into place. The worlds of religion and daily life are inseparable from one another:

Through their unrural paths the saints walked
To Salem and Zion, morning afternoon and evening,
Seeing the tips transformed in sun and rain
From diamantine shine to total aridity.
Birth, marriage, living and dying humanized this place:
Play and love and religion civilized its ways.
In truth, they have become beautiful for us through human transit,
Turned fresh and green by all life's experiences.[40]

Gwenallt's *œuvre* may be seen as including a prophetic challenge to those spiritual – and spiritualizing – traditions in Wales which have historically undervalued the religious importance of place. There is no doubt that, for Gwenallt, the geographical reality of his country is potentially sacramental, and that holiness shines forth in specific places. The physical realities of Wales, the material element essential to Wales's sacramentality, interest him greatly, but they are places which are interpenetrated with the life of a specific people. In the whole country of Wales, as in specific locations within it, the holiness of the lives of the past have made the land holy, consecrated by contact. As Jonathan Z. Smith asserts, 'The shared history of generations converts the land into the Land of the Fathers.'

The dust of all the saints of the ages
And the martyrs lies in your bosom;
It was you who gave them breath,
And you who took it from them.[41]

The relationship between place and people is interpenetrative, and the land derives its holiness from the holiness of the lives of those who have inhabited it over the generations. As a quasi-sacrament, in some way Wales contains the possibility of sanctifying the lives of those who currently inhabit it – on condition that they are aware and capable of interpreting it in the light of the religious and cultural tradition and inheritance handed down to them. In the above stanza, Wales is addressed, and it is noteworthy that here it is the country – symbolizing God as in the typology of Ellen Ross – rather than the nation which functions sacramentally, dispensing life. Does this imply that the land itself somehow contains essential spiritual qualities?

> It was Wales who gave this Cardiganshire man his morality
> She who lifted him up from the devilment of sin;
> It is difficult to walk any of the paths of Wales
> Without coming up somewhere against God.[42]

In such assertions as these and, indeed, throughout his poems, Gwenallt is not applying a systematic theologian's precision. Nevertheless, such poetic insights have their own theological value, in that they express a collective – and therefore, in the terms of J. R. Jones, an objective – experience of place. If the land is guarantee of morality it is because of its associations with the Christian past and tradition of the nation. In the poetry of Gwenallt, the country of Wales is symbol and *anamnesis* of God's action in Wales in the past. It therefore sacramentally unites symbolic and real senses of land. A land-ethic and land-awareness, typical not only of biblical Israel, but of modern indigenous peoples, survives quietly in the Welsh tradition. Gwenallt's Carmarthenshire finds interesting sympathetic resonances in far-away places:

> The Apache landscape is full of named locations where time and space have fused and where, through the agency of historical tales, their intersection is made visible for human contemplation. It is also apparent that such locations, charged as they are with personal and social significance, work in important ways to shape the images that Apaches have – or should have – of themselves . . . Apaches view the landscape as a repository of distilled wisdom, a stern but benevolent keeper of tradition, and an ever-vigilant ally in the efforts of individuals and whole communities to put into practice a set of standards for social living that are uniquely and distinctively their own. In the world that the Western Apache have constituted for themselves, features of the landscape have become symbols of and for this way of living, the symbols of a culture and the enduring moral character of its people.[43]

In the names of Apache locations are condensed universes of meaning. Similarly, the Old Testament concept of name is that it encapsulated something of the essence of that to which it refers, Yahweh's name being held to be so holy that it could not even be uttered with impunity. Many of Gwenallt's poems follow the ancient Welsh poetic practice of naming specific places and people: 'Rhydcymerau' names the Carmarthenshire farms of his ancestors, now swallowed up in the English forest. Such an *anamnesis* has a liturgical quality, the poet-as-priest representing the past. Lane notes that 'sacred place . . . becomes recognized as sacred because of certain ritual acts that are performed there, setting it apart as unique' (*Landscapes of the Sacred*, 15). If ritual is understood as a mechanism for maintaining the order of the cosmos, then naming places in Wales can be seen as a quasi-liturgical function of the poet-as-priest, an act which maintains a sense of nationality, and which symbolically prevents the places of Wales from degenerating into mere space.

Glamorgan and Carmarthenshire are the two poles of Gwenallt's personal symbolic universe. In the case of Glamorgan, the human values which remain after the evaporation of the Marxist dream are similar to those which he finds in Carmarthenshire: 'family and neighbourhood, man's sacrifice and suffering'.[44] His Christian optimism allows him to see the possible fusion of the values of these two worlds: recognizing on the one hand the pietistic spiritualization of chapel religion, and on the other the reductionism of Marxist materialism, Gwenallt offers a wider Christian synthesis which includes and transcends both the pietism of Calvinistic Methodism and the political traditions of the valleys. In his vision, the material and the spiritual are united, in a coincidence of opposites:

> The span of the Cross is wider by far
> than their Puritanism and Socialism,
> and there is a place for Karl Marx's fist in His Church;
> farm and furnace live together in His estate,
> The humanism of the coal mine, the godliness of the country,
> Tawe and Tywi, Canaan and Wales, earth and heaven.[45]

Yet balance between 'earth and heaven' is elusive, and the nation-church, in which Canaan and Wales frequently become confused, reasserts itself. In 'Llywelyn our last Prince', writing of the place where the last Prince of Wales was killed by the English in 1282, he hints at a more tangible, permanent and objective connection between history and place. If there is potential ambiguity about Gwenallt's attitude towards places, then there is evident ambiguity over the linguistic and theological registers employed in his most strident patriotic voice. Here the national political hero is transferred to the pantheon of the communion of saints of a civil religion. The familiar image of Wales as shrine appears, the place hallowed by the blood of a national martyr:

> He bled to death like a pelican of disaster,
> And independent Wales with him . . .
> We come today like an army to the place in Cilmeri
> Where not one bone of our Prince remains;
> But here is his blood, and the blood of his Wales,
> The Wales of St David and King Hywel and God.[46]

Gwenallt does not apply constant theological precision to this theme. That the Christian saints of the Welsh past should also be seen as national heroes is not surprising, at least in a Wales-as-Israel paradigm. An interesting ambiguity surrounds the nature of Gwenallt's saints: they are at once the 'saints' of New Testament and Welsh Nonconformist parlance, the community of believers, who may or may not be gifted with individual holiness. But they are also the official – and non-official – saints of the Church triumphant, whose holy lives have made the places they inhabited become, by association and contact, correspondingly holy. Throughout the work of Gwenallt, there is continual reference to such a communion of saints, personal, national and ecclesial, uniting the past with the present, and the family and the nation with the Church – a *communio* whose ranks are filled with political as well as religious heroes. Insofar as the functions of the canonized saints (in the Catholic usage of the word) include acting as models and inspiration, then, given the moral remit of the nation, there is much of value in national saints. Theological tradition sees the Church triumphant in heaven as the fulfilment of the Church militant on earth. Yet amongst the side-effects of Gwenallt's commingling of Church and nation in his vision of Wales-as-Church is that both the embattled Church on earth and embattled Wales have their fulfilment in heaven alone. A truly incarnational national identity proves a difficult prize to gain.

On his visit to modern Israel, Gwenallt came face to face with the Holy Land *par excellence*, with multiple levels of awareness and significance: the biblical places which, through scripture, hymns and literary tradition, were part of Gwenallt's imaginative universe; the contemporary concrete reality of those places; and the modern Zionist state. Gwenallt admires the fact that, for the Israelis, a sense of place functions to make unity out of the different levels of the palimpsest of national consciousness. In Israel as in Wales, the memory of a nation serves to incarnate the whole of its tradition, history being made present, quasi-sacramentally, by means of an awareness of the past.

> It is a nation which has kept its past,
> Its faith and its old traditions.
> Its land today is as it was centuries ago,
> Its sun historical, its lightning and wind.[47]

For Gwenallt the interpenetration of memory with specific location is the means by which the identity of the Jewish people is anchored. Land is a mnemonic of the past, and from the security of that association national survival is made possible. Being intimately connected with their future, the question of place bears for the people of Israel, ineluctable political repercussions:

> Though so old, the history of the Jewish nation is so new,
> Some twelve months past David was placed in his tomb,
> And three months past
> Judas Maccabeus conquered his nation's enemies.[48]

In the Welsh-Israelite tradition, Israel is typologically connected with Wales. It is reasonable therefore to extrapolate from Israelite and Israeli experience the significance of places in Wales for Gwenallt: repositories of memories for the whole nation, guide for the present, guarantee of the future. Moreover, the specific places of Wales – considered as social and geographical realities – anchor in geographical reality a Wales which continually threatens to evanesce into a memory of a golden past or a dream of a splendid future. Gwenallt's poetry variously draws from the Welsh-Israelite notions of election, and from a *pars pro toto*, New Testament model of Church, but in both cases, his is a nationality with a fundamental religious aspect. Belonging, like the Church, to the spheres of both nature and grace, creation and redemption, the nation is portrayed as divine gift and human challenge. The specific responsibility of the nation of Wales is to be incarnate in the place of Wales, consecrated to the service of God in his sanctuary:

> God chose you for his handmaiden,
> And called on you for witness;
> And He inscribed His Covenant
> On your doors and on your doorposts.[49]

Yet Gwenallt realizes that there must exist within Christianity a perennial tension between placedness and placelessness, between intramundane history of which nationality is a part, and eternity. A fully realized sense of place has an inseparable religious aspect, but its various material and transcendent elements must be held in balance. If place functions as an icon, then an important element in the experience of a sense of place is that of being led into contemplation of the transcendence which that place expresses. In the poems of *Y Coed* the Gwenallt of old age finally considers that transcendence to which placedness points. It is, he says, 'the Supper which is important, not the place'.[50] An excessive concentration on the materiality of place or holy place can lead to neglect of that transcendence to which they point, with practical repercussions: reducing the interpenetrative union of spheres to a plane in which sacred and secular are confused one with another, a spirituality of superstition; deifying holy place, a spirituality of idolatry; or ignoring any transcendental reference whatever, an anti-spirituality of commercialism, colonialism or imperialism.

> It is natural for Christians to make beautiful the holy places;
> But let us not forget the stable of old,
> The animals' dung on the straw.
> We were pilgrims there; sinful pilgrims;
> Important sin; distant sin.[51]

Belden Lane teaches that 'the impulse of sacred places is both centripetal and centrifugal, local and universal. One is driven to centredness, then driven out from that centre with an awareness that God is never confined to a single locale' (*Landscape of the Sacred*, 15), an insight which is similar to that of the poems of *Y Coed*. Gwenallt's final view of the holy places is realistic and catholic, underestimating neither sin nor the goodness of the world, and in such an elusive balance. Gwenallt expresses the ideal of both a sense of place and national identity, in which the specific is held in equilibrium with the universal, the placed and the historic with the transcendent and eternal.

Conclusion

Gwenallt's work varies widely in literary value; certainly some of his published poems are underworked, and tend towards the banal. Nevertheless, within the history of twentieth-century Welsh spirituality, Gwenallt gave poetic and prophetic voice to what have been widely held, if inchoate, convictions for many Welsh Christians concerning the relationship between their religion and their sense of national identity. This is the role of the national *bardd gwlad*. But does Gwenallt's work offer any wider, more universal interest?

This book opens with a discussion of the deeper theoretical issues which underlie discussions of place and nationality: the relationship between the particular and the universal, the sacred and the profane. Gwenallt's work invokes several of these problematic areas, not least the relationship between the religious and the social aspects of national identity, the nature and function of land in Wales, and the relationship between national identity and place.

Gwenallt's distinctive note in the Welsh spiritual tradition is, I believe, his emphasis on the Church and his sense of sacramentality. From a theological point of view, the Wales-as-Church image which appears in so many of his poems is potentially problematical. It contains several advantages: reminding Welsh people of the religious remit of nationality, avoiding a radical separation between political and religious spheres and introducing the element of morality into political concerns. Depending on precisely which notions of sacredness and which particular ecclesiology – missionary or introspective, sacramental or scriptural, dynamic or essentialist, inclusive or exclusive – it is informed by, it can offer us a universally engaged or a radically separated-out Wales. The great disadvantage of Gwenallt's model is that, just as much as the Wales-Israel paradigm, it effectively contradicts the first of the Chalcedonian adverbs, confusing nationality with religion, with all the consequent dangers. A sacramental notion of nationality has the powerful advantage of clarity, by illuminating how different elements, human and divine, may coincide. Questions of national responsibility and rights are also present in Gwenallt's poetry, the one or the other receiving differing emphases according to his poetic stance. His poems addressing the Welsh are generally essentially religious in nature, and in these, Gwenallt often employs a prophetic mode which stresses national responsibility. But the rights of the nation are also expressed by Gwenallt in the mode of Moses addressing Pharaoh. The poems in which Gwenallt speaks on behalf of, rather than to his nation contain more than a suggestion of a purely nationalistic use of biblical imagery. Bobi Jones points out that Gwenallt's religion and his politics often coexist in the same poem – and they are not always clearly distinguished one from another.

In his most theologically cogent poems Gwenallt expresses a consciousness of Church separate from but in intimate association with national identity. With this perception, Gwenallt frees us from the inherent danger of both Welsh-Israelite and Wales-as-Church paradigms: the tendency to maximize the historical and spiritual sense of Wales, but to underplay the significance of national or local land, in a compensatory national docetism. Gwenallt's contribution to the theology of nationhood is to place the nation within both the ambit of creation (nationality as gift) and the history of salvation (nationality as responsibility). Separating Church and nationality also thoroughly obviates the theological and political dangers of exclusivism, in that national identity is not patterned on an ecclesial model.

Gwenallt's sacramentalist understanding is based on an awareness of the potential translucence of human action and the material world to the sphere of the eternal. Such transparency is especially perceptible in holy places – and prime amongst these in Gwenallt's universe is the land of Wales. It is true that Gwenallt's *œuvre* contains many poems of particular places, but there is a sense in which the materiality and individuality of such places is less important than the fact that they are parts of Wales. The theological issue which thus remains unresolved is that of the universal and the particular: we are still left with the question of the relationship between the place of Wales, and the individual places which constitute it.

Gwenallt does, however, provide a valuable contribution to a specifically Christian consideration of place. Sacred place for Gwenallt is not related to a generalized and vague numinousness, but to the specificity of the Incarnation, the Passion, and the Empty Grave. The sacramentality of such places derives from and finds its fullest expression in the sacramentality of the Church, understood as the continuation of the Incarnation. It is this quality of specificity which is also part of the *human* value of place. Although the Incarnation has transfigured matter, and made all places potentially sacramental or at least revelatory, for Gwenallt, as for the majority of twentieth-century Welsh nationalist religious writers, places are sacred by virtue of historical contact with a *specific,* transgenerational community of people, and that sacredness is only fully realized when that close association is in operation.

Since it works within a Protestant theology in which holiness is generally perceived as non-mediated, the tendency of the Wales-Israel tradition has been to flee from attributing any holiness to place, for fear of the idolatry which arises in response to considering such holiness as essential and unconditional. Gwenallt, too, understands the holiness of the land of Wales as a derivation of the call to morality of the Welsh, and thus he lays emphasis on divine transcendence rather than presence, history rather than place. Sacramentalism and other elements of Catholic-local spirituality and *pars pro toto* understandings of nationality are major elements within Gwenallt's work but in constant danger of being dominated by his political sympathy for the Protestant Welsh-Israelite tendencies so closely associated with Welsh Nonconformism. To Saunders Lewis is attributed the comment that 'Gwenallt never really left the chapel', and to the extent that the literary and cultural tides of Wales carried Gwenallt back to his beginnings, it is a fair comment. The combination of sacramentality, Methodism and Calvinism which Bobi Jones identifies in Gwenallt's work is a risky recipe: potentially rich, but in danger of being indigestible. Yet if the lack of intellectual resolution makes Gwenallt's work less theologically cogent, it has the effect of making it all the more creative and complex.

Like the writers of the previous chapter, Gwenallt wrote to address the *ad rem* questions of his nation, the poet functioning as pastor. The Welsh-Israelite tendency tends to understand nationality in an exclusive sense, and so some of the output of Welsh writers could not unreasonably be accused of being introspective, concerned exclusively with local and national issues, and therefore of betraying a lack of any wider catholicity or universal relevance. But is a concentration on specific local issues necessarily inimical to and incompatible with wider theoretical issues and a more internationally minded constituency? The theoretical issue of the relationship between the particular and the universal remains a difficult one to solve. The Welsh *pars pro toto* tendencies of national understanding have already pointed us in the direction of a universally engaged local spirituality, but there is one twentieth-century Welsh writer whose combination of sense of local place and of country, of nationalism and universal brotherhood, stands as eloquent proof not only of their complementarity but their mutual necessity: Waldo Williams.

6

Apocalypse of tradition: Waldo

In Welsh-speaking Wales of the twentieth century, few writers have been more esteemed than the Pembrokeshire poet Waldo Williams. The general affection in which the singular person of Waldo is held, even some thirty years after his death, has always made critical evaluation of his work rather difficult. The critic Tony Bianchi points out 'the amazingly potent myth-making capacity of the contemporary Welsh-speaking community' – a deeply rooted historical tendency which has in its turn embraced Waldo.[1] Various critical responses have given us Waldo, *inter alia*, as the Christian humanist, as the poet with an awareness of original sin, as poet-preacher of the social gospel, as mystic, as *bardd gwlad*. More emotional personal and political responses towards Waldo's life and work made him into something approaching a patron saint for Welsh-language activists in the 1960s and 1970s. This, and the fact that J. R. Jones quotes Waldo's poetry in his discussions of the interpenetration of land and language, further illustrates that the historically intimate connections between spirituality, politics and literature which this book discusses continue to be a distinguishing feature of Welsh-speaking society in the late second millennium AD.

The proliferation of different critical Waldos is explained to an extent by the 'open', imagistic, non-dogmatic nature of his poetry, a comparatively slim corpus[2] which includes occasional and humorous poetry, as well as several major poems which are amongst the masterpieces of twentieth-century Welsh poetry. Accepting the inevitability of showing only a few of the many possible faces of Waldo, this chapter will concentrate on those poems which are most directly relevant to the themes of place and national identity in Wales. In his engagement with these issues, Waldo's poems show both continuity and discontinuity, tradition and innovation.

The singular nature of Waldo's life and convictions goes some way to explaining these similarities and differences. Son of a

Welsh-speaking schoolteacher father and an English-speaking mother of Welsh parentage, Waldo was born in 1904 into an English-speaking household, and brought up for the first seven years of his life in Haverfordwest in English-speaking south Pembrokeshire. His father's religious roots were in the socially radical Baptist traditions of eastern Pembrokeshire. A letter written to Waldo about his intention to seek baptism illustrates the influence of J. Edwal Williams on his son's religious originality and independence of thought:

> [Some people] have misunderstood religion taking it to be a thing of a day and a place . . . They take the sign for the real thing. These petty notions and narrow material aims have lowered the ideals of the Church and crippled its effectiveness for good.
>
> The Highest Religion I have had glimpses of is that which makes man a brother, Life a Sanctuary and the common deeds of life sacred by purity of motive. It makes a man sensible to the claims of justice upon himself and to all noble impulses. It also makes him lenient at heart to the failings of his neighbour through weakness.[3]

The family's move to the Welsh-speaking village of Mynachlog-ddu wrought a fundamental change in Waldo's life. In this society of farmers on the slopes of the Preseli Mountains the young Waldo discovered a new geographical world: one in which place and society were intimately connected in anciently rooted contact with the land. Equally importantly, through his schoolmates he learnt Welsh, entering into a new cultural universe of words, images and literary tradition. In this closely knit, mutually supportive community of strong religious and social traditions, Waldo found his spiritual home and the generative matrix of much of his imagery. While Waldo's family were living in this area, his elder sister Morvydd died at the age of thirteen, the first of the experiences of pain and loss which were to mark his life. Like Gwenallt, Waldo studied at Aberystwyth, but English literature, rather than Welsh, was his field. In his studies, Waldo came under the sway of the English Romantics; he also threw himself into the Welsh-speaking cultural life of the college. His early published work dates from this period, humorous poetry and prose already showing a delight in word-play and a mastery of language.

Periods of work as a schoolmaster followed. Soon, however, conflict with educational authorities over his registering as a conscientious objector led Waldo to move to Llŷn in north Wales. There, after a very short but intensely happy marriage, his wife Linda died in 1943. For a period of years Waldo taught in England – in Huntingdonshire, Chippenham and Lyneham, and it was during this period of exile that some of his greatest poetry was written. Returning to Wales in 1950, Waldo took up employment as an extramural lecturer, in order not to have his tax deducted at source (as was the arrangement with schoolteachers) and thus contribute to the militaristic policies of the Westminster governments. In 1951, he became a Quaker. The period of the Korean War and the Cold War and of continued military conscription in Britain – a practice which had struck Waldo as horrifyingly immoral – led him into practical protest. His refusal to pay tax led to his imprisonment on two occasions.

Waldo's political peripateia led him from an early sympathy for the religiously informed socialism to which the young Gwenallt had also been attracted, to a nationalism of a particularly internationalist flavour. In the independent Labour circles in which he moved as a young man, the religious radicalism of Nonconformism coexisted comfortably and sometimes merged with social radicalism, and consideration was sometimes given there to a measure of independence for Wales. Disillusionment with the post-war Labour government's failure to provide any recognition of the distinctive needs of Wales led many former socialists, including Waldo, to change their allegiance to Plaid Cymru. In 1947, the Labour government proposed evicting the people of Waldo's beloved Preseli Mountains and turning their homeland – one of J. R. Jones's 'footholds' of interpenetration between the land and language of Wales – into an area for military manœuvres. It is from this period that most of Waldo's most patently nationalist poems date – a period when he was still in self-imposed exile in England. Returning to Wales, in 1959 Waldo stood, unsuccessfully, as a very singular Plaid Cymru parliamentary candidate for Pembrokeshire. The end of conscription meant that he could return to teaching at the beginning of the 1960s. Failing health in Waldo's last years led to a stroke in 1970, and he died in 1971, mourned by many friends and admirers from all strata of Welsh society.

The poems

Waldo's avowed purpose in publishing *Dail Pren* was to be of practical assistance to his nation – a stance which evokes the poet and the mystic as national politician, in the line of Tagore and Gandhi. The poetry of Waldo Williams is a dense and rich landscape, containing compressed within itself a whole world. It is as elusive as those glimpses of otherness which landscape sometimes affords. At times, Waldo's language and beliefs can appear naive or even facile, but the process of becoming familiar with Waldo's world, a process which demands time, reveals unexpected riches. Like the Pembrokeshire landscape it invokes, it is full of strange light: the light which is the subject of Waldo's images, but also the light which his poetry sheds on notions of place and national identity, and the human condition in general.

Just as the poems of Gwenallt both reflected and created the history of his age, so Waldo too, as man and as writer, is part of his generation's history. There is a sense – to be fair and not to judge too harshly, only a sense – in which Gwenallt's religion is a function of his politics. In much of Waldo's work religious and political interest similarly coexist, but it would be more accurate to see Waldo's political concerns as expressions of his religious and artistic convictions and experience. Many commentators describe Waldo's 'mysticism'.[4] Whatever definition one offers of 'mysticism' – and there are almost as many as there are mystics – one can affirm at the very least that Waldo was a man of acutely refined religious sensibility, if not genius. Two major poems, 'Cwmwl Haf' (A Summer Cloud), and 'Mewn Dau Gae' (In Two Fields) describe intense spiritual experiences, but the entire corpus of Waldo's work is scattered with such classical religious *topoi* as inner light, and the essential unity of all things. First among Waldo's religious convictions is universal brotherhood, and the political stance of pacifism which inevitably issues forth from this:

> I believe all men to be brothers and to be humble partakers of the Divine imagination that brought forth the world . . . War to me is the most monstrous violation of this Spirit that society can devise . . . I believe Divine Sympathy to be the full self-realization of the Imagination that brought forth the world. I believe that all men possess it obscurely and in part, and that it has attained its perfect

expression in the life and teaching of Jesus . . . It tells us that oppression is not shortly to be eliminated from the world. It tells that it is the Christian duty to bear it patiently, whereby it is transmuted from its passive state into an active principle in the fight of good against evil.[5]

Despite his appeal to Jesus, to classify Waldo as a conventional, orthodox Christian would be to do him a disservice. Waldo's conviction that the Divine Imagination is to be found in all people is foreshadowed in his own father's set of beliefs, and found a natural home in Quakerism. Another major source of influence was his wide reading, particularly in the ideas of the Russian existentialist writer Nicholas Berdyaev that spiritual values are innately embodied in both the individual and in society. This deep sympathy for the common divine spark in all humanity produced poems on a wide variety of people, from Gandhi – whose pacifist activism he profoundly admired – to the Catholic martyrs of Elizabethan Wales.

Derec Llwyd Morgan's observation that the Welsh literary tradition is fundamentally Christian includes Waldo, despite his singular independence of thought. Waldo does not entirely escape the weight of the Welsh-Israelite application of biblical imagery to Wales, but it is especially the apocalyptic stratum of the Bible – the Book of Revelation in particular – which inspires his language, the very title of his one published volume, *Dail Pren* (Leaves of the Tree), deriving from Rev. 22: 2. Bianchi points out that Waldo's apocalyptic stance is not limited to a use of biblical language: rather, an apocalyptic attitude informs the whole of Waldo's work.[6] In his quarrying of scriptural material Waldo continues the Welsh literary-spiritual traditions, but the particular emphasis on apocalyptic elements, and his development of an apocalyptic universe, is part of Waldo's creative innovation within and rupture with those traditions.

The genre of apocalypse developed in the difficult political world of late Judaism, and although both New and Old Testaments contain apocalyptic elements, it finds its natural home in the literature of the intertestamentary period. Typical of the apocalyptic vision is disillusionment with the hope that the current world can provide salvation. Such is the difficulty of life that God is now felt neither to act through history – the prophetic vision of time-as-providence to which Eusebius, Orosius and Charles Edwards subscribe – nor even within history. Redemption therefore is reserved for some future existence. For the moment, the skies are closed, the membrane between heaven and earth remaining impermeable, with one exception: the apocalyptic seer's revelatory vision of the future, which provides sufficient hope and consolation to make the world habitable for the time being. The apocalyptic mode functions by the concept of diametrically opposed and conflicting powers engaged in cosmic struggle – in the biblical book of Revelation, the power of the Lamb and that of the Beast.

Given the ways in which Welsh-Israelite spirituality operates on a twofold embattled polarity – Christian Britain versus pagan Saxons, Welsh Christians versus the nationalism of the imperialist British state – it is not surprising that the hillsides of Wales should keep a welcome for the apocalyptic genre. Bobi Jones[7] notes that apocalyptism has a deep tradition in Welsh literature, spirituality and politics: over the centuries, the hope of a national redeemer and the coming of a golden age where goodness and godliness will thrive under the guidance of the saints has been a familiar and recurrent theme. Both Welsh national and Christian 'myth' function along the shape of A-B-A, in which the protological vision (Eden, medieval independent Wales, the land given) shapes the eschatological vision (Paradise, independent Wales of the future, the land restored) during a middle period of misfortune ('this vale of tears', political subjection, exile, the desert).[8] Between deuteronomy and apocalypse, however, lies a significant difference: the deuteronomic vision functions by an emphasis on the lost past, the difference between past fullness and the present decay urging the creation of a future understood as restoration. This is certainly a strong thematic strand in Welsh spirituality, and includes the vision of Gildas, to a certain extent that of Charles Edwards, of Saunders Lewis and Gwenallt.

In Waldo's apocalyptic stance, however, the future is conceived in terms of transformation and liberation. Hope in that future arises out of and as the only solution to current despair. It is an existential attitude, an act of will to choose to circumvent both fossilization through nostalgia and paralysis through fear, demanding instead a responsible engagement with one's own here-and-now.

Given the permeability of social and religious concerns in the Welsh traditions and in Waldo's own life, his evocative and shimmeringly ambiguous use of apocalypse should not surprise us. Waldo's long poem 'Y Tŵr a'r Graig' (The Tower and the Rock) fits well into the polarized model of apocalypse: the poem takes as its symbolic stanchions the tower of Roch Castle and Plumstead Rock near Waldo's home, which stand for a number of such struggles. Bobi Jones holds that

> the rock may be interpreted as the good and the just; Wales; the old and the rural; peace; the peasant . . . [whilst] on the other hand, the tower can be understood as meaning evil; the oppressor; England; the new and industry; war; and the upper class.[9]

The natural element of the rock, which Waldo associates with the *gwerin*, the peasantry of Pembrokeshire, suggests that the values of goodness have a permanent, time-transcending value. But one possible effect of such a concatenation of values, ways of life and nations is to associate Wales, whether as place or nation, *unconditionally* with goodness. Whilst this latent tendency is yielded to by some Welsh writers, it does not sit comfortably with Waldo's sense of universal brotherhood and his love for English literature. The Gospel according to Charles Edwards is fundamentally pessimistic. Waldo's universe is one in which the principles of good and evil are similarly embattled against each other, but with the assurance of hope. Whereas the Wales-Israel notion tends towards an exclusivist holiness – deriving an exclusivist national identity from this – in Waldo, a keen awareness of the fundamental cosmic struggle issues into a sense of identity which stresses common humanity, rather than separation. And since Waldo's vision does not function on an exclusivist understanding of salvation, then as Ned Thomas points out,[10] Waldo's hyper-ecumenical vision of universal brotherhood may find sympathy amongst both Marxists and orthodox Christians, humanitarian concerns being common to both.

Categories such as 'religious', 'mystical' or 'political' are often as misleading as useful when applied to Waldo. Certainly, Christian symbols and patterns are present in Waldo's poetry, but in the same way as Waldo reworked the symbols of earlier Romantic writers – mist, other-world, the search for a *locus amoenus* – religious referents are reworked and refined into a unique and personal symbolic universe which both continues and ruptures the Welsh tradition, taking it into territory which is both familiar and strange. God is rarely named as such, even more rarely Jesus – but addressed in such terms as Divine Imagination or Inspiration or Light, plus a plethora of more original epithets, in a stance which is at once highly personal and communitarian, in that it allows for access to and great freedom of interpretation to readers of differing ideological viewpoints.

Waldo's predilection for Romantic poetry goes some way towards explaining the polysemic nature of his symbolic universe. The nature of the symbol is that it allows for unlimited interpretation, containing a whole universe of potential meanings, each of which will depend on the interaction between the symbol and whoever perceives it, a process which allows space for contradictory interpretations to coexist. At heart is the concept of relationality: the creative interaction between the poet's imagining and the reader's response and the symbol itself, reveals the symbol's potential to be a distillation of meaning, intelligibility and order – in short, a *kosmos*. John Rowlands notes that

> [t]here is something attractively vague in Waldo Williams' use of abstract terms such as 'brotherhood', 'friendship', and 'knowledge'. He uses them in a way which is wide enough for both the Christian and the atheist to be able to respond to them. We can understand their significance intuitively, rather than theologically. [11]

Waldo's poetic style evokes the density of meaning which a symbol may contain. The syntax of Welsh, the style of Welsh classical poetry, and the literary tradition all allow for a compression of whole worlds of meaning in few words, a process which Waldo pushes to an extreme. *Cynghanedd* – alliterative consonantal chiming – creates a soundscape within each poem, analogies of the physical landscapes which they invoke and the symbolic landscapes of Waldo's imagination. Centre of this symbolic universe is Waldo's Preseli:

> Wall of my boyhood, Foel Drigarn, Carn Gyfrwy, Tal Mynydd
> Backing me in all independence of judgement,
> And my floor, from Witwg to Y Wern and down to the smithy,
> Where from an essence older than iron, the sparks were struck . . .

... For me a memory and a symbol – that slope with reaping party
With their neighbour's oats falling four-swathed to their blades.
And a single swift course, and straightening their backs,
Flung giant laughter to the sun, one cry in four voices.

My Wales, land of brotherhood, my cry, my creed,
Only balm for the world, its message, its challenge, shall be
  brotherhood alone.
Pearl of the infinite hour, a hostage to time,
Hope of the long journey on the short winding way.

This was my window, these harvestings and sheep shearings,
I beheld order in my palace there.
Hark! A roar and ravage through the windowless forest.
Let us guard the wall from the beast, keep the wellspring free of this
  beast's dirt.[12]

For the Western Apache, the physical landscape is the keeper
of a moral landscape. Likewise, for Waldo, the places of Preseli
both create and sustain 'independence of judgement', radical
freedom and unwillingness to subscribe to any dogmatic system
which would deny the human values embodied in the people of
Preseli – precisely those values which make 'space' into place.
With the mountains as walls, and the whole landscape as its floor,
Preseli is a homeland, a confirmation of Bachelard's observation,
that 'All really inhabited space bears the essence of the notion of
home.' In Waldo's poetry, the house is 'the great symbol of the
dependence of the temporal upon the eternal',[13] a symbol which
invokes Preseli as a harmonious and habitable place of shelter.
The whole of Wales is symbolically compacted through the prism
of Preseli.

The relationships between Preseli and the whole of Wales, the
Welsh nation and the whole of humanity evoke the question of
the particular and the universal. Nationalist and local consciousness might be thought surprising in a writer for whom universal
brotherhood is so crucial a part of his convictions. Yet for Waldo,
brogarwch (the love of one's native area) is the foundation of
gwladgarwch (the love of one's country). In this way, Waldo's
Preseli is an expression of the complementarity and connection
between the Catholic-local tradition and the Wales-Israel tradition. The love of one's own place and of one's country are in turn

the seeds and concrete expression of a universally orientated brotherly love: the love of place and the love of humanity are revealed as being intimately connected. Waldo's perception of his own homeland is a social and geographical one, that of human beings in accord with one another and with the land. A favourite theme of Waldo's is the beatitudinous connection between the rough starkness of the landscape and the often difficult living conditions, and spiritual and social richness: 'My nation is a poor one. She has been given fullness.'[14] In 'Ar Weun Cas' Mael' (On Weun Cas' Mael), Waldo addresses the land itself, seen as vehicle of human values and creator of moral living:

> In your own beautiful severity
> You awoke the favour of man to man.
> You brought their society to one accord,
> with your strength behind them.
> Their slow order
> flourished with no slavery.[15]

Preseli is described as 'my window', implying that insertion in such a society and landscape becomes the precondition for viewing the whole world as *kosmos*: from the security of such a house, of a sense of belonging to a specific society and place, it is possible to look on life as order, rather than chaos. Through the window of that society, Waldo glimpses something of heaven, 'order in my palace there'. Most of the poem exists in a timeless 'now', the secure world of the child. The last verse of 'Preseli' moves us into a different plane, expressing the passing of time and the potential crisis of meaninglessness now posed by the apocalyptic beast – who is neither named nor defined. Such a biblically worded dramatic call to action, to a national salvation based on human works, might be perhaps more expected of Saunders Lewis or Gwenallt. Despite its essential optimism, Waldo's vision is not eirenic: human action is a necessary expression of hope.

Waldo is described by many commentators as a poet of hope, his poems including many assurances that, come what may, all shall be well, at a time and in a manner we know not:

> The day will come when the small shall be great
> The day will come when the great shall be no more

The morning will come which will see only brotherhood
Gathering together the families of earth.[16]

Unlike classical apocalyptic visionaries, Waldo does not seem to suggest that this cosmic reconciliation will come uniquely via the actions of a *deus ex machina*. The implication of the value of Preseli, for Waldo, for its inhabitants, for Wales and for humanity, as guarantors of brotherhood, is that such places must be defended, actively. In the face of potential chaos and meaninglessness, hope is an existential attitude which demands affirmative, peaceful action as a means to sustain that very hope and order embodied in Preseli.

Although many Welsh writers have been happy to echo prophetic condemnation and consolation, fewer have been able to engage in the prophetic gesture, Saunders Lewis and Waldo Williams being eminent among this latter group. Waldo's sensibility led him to take his own symbolic and practical actions: registering as a conscientious objector when he was too old to have served in any case, standing as a Plaid Cymru parliamentary candidate, and refusing to pay taxes to a government which obliged Welsh soldiers to fight in Cyprus, and accepting a prison sentence – an experience which he claimed to have enjoyed!

'Tŷ Ddewi' (St David's) is the poem which probably best expresses the religious faith from which issued such prophetic gestures. The poem expresses a unity and continuity of faith, sustained in the expanses of time by the sense of belonging to one particular place, namely the geographical location of St David's ('David's house' in Welsh). The poem spans three distinct eras – the time of David, the Middle Ages, and the time of Waldo. David is portrayed as being intimately in communion with his 'house' – the place of his hermitage. Here, the world of nature and the world of grace come together in an evocation of Edenic, cosmic harmony, a sympathetic union of the world of timeless creation and of divine redemption which takes the intramundane world as its platform, salvation being coextensive with creation:

The insistent waves break on the shore,
And again with quieter voices, where they whisper.
'It is David', they say – their open lips
so loving around the name they love.[17]

Waldo places in David's mouth the assurance that the values of ancient pagan Celtic culture will survive and receive their fullness of expression in the new Christian faith, in a continuity linking the past of Wales with the present.

The second section describes the noise and busyness of medieval pilgrimage, but a mason, a craftsman-builder of 'David's house', expresses a desire for the original contemplative peace of David. The mason's desire for stillness and peace points not so much to a nostalgic return to the past, but to a transformed future:

> I behold yonder a city
> On Jerusalem's foundation.
> Let us go, beloved carpenters, and join her seraphim,
> Our hidden image will be made plain.
> Time and oppression will not penetrate there to cast us out
> From the youth cloisters of her holy temple.[18]

In each of the first two sections, the material world carries some transcendent reference – the world of nature remitting us to Christ, the world of artistic craftsmanship and inspiration pointing towards the heavenly Jerusalem. And both of these point to the third section where a window into this world of transcendence opens up as Waldo describes a mystical experience he underwent on Carn Llidi, a rocky outcrop which overlooks the whole area of St David's. The revised version of this section, published in *Dail Pren*, differs substantially from Waldo's original version of 1936, but in both versions, the central concern is the transcendence of time and the unifying of the past, the present and the future through the poet's vision.

The 'mountain', unchanged through the centuries and through the faiths, on which Waldo stands is the poem's symbolic centre of meaning. In the 1936 version, Waldo attributes to the mountain something more than symbolic value:

> You conceal in your heart a name
> for the true God unknown with the notes of men.[19]

Robert Rhys notes that in the original version 'Any dogmatic faith capable of defining itself in the terms of a confession of faith is rejected in favour of exalting natural objects, the river Alun and Carn Llidi mountain, as vehicles of the truth and as spiritual transmitters which God hears.'[20] There are within Waldo's work traces of attribution of inherent value to places, but the later version of the poem retreats from a stance of Romantic nature-mysticism (a vision which is essentially individual and individualist). The view of the landscape becomes the canvas on which the mystic and the poet's vision is painted, but the vision has a social destiny: an understanding of place as mnemonic and guardian of moral and spiritual values, a sphere which is essentially communitarian. And it is the vision, rather than the cathedral or area of St David's itself, which is the ultimate focus of Waldo's gaze and interest. In his most mature poems, Waldo's interest is not in the places of Pembrokeshire in and for themselves: it is in light of their social and religious significance that they are important. Just as the individual's religious experience has a social remit, so the fullness of meaning of place resides not in the individual's reaction to a particular locality alone, but must expand outwards to embrace social experience. An awareness of place necessarily involves experience of a concrete and historical community of people, in a particular piece of earth, and with reference to a world of transcendence:

> Older than his house is David's muse
> And older still her workmanship.
> And a stronger stone that the heavy blow
> of death is his word amongst us.
>
> . . . Good night, David's favour,
> and the land of his patronage. Grant to us
> The same face, the old promise
> And a people's house which is not the work of human hand.[21]

The same quality of concrete and earthed specificity acting as window on eternity applies to the whole of Waldo's Wales. Far from being an abstracted, disincarnate moral state, Waldo's Wales is a unity made up of individual, specific places, in each of which the idea of Wales is embodied in landscape and community in age-old partnership with each other. 'Cymru'n Un' (Wales is One) at one level describes Waldo's own ancestry in different neighbourhoods of the country:

> Within me, Wales is one. The manner, I do not know.
> I searched through the long chamber of my being, and found
> The material of neighbourhood there – from this Hiraethog,
> And its literary hue; and this same way and without fail
> Some old bygone shepherds cherished me,
> Before they went in a group over the shoulders of Mynydd Du,
> and by the tillers of the soil of Dyfed. Above my course
> The awakener of each part, my beloved Preseli.[22]

At another level, the poem is an attempt to fuse those different places which constitute of Wales into a national unity which is greater than the sum of its parts – a unification which takes place initially in the individual's awakening to national identity. Waldo's poems about such specific places as Cas'Mael or St David's function to create Wales, Waldo's Preseli being 'my Wales', the microcosm making the abstract macrocosm concrete:

> And that is why perhaps, I wish to be
> Amongst those who wish to make Wales pure
> For the name in which there is no division;
> to shatter the alien sky
> which mocks the inspiration of their people;
> to give to the bruised the ease of their lineage's order.
> May hope be our master, and Time be given us as our servant.[23]

In the crucible of the poet's imagination, specific place becomes genetrix of a sense of nationality for others:

> Literature has a strange power to bind neighbourhood and place to our awareness of what Wales is . . . 'In me, Wales is one', Waldo Williams began one of his sonnets, 'the manner, I do not know.' Certainly one manner, one answer, is that Welsh writers, by strengthening our ties with one patch of land, maintain those places in the totality of our experience of Wales. And part of Waldo Williams's contribution is that in his poems, he has bound Pembrokeshire more tightly to our idea of Wales.[24]

A series of analogous relationships may be observed here: the relation between each singular human life and human society is mirrored in the relationships between one's neighbourhood, and one's nation. Waldo's Preseli is 'his' Wales, local place making national place real, a politically useful corrective to the serious risk of the spiritualization run by the Wales-Israel tradition.

Brueggemann's understanding of Israel is that it combines symbolical and real values – being a place of identity and a material place of shelter. Bachelard's observation is that each inhabited place bears the imprint of home. For J. R. Jones, human beings have an inherent need for a 'foothold', a concrete piece of land to anchor them in the limitless expanses of the universe. Jonathan Z. Smith's and Yi-Fu Tuan's observations on the concept of homeland also shed light in that, for Waldo, Wales is quite literally, a home-land – a place which involves values of meaning, identity, and order. The microcosm of the house, one of Waldo's key symbols, contains within it the macrocosm of the whole world of Wales, and indeed of a world beyond. Evoking both biblical and medieval Welsh usage of the word 'tŷ' (house) to mean lineage, the symbol of the house not only contains a spatial macrocosm but also a diachronic one, for compressed into it are all the protological associations of past inhabitants and the eschatological vision of the future. A rich web of relations emerges – between the microcosm (the individual, the house, local society and place, Welsh nationality and land) and the macrocosm (universal brotherhood and the whole earth, the Welsh nation and Wales, local society and neighbourhood). The relationship between each of these contains a temporal element – the past as inheritance and gift, the present as arena of responsibility and moral action, and the future as apocalyptic revelation of the Divine Imagination inchoately present in all reality, and in which all concrete reality and all truly human society shows forth, if only as in a mirror darkly.

Acting as transmitter between the different levels of microcosm and macrocosm is the experience of the divine. This web of meaning-giving relations – *adnabod* – is only possible when God is present. Wherever the divine is not involved, the result is Chalcedonian separation and division: twentieth-century existential isolation, and a crisis of meaninglessness, fragmentation and loss. But when God is present, then divinely sustained mutual involvement of the spheres of the specific and the universal means that human existence can be perceived as order rather than chaos.

But Waldo's vision of brotherhood and *adnabod* coexists with expressions of the counter-experience of despair and erosion of identity. John Rowlands rightly points out that 'to describe Waldo Williams uniquely as the poet of national hope is superficial . . . his poetry has to do with the terrible battle which faces humanity: the battle to remain human in an increasingly inhuman world.'[25] The political and historical experience of such themes in Wales – rooted in the dismay at the loss of Christian Britannia and the gradual diminution of national identity or pre-eminence – finds frequent expression throughout the literary tradition which Waldo inherited: if his personal religious tradition leant towards a fundamental optimism, much of his literary background arises from the darker reality. Ned Thomas notes that the notions of 'belonging' and 'roots' and nationalism itself are all products of the experience of exile and loss.[26] But in that the search for roots and for belonging as purveyors of meaning typify mid-twentieth-century existential concerns, Waldo's own personal concerns are emblematic of the concerns and fears of a far wider humanity.

'Cwmwl Haf' (A Summer Cloud) was written during Waldo's exile in Lyneham. That the biblical notion of exile should have resonance in Wales is already obvious from our study of the sense of place in Israel. A New Testament understanding based on a notion of Jesus' incarnation as separation from the Father considers earthly life as a 'time of exile' (1 Peter 1: 17). The Welsh-Israelite psychology of internal national exile combines religious convictions with the specific political experiences of the early British and the Welsh. In the case of Waldo, part of the apocalyptic world-view sees this world as a place of exile, alienation from its true self. In this poem, written some forty years after the experience it describes, Waldo's personal experiences of bereavement and of grief were crystallized. It is structured along the pattern of a classic rite of passage – primeval innocence, death, and rebirth into a new identity – part of that same pattern which lies at the root of both deuteronomism and apocalypsism. At the centre of the poem, lost in a cloud of unknowing, in which there is no *adnabod*, isolated from others, from any recognition of the land, himself or the transcendent, Waldo presents the existential nightmare:

> The rushes grew like trees and perished
> In a world too enormous for being.
> No over there. Only me is here.

Me
With no father or mother or sisters or brother,
And the beginning and the end closing about me.

Who am I? Who am I?
A stretch of my arms and then, between their two stumps
The dread of thinking about myself,
And the questions that is the ground of all questions:
Who is this?
The sound of cold water. I wade it for an answer.
Nothing but the cold current.[27]

Gwenallt had offered the Church and its sacraments as source of healing for the nations. Waldo's resurrection-experience comes instead via a reconnection with the material realities of the earth. The 'Exiled King' of 'Mewn Dau Gae' exiled from this earth, and his return is seen as the fulfilment of hope. Homecoming to a world experienced as a habitable *kosmos* is made possible by means of tangible and localized realities. Such specific and apparently secular experiences as Waldo's boyhood and his physical journeyings are guarantee and expression of the universal and the transcendent. If the world's existential crisis is experienced within that microcosm which is the individual person, then also it is within the individual and through his contact with the specifics of his here-and-now, that the world can be re-established and the nations healed. The poem's homecoming to the world of the senses was echoed by Waldo's return to Pembrokeshire in 1950. Waldo expresses Everyman's crisis of meaninglessness, and discovers its remedy in the familiar, now seen in transforming light:

Through the ditch homeward if it is homewards.
I hefted the gate-post, still doubtful,
And O, before I reached the back-door,
The sound of building a new earth, new heaven,
Were my mother's clogs on the kitchen floor.[28]

Christian mysticism, rather than being a totally other-worldly experience, sometimes involves a heightened awareness of this world. St Teresa of Avila's observation that 'God is found amongst the pots and pans' finds echo in 'Cwmwl Haf'. In this model of holiness, transcendence and immanence are not spheres totally isolated from and opposed to each other, but meet and interpenetrate, an expression of belief in the Incarnation. Waldo implies that transcendence *can only* be experienced this side of death through the specific – an expression of Matt. 25: 31–46. The physical (hefting the gate-post), the material and the homely (the sound of clogs on the floor) are thus the vehicle and place of embodied encounter with the transcendent. Eliade's concept of located holiness as the piercing of the membrane between these two spheres thus makes sacred space of the kitchen of Waldo's boyhood. The house – be it understood literally or figuratively as lineage, church, land or nation – is microcosm and pattern of the world to come.

Waldo wields an Ockham's razor against abstractions and universals. The Kingdom is built up in and through the specific, the concrete and the local. In Waldo's terms, there is no brother-hood, unless individual, specific people live practically as brothers and sisters in their own particular circumstances. Only in the proximity of the *bro* – the place of one's own neighbourhood – may national identity be made real and experienced. There exists no tension between his love for Preseli and his love for Wales. Wales, as place and as nation, can only be experienced in the local – so much so that Waldo's poetical vocabulary sometimes needs some explaining even to Welsh-speaking readers not fully conversant with the dialect and old agricultural practices of Pembrokeshire. Within the narrow walls of Wales, there is a wide hall of *koinonia* which may be home both to its Catholic martyrs:

> Welshmen, were you a nation, great would be the glory
> These would have in your story.[29]

and the values of Nonconformist Protestantism:

> The people knelt
> At the sturdy bench of the yard of their neighbourhood farm,
> With easy generosity, it gave them
> A barn to shelter against bishops.
> The resolve of its children will not bend
> neither to a lord nor all his machinery.[30]

In exactly the same way as there is for Waldo no opposition but mutually necessary complementarity between the local and the national, nor is there any contradiction between love of one's nation and universal brotherhood. Nationalism and internationalism are mutually inseparable and interpenetrative elements of Waldo's creed. His nationalism, it is true, is reactive, but finds its place in the *pars pro toto* understanding of nationalism that so typifies Welsh writers of the twentieth century. In his lecture 'Monarchy and Brotherhood', Waldo justified political nationalism in Wales as a religious act, a breaking free from the shackles of the militarism of the British empire for the sake of the Christian humanistic values of the Kingdom of Heaven:

> Here in Wales, what can we do? We should work to make Wales free. A small country without the temptation of power, with no hope of lording it over other countries, with its good in the friendship of countries, and its society as unpretentiously of the people as only the society of small countries can be.[31]

Although much of his work treats local issues, a small group of poems shows the explicit concern for national issues found in the Wales-Israel tradition. But in these most outspokenly nationalist poems, 'he comes nowhere near worshipping Wales and Welsh. For him they are not absolute principles. They embody principles.'[32] Waldo avoids many of the spiritual pitfalls inherent in the Wales-Israel tradition, including the familiar one of attributing unconditional spiritual value to Welsh nationhood.

The theological implications of these poems are complex. The Welsh language – for Waldo, an essential component of national identity – is divine gift. As such, it bears the imprint of transcendence:

> There is nothing in the world which can capture your mystery,
> No equal in God's creation.
> And I hear, as I kiss your lips
> The life-filled high-water of all that lives.[33]

The association of the divine with the created, particularly when poetical imagery is employed, might raise the fear of idolatry, but the concept of interpenetration allows us to make distinction between the divine and the sacred. In 'Cymru a Chymraeg' (Wales and the Welsh language), the territory of Wales and the

Welsh language are inseparably interpenetrated with one another. Waldo brings together the spheres of the natural world and cultural history, a union which suggests that the language has some essential, eternal value. In 'Tŷ Ddewi', Carn Llidi, the place of Waldo's vision, is the symbol of human encounter with the divine. In 'Cymru a Chymraeg' the mountains symbolize the physical and spiritual abiding of the Welsh language, a complex association of political, geographical, social and linguistic realities:

> Here are the mountains. One language alone can raise them
> And set them in their freedom against a sky of song.
> One alone penetrated to the riches of their poverty
> Through the dream of ages, the visions of small minutes.
> . . . A worthy house for their interpreter![34]

Just as the places of Preseli are inseparably interpenetrated with the lives of generations of people who have lived there, a people to whom the land belongs and who belong to that land, so the whole material world of Wales is interpenetrated with the Welsh language. Like Gwenallt's nation, Waldo's Welsh language stands in the two fields of nature and grace, creation and salvation. Creation emphasizes elements of presence, immanence, contemplation and eternity. Yet the relationship between national language and national land can no longer be taken for granted. In 'Preseli', Waldo's spiritual home is described as 'challenge' as well as 'Wales'. The nation's existential crisis now demands decisive work – 'let us keep the beast from the wall, the mud from the fountain' – so that there may be a future. Welsh thus belongs also to the sphere of salvation, stressing action, both divine and human. Interpenetration of the land and the language of Wales reveals itself not only as a matter of fact, in a world of faith and nature. Like its related concept, *adnabod*, interpenetration shows itself to be a responsibility and a task, in a world of works. The dynamic principle of perichoresis illuminates this intrahistorical aspect of interpenetration:

> We did not notice her. She was the light, without colour.
> We did not notice her; it was the air that brought her perfume
> to our noses.

The water of our mouths, the light of taste.
We did not feel her arms around her danger-free land.
But there is a land where the lark does not climb back to its sky,
A longing-less yesterday separated them.
This is the winter of a nation, the cold heart
Which does not know that it has lost its five joyous mysteries.[35]

Waldo's concept of Wales is that of a historic, human reality, one which involves a process of human commitment and action. His small corpus of poems celebrating Wales can be read as a call to arms, facing the future. And the fact that in his works, albeit through the lens of a fragile hope, Waldo *can* envisage Wales as a future, as well as a past and present reality, is highly significant.

Charles Edwards's address to the nation at the end of *Y Ffydd Ddi-Ffuant*, Saunders Lewis's Vineyard speech, and much of Gwenallt's *œuvre* are all based on the deuteronomical understanding of the future as restoration of something either lost or in grave danger of destruction. The psychological experience of this world-view is that of grief or fear. The starting-point of any deuteronomically inspired reaction is that of the encircling threat of chaos. The Welsh-Israelite tonality is generally defensive, essentialist in its notions of national identity, and reactive against English imperialism. But although Waldo expresses eloquently the potential threats to humanity, his poems look forward prophetically to the revelation of something not yet in full existence, in a sense of holiness understood as universally engaged being in process. Just as his understanding of holiness is dynamic, his vision of national identity is that of intrahistorical, moral enterprise:

We must demand that Welsh lives here
without asking the price[36]

In his many less sanguine poems, Gwenallt had placed the moral burden of the survival of Welsh nationality on the shoulders of his pusillanimous compatriots, in a national spirituality stressing the need for works. There are echoes of this sense of frustration within Waldo's work. Admittedly, Waldo's hope is born out of the threat of despair, a hope which would be fragile if it were to depend on human will alone. But it is hope strengthened by the faith-filled assurance of success and inchoate immanence:

> No! Spring will return to one who gave succour
> To the awakeners of nations before their summer.
> Generously, she poured out her wine for them.
> They rose from her tables, bold for all beauties.[37]

Here, the future existence of the language is caught up in the natural cycle of the seasons – a potentially problematic image if followed through to its logical conclusion that Welsh is of the order of divine creation, irrespective of human actions and association. However, what Waldo seeks to assure himself and his readers is that this success will come, as surely as the Exiled King. 'Divine Imagination' is innate in humanity, and part of the cosmic order. Hope may thus survive in the face of apparent individual or national disaster:

> There is in the root of Being no withering.
> There the heartwood grows still.
> There is the courage which is the gentleness
> of life of every fragile life.
>
> There the heart retreats after every storm.
> The world is in ruins.
> But in the low stronghold, the squirrel of enlightenment
> Makes its nest tonight.[38]

The apocalyptic mentality arose out of a combination of despair and hope: a pessimistic evaluation of current political circumstances produced an existential need for hope in order to remain human in those circumstances. Waldo's Quaker belief in the immanent Inner Light, and his mystical awareness of brotherhood as divine gift and human task, his insistence on the here-and-now as well as on the future, all point to a more hopeful and practical vision of redemption already achieved, if only obscurely and in part, and assured. The classical apocalyptic vision is posited on complete transcendence over time, and the denial of the significance of intramundane history, but Waldo's apocalypticism has a place for history, understood as the platform of divinely inspired *human* action:

> For there will be a stirring of the memory, the cavern will open,
> There will be support for our strength, and following of Arthur
> There will be demanding-back of the house, and calling-back of
> the roofers
> There will be claiming of the builders' inheritance.[39]

Biblical and national resonances working together in such verses suggest a synergy of divine and human energies in the sustenance and future of the nation. Based on a psychology more optimistic by far than that of the Wales-Israel tradition, or of the classic apocalyptic vision, Waldo's conception recognizes the re-assuring immanence of God within all. From within the security of that embrace, human energies are set free to build a new heaven and a new earth – and a new, redeemed Wales, whose king is currently in exile:

> Henceforth our freedom
> Is to be found in the ground of your mystery.[40]

Exactly *how* this will happen, Waldo does not make clear. What is clear is that the survival of national identity is dependent on the spiritual awareness of each individual member of that nation. And in the same pattern, the precondition and vehicle of 'a new earth, a new heaven' of international brotherhood is a strong sense of national identity.

Conclusion

The two streams of place and nation have run throughout this study, sometimes parallel with each other, at other times diverging from each other or meeting. Within the Welsh tradition, they have not flowed with equal bodies of water, nor always with clarity and purity. Spiritualities of both place and national identity are capable of expressions which are variously whole-some or dangerously reductionistic, inclusive or exclusivist, essentialist or dynamic. The fact that an interest in these two fields of experience typifies Welsh spirituality is incontrovertible, as is the fact that they often exist in close association with each other. There remains, however, the theological task of exploring this relationship, and the practical task of considering its possible repercussions. Waldo's vision contributes considerable light to the path through these complex issues.

In the work of Waldo Williams, unity occupies a central place: the unity of universal brotherhood; the unity of the material and transcendent aspects of the symbol; the unity of the individual with the social, the local with the national, the national and the international, the specific with the generic; and the close connections between hope and despair, faith and works, nature and grace. All these may be seen as Waldo's experience and resolution of the theoretical tensions presented in Chapter 1 of this book. A synthesis of what Waldo evokes imagistically (*adnabod*, experience of the divine, inspiration, brotherhood) and what J. R. Jones describes in a philosophical mode (interpenetration) provides ways of understanding the paradoxical harmony of such potentially jarring opposites.

Armed with this hermeneutical battery, we can begin to elucidate a possible theology of the relationship between place and national identity. Taking Chalcedon as its model of interpenetration, a balanced Christianity sees no contradiction between a spirituality of creation and a spirituality of salvation, between immanence and transcendence, faith and works, history and eternity. Both are necessary, each sphere existing in an interpenetrative perichoresis, inseparable but distinct from each other. Chalcedon warns that the person of Christ may *only* be acknowledged as a differentiated unity of human and divine natures. What Waldo's vision implies is not only that such relationships as I have noted above *may* exist, but that if each element is to find its full meaning, and be expressed and experienced fully, they *must* necessarily exist in creative tension with each other.

Waldo's mystical appreciation of the essential unity of opposing forces suggests that the two strands of nation and place are not separate, but necessarily complement and complete each other. An active, Protestant spirituality such as Welsh-Israelitism, with an interest in history, divine and human action (salvation through works of morality), will be balanced and complemented by a more contemplative Catholic-local spirituality of place, with a preference for divine presence (salvation through faith). Action and being then show themselves to be mutually necessary, without ontological or chronological primacy being afforded to either concept.

For Waldo, a major component of human existence is a sense of place, understood as a social-geographical unity. Ancestral experience of place binds people together, not only horizontally in the present, but vertically, over the generations of a society who have lived in a land interpenetrated with their language. Likewise, national identity is inseparable from, but not identical to inhabitation of national place, its own land. To the wounds inflicted on the Welsh nation by the moral lash of Gwenallt and Saunders Lewis, Waldo applies the balm of insisting on the beauty of the place of Wales, and its essential connection with the Welsh language. All three writers attribute a high degree of sacramentality to the land of Wales. In Waldo's case the assurance of God's immanence in Wales is coupled with an apocalyptic optimism stressing the transcendence of the divine, an association which considerably reduces the existential pressure and sense of responsibility for 'keeping the beast from the wall, the filth from the fountain' which looms in the works of the other two writers. But an appreciation of the beauty of Wales does not mean a descent into the reductiveness of aestheticist individualism. The fundamental optimism of this contemplative act of faith does not obviate individual and social responsibility. The task for Waldo, rather than maintaining a status quo or regaining lost territory, is that of bringing into fuller existence that which as yet exists only inchoately. In biblical terms, both the contemplation of place (faith) and the intrahistorical, moral task of creating, sustaining and sanctifying identity (works) are necessary. Place and time are bound up together:

> 'Durham', 'Devonia', 'Allendale', – there are their houses,
> and every name is the same name,
> the name of the old place and the slow place where time
> springs from.[41]

Of these words of her brother, Miss Dilys Williams noted that 'I think that (they mean that) time is an accompaniment to place – and that they both dissolve into one another, forming a new whole.'[42] In more philosophical terms, we might say that 'time and place interpenetrate with one another', in the terms of Chalcedon, 'without any commingling or change or division or separation'. The implication of Waldo's words is that any sense of place which does not take into account its historical human significance is deeply insufficient. Against an individualist reaction to place, Waldo's vision posits the inseparability of the individual, local, national and universal strata of identity: an individual's sense of place, be it local or national, is only ever experienced authentically when it integrates social significance. And inevitably involved with social considerations are political ones. The concept of perichoresis applied to interpenetration means that such relationships are dynamic, rather than static, involving questions of maintaining a healthy balance between the various elements. An authentic, integrated sense of place then reveals itself to be a task, demanding human commitment and responsibility. Such is the message of Waldo's 'two fields' where the individual vision, rooted in one place, issues via the still meeting point of the One and the Many, into a vision of the whole humanity.

Waldo's argument thus agrees with the views of phenomenologists of religion that holy place is an experiential, not an essential category. In tune with the understanding of Old Testament Israel, Waldo presents land as a sacramental category, mediating the relationship between humanity and God. Against all faux-naive or colonialist assumptions that particular places inherently contain universally perceptible values, Waldo offers us the value of the specific place, interpenetrated with a specific people. The quest for meaning, the search for roots, is answered by a sense of place in interpenetration with each individual and each neighbourhood, the divine spark being present in all. The application of interpenetration distinguishes between the divine and the sacred, allowing us to venerate place, without worshipping it.

The Wales-Israel and the Wales-as-Church paradigms both portray Wales as 'a chosen people, a royal priesthood, a nation set apart' (1 Pet. 2: 9), pressing questions of national survival meaning that the difficult issue of the spiritual role of other nations and their relationship to the Welsh is left pending. Waldo's understanding offers us instead an apocalyptic vision of humanity as *koinonia*.[43] If the Wales-Israel tradition stresses the corporate, national element of human identity and spirituality, Waldo's vision represents a return to the personal, the interior, and the concrete. Towards the construction of a healthy spirituality of national identity, Waldo offers us the supreme importance of the individual human person, and the recognition of the divine spark in all human beings as the basis for universal brotherhood – his corrective to any form of collectivity which would seek to subjugate the individual to the system. Waldo extends the Romantic notion of individual inspiration to include the social. Transcendence over time is achieved, not uniquely by means of divine action, but also through the individual's subjective mystical-poetical vision. In such moments of insight, the individual partakes of the Spirit indwelling and underlying all reality, but the dynamic of this individual experience of the 'divine imagination' radiates out into the spheres of the local and national societies. The duty of making possible the practical, lived experience of universal brotherhood is incumbent in all individual interior experiences of the intimate connection of all that is.

Waldo's espousal of both nationalism and internationalism illustrates the mutual necessity of both creeds. The negative understanding of nationalism exemplified by Pfaff and others in Chapter 2 of this book is gainsaid by the *pars pro toto* nationalism of many modern Welsh writers, Waldo among them, which stresses responsibility and national distinctiveness rather than national rights or distinction. Within Waldo's view, there is no place for Israelite, Welsh or any other pre-eminence, spiritual, racial, linguistic or cultural. What is true of the Welsh nation within its own land must also be true of all other nations: as Simone Weil points out, it is false to assume that a nation has no purpose unless is can be shown to have purpose 'within History'.[44] Within the Welsh-Israelite tradition, a sense of national identity derives from notions of cultic purity, in which the mighty stronghold of divine election is in reaction to the world. Inevitably correlated ideas concerning holy place, national territory and political nationalism all tend towards a defensive stance. Waldo's understanding of holiness offers a different model, one based on the Incarnation, in which the sacred is understood as salt of the earth and light of the world. The spirituality deriving from this is universally engaged, and fully incarnational. The sense of national identity and the political nationalism based on this spirituality will present themselves as challenges to nurture the seeds of the Kingdom present in the world.

In that he sees the nation as a vehicle of deep spiritual values, Waldo's understanding of nationality is a sacramental one. As sacrament, the nation brings together the two fields of nature and grace, humanity and divinity. Different understandings of holiness produce differentiated national psychologies: cultic purity nationality will tend towards understanding culture and faith in static, essentialist terms, and time as agent of decay, in a worldview which is fundamentally conservative and pessimistic. In the world as envisaged by Waldo, culture and faith are bound together in a mutually necessary, dynamic union: time is the vehicle of hope and transformation of the world into its own truest self. In the words of the scholastic dictum: *novum in vetere latet, vetus in novo patet:* 'the new has its roots in the old, and the fullness of the old shines forth in the new.'

Waldo's unitive understanding of the necessary relationship between national identity and international brotherhood strongly suggests that an internationalist outlook needs to be incarnated in particular nationalisms. Just as political nationalism is capable of healthy and more sinister variants, internationalism is likewise morally variable. The unity between an individual and a local society, between a local society and a national one, and between nations and a universal brotherhood demands that each of these elements be held in balance with one another, in a process of active and responsible perichoresis. Applying Chalcedonian canons to Waldo's insight, we arrive at an ideal of universalism close to *koinonia*: one in which 'one world' attitudes do not ignore or seek to abolish necessary national differences in the misconception that such distinctiveness is a threat; one in which no nation subsumes another, as in the tragedy of cultural or territorial imperialism or the universal cultural supermarket in which attractive elements of poor cultures are arrogated by the rich; and one in which national identity becomes the specific and local embodiment of international identity. Waldo's Preseli is 'my song' – his contribution to what J. E. Daniel refers to as 'eternal Pentecost', 'perfect harmony in mutual understanding and singing together'. Like perichoresis, such a vision of universal communion is based on a linguistic model, in which relationality is expressed as dialogue. The prerequisite and the fruit of all meaningful dialogue is a secure sense of identity and accurate self-worth. The international brotherhood preached by Waldo demands an openness to the other, a vulnerability and a willingness to change not easily attained in many national psychologies.

An internationalism which sees distinctiveness as gift to the world opens up new horizons.

I have referred to Waldo's operative spirituality as being incarnational and sacramental. In both the Incarnation and the sacraments, the material and the localized are the guarantors and expression of the universal. Waldo offers a spirituality which pays significant attention to the specific context of experience: to the geographical context of land, and the social context of local community, nationality and universal humanity; to the historical context of one's present reality and the transgenerational community to which one belongs. Gwenallt sees the specificity of Jesus' nationality and, following him, all national identities as being part of Incarnation. Waldo's insistence on the solid, the specific, the material and the local, argues that the answer to the universal search for meaning is to be found in due attention and commitment to one's geographical and social roots: his mother's kitchen is the place of transfiguration revealing a new heaven and a new earth. As such, Waldo's spirituality is both local and catholic: catholic, not in spite of its insistence on the local, but precisely because of it. In very practical terms, the implications of Waldo's perception is that a sense of place involves a commitment to the rich and many-layered associations – social and national being prime amongst these – of one's here-and-now. Diversities and particular perfections, then become 'the mirror of divine justice, the cause of our joy, the spiritual vessel'.[45] In the particularity of places and of nations lies their universality.

The vision of universal brotherhood and the idea of *adnabod* share the idea of family relations, in which there is unity and diversity. The Welsh word *perthyn* enshrines two meanings: that of belonging and that of being related to. Both meanings involve questions of identity, rights and responsibilities. For Waldo, individuals, neighbourhood societies, nations and the whole of humanity belong to each other. A constituent part of that national sense of identity which makes international peace possible is a sense of place. Just as a people belongs to its place, a place belongs to its people.

Epilogue

That the glory that was may be kept for the ages to come[1]

In the foundations of a sense of place or of nationality lies a search for identity, relationality and meaning. The concepts of interpenetration and sacramentality, typology and tradition, which have been so much part of this book all share a conviction that particular identity – of individuals, societies, nations, places and national territory – and universal context involve each other. Only by means of its connection with the whole can the identity of each part be illuminated, and vice versa. In this paradoxical relation, individual and universal aspects of identity reinforce each other's meaning. Welsh spiritual and political traditions have often arisen out of wrestling with *ad intra* questions of identity, the internal discourse in answer to Waldo's anguished cry in 'Mewn Dau Gae', 'Who am I?' Much of the Wales-Israel tradition has sought identity vertically, by exploring national relationship with the divine. Equally, particularly in their *pars pro toto* preferences, Welsh traditions have attempted to place themselves in a wider, horizontal context – the world of the nations – in a search for the meaning of Wales and Welshness. These quests involve looking for both distinctiveness and similarity – the building-blocks of relationality.

This book has partly been written as a response to my own internal discourses: as a Welsh-speaking Welshman living in a place which has for fifteen centuries been Welsh-speaking but which now is also home to a large number of recent English immigrants; as a Welsh Catholic in a nation whose images, *ad intra* and *ad extra*, have been so profoundly affected by Protestant spirituality; and as a Welsh-speaking priest serving a largely English-speaking diocese. I have also had in mind other discourses: the national internal audiences of this book are fellow-Welsh citizens, speakers of both languages. But this book has a wider range of possible, more exterior interlocutors: people who live in Wales but who are not Welsh; people in Wales and outside who are either non-Christians or who profess no official religion; people in other countries who have no experience of Wales, but who are interested in it; and people concerned by what is meant by 'a sense of place' or by the connection between nationality and religion.

Welsh experience has a number of features which are unique, obviously paramount amongst them the geography, demography, and political history of Wales, all of which have shaped the spiritual traditions explored in this book. A sense of place and an awareness of national identity, or even a sense of divine election, are by no means unique to Wales. The particularities of Welsh experience find echoes in far-away peoples such as Australian Aboriginals, Orthodox Russians, the Boers and the Western Apache. But within Western Europe and Northern America, the Welsh traditions of place and national identity are unusual ones: the intimate connection between individual, society and place portrayed in Gwenallt's Carmarthenshire or Waldo's Preseli is diametrically opposed to the experience of many people, particularly those living in urban and cosmopolitan environments. The 'crisis of meaninglessness' identified by J. R. Jones has expressed itself in the latter part of this century as a crisis of roots – geographical, social and spiritual. The search for a sense of place and certain forms of nationalism may be seen as attempts to fill that existential vacuum. What then can a Welsh sense of place, inseparably connected as it is with a specific, largely rural land, and a specific diachronic community, have to say to people long uprooted from any such generational contact with the soil?

An emphasis on the importance of national identity is a common concern of subject peoples in either colonized or post-colonial phases. The rise of the theory of the nation-state has inevitably affected Wales. The specifics of Welsh history have brought the Welsh nation into frequent contact with the English, a process that – on the Welsh side at least – has made nationality an important component of many people's sense of individual identity. But in a world tending towards cultural homogeneity, is the Welsh experience of nationality – and nationalism – anything more than a freak survival of a primitive and conservative outlook? What psychological or spiritual density can we attribute to national identity? Given that many writers look forward to the demise of nationalism as a dangerous ersatz religion, should not the ironing out of national distinctiveness be encouraged, as part of building international peace?

Welsh spiritual traditions, I would wish to argue, are bound together by their awareness of – or search for – unity as the source of identity and meaning. In Eusebius' typological understanding, the constancy of God is the basis for seeing the flow of time as history, namely a process which contains order, direction and meaning. In the development of history, the old is present in the new, the part in the whole, and vice versa. This is the conception of time inherited by Gildas, Charles Edwards, and the whole Welsh-Israelite tradition, and in which their deuteronomic understanding of the nation is placed. Saunders Lewis's notion of Welsh nationality is that of a tradition, a world-view in which there is organic connection between the parts of the whole, and in which particular diversities are held together within a deeper catholicity of unity.

J. R. Jones's idea of the interpenetration of language and land in certain 'footholds', and his understandings of the functioning and purpose of nationality are all taken from a view of the world as potential, if not actual *kosmos*. Within this, micro and macro expressions all contain the same significance, irrespective of their size: in the small worlds of Wales, whole universes are contained. Expressions of the concept of sacramentality – of place and of national identity – have arisen throughout this book. In the sacraments, the thoroughly disparate spheres of the material and the spiritual, the divine and the human, are brought into relation with one another, acting as channels of meaning to a world which continually threatens to break down into meaninglessness. The pattern of microcosm and macrocosm is also at work within sacramentality, for the limited physical matter of the sacrament contains the whole of the divine essence, the fullness of God being a real presence in each fragment of the eucharistic bread. The other element of sacramentality implicit in place and nationality is the unity in one reality of symbolic and material natures. Waldo's world of brotherhood and his insistence on the local, the specific and the concrete are likewise bound together with the conviction that there is 'order in my palace there', the indwelling presence of the 'divine imagination' being that which holds them all together.

The different strands of spirituality present in the Welsh tradition all contain a unitive understanding, and it may be that this is one of its main distinguishing notes. These statements of faith derive from an experience – or the hope for experience – of life as having form and meaning, and as containing a fundamental unity between all its aspects. In this, Welsh spiritual traditions offer a comforting, integral vision. They are also a dissenting voice in a late twentieth-century world-view. In many European and North American paradigms, largely urban in context and inspiration, existence is experienced as fragmentation, in a world of absolute relativism. Such patches of unitive existence as may be found extend in time and space only to a small extent, to the effect that they are relative only to another, not to any wider reality. Whereas Welsh spiritual traditions proclaim an ideal (admittedly sometimes confusing the ideal with the reality), many postmodern philosophies seek merely to describe, without attributing ultimate or absolute value. A scholastic theology defines the reality of divinity as being ultimate truth, goodness, and beauty. What I have argued in this book is that a true sense of place and national identity must integrate moral as well as aesthetic considerations.

A postmodern sympathy veers away from any grand unified theories, and that distrust may contain considerable wisdom. Just as all the different phenomenological understandings of sacred place may be seen as possible expressions of a complex reality, it is probably wiser not to posit in this book any all-encompassing grand unified theory of place or nationality, particularly in such a multi-disciplinary area. The notions of sacramentality, or interpenetration, that I have described are thus best regarded as possible approaches to this field-encompassing field. I write, however, as a Catholic, and a believer, if not in grand unified theories, then in the grand and unified reality of the Incarnation, in whom Christian theology sees the source and summit of all realities. If postmodernism offers fragmentation and separation, the Incarnation offers 'the healing of the nations'. The author of Ephesians presents Christ as *theios aner*, the macrocosm to the microcosm of each individual person. Christians find their identity, the significance of their own microcosm, in relation to Christ, the 'perfect human being' (Eph. 4: 13).

Significance, identity and relationality, the base-questions of land and nationality, are at the root of the two central dogmas of the Incarnation and Trinity, both of them relationships in which the internal economy is that of love. The four Chalcedonian qualifying adverbs provide a detailed description of divine love for humanity, a relationship internally embodied in the one person and two natures of the hypostatic union. The adverbs, as I have shown throughout this book, can be exported to describe ideal balanced and healthy interpenetrative relationships. Prime among such relationships is love between individual persons: in a relationship which functions *inconfuse* the partners do not lose their separate identities but rather their sense of identity is strengthened by their union, and vice versa; in love which is *immutabilis* one partner does not dominate the other to the extent that the distinct sense of self of the dominated partner is extinguished. *Indivise* describes a relationality in which every single aspect of the identities of both partners is included in their union. *Inseparabiliter* witnesses to the fact that unconditional commitment is an essential part of mature love.

Included in the different levels of identity we may include the social and the national, both of which are called to be 'rooted in love and grounded in love' (Eph. 3: 17), divine love being made manifest in Jesus Christ (Rom. 8: 39). Incarnation therefore provides a basis and model for societal relations. Chalcedon may certainly describe the ideal relations between an individual and the nation of which he or she is a member. International relations may also use Chalcedonian union as an ideal, taking the family or the Church as the model for universal brotherhood, all of them situations in which there is unity amongst diversity, diversity being the necessary condition and expression of unity.

For Waldo, *adnabod* is a process which he sees largely as taking place between people. But the concept of *adnabod*, informed by Chalcedonian guidelines, can also serve as a Christian land ethic, describing a Christian ideal of the experience of place, both local and national. The biblical roots of this lie in the understanding, present also in Ephesians and Colossians, of Christ as macrocosm of the whole universe. The theology deriving from this includes the insight of the Eastern Church that all matter has been pervaded and transfigured by the Incarnation, Teilhard's Omega Point, and the 'christification of the universe'. Strictly speaking, in such a relationship, it is only the human partner which is active. But in this application of interpenetration understood as equilibrium, the Chalcedonian adverbs may be used as a corrective to a partial or unbalanced sense of place. In the light of divine-human love in the Incarnation, Yi-Fu Tuan's two neologisms lend themselves to a deeper appreciation: *topophilia*, 'the affective bond between people and place', and *geopiety*, 'reverence and attachment to one's family and homeland, attachments to place, love of country and patriotism'. In these human relationships with place, the potential of identities and significances is made manifest by means of association, to the effect that one's place, local and national, plays an integral part in one's identity, and vice versa; physical, historical, social and religious significances are all integrated, in due proportion with each other, escaping such extremes as spiritualization and reductionist materialism; all the various aspects of place, and all levels of human identity are involved, thus avoiding stances which ignore historical and social significance of place such as individualist-aestheticism, or 'deep ecology'; and in this model of place as love, in a recognition of the moral and political aspects of land, an authentic sense of place involves a sense of commitment to one good place.

In Tuan's two concepts, social identity is an essential aspect of the understanding of place. This may be understood synchronically, as relationship with the people who share land, or diachronically, as relationship with one's forebears in that place. For Jonathan Z. Smith, it is the intimacy of whole generations with land that turns into 'the Land of the Fathers'. In their preference for deuteronomical understanding of time both the Wales-Israel and Wales-as-Church traditions stress diachronic relations. They also contain strong synchronic aspects. However, since their understanding of nationality derives from an abstract, essentialist understanding of holiness, they are not well equipped to deal with the complex earthly realities of place, in which the Church or the nation have their physical existence in a mixed society. Geographical proximity does not equal identical social allegiance or spiritual identity. Neither the Church nor most nations live in discrete geographical spheres: the issue of the relationship between spiritual and social identities addressed in Augustine's *City of God* remains a perennially thorny one. Attempts to harmonize the theological vision with political realities have led to a vast variety of historical manifestations, including emigrations in search of new and pure lands, certain varieties of colonization, the monastic tradition, and ethnic cleansing.

The Wales-Israel model of place and nation then is widely or easily exportable: many people in the rich world do not live in the place of their ancestors, and those who do are frequently in a situation of sharing it with those who have considerably shallower social and family roots. The fact that people who experience the same place have varying depths of diachronic social identity makes a consolidated synchronic social identity a harder prize to gain. The insight that holy place is discerned experientially applies to all land, given that different levels of awareness will give rise to different senses of place in the same location. And since social identity is interpenetrated with place, the implication of this is that an inauthentic, fragmented social identity will give rise to – and derive from – a socially incomplete sense of place. The logical outcome of the connection between individuals, place and people, is that a partial sense of place will be produced by and confirm an inauthentic personal identity. Here lie the roots of individualist-aestheticist attitudes to Wales and the psychology underlying many forms of colonialism, including that of the popular search for rural utopias.

The current experience of nationality and place in Wales is involved in this potential dilemma. The Welsh-Israelite tradition does not discuss the spiritual identity of other nations (apart from as vehicles of divine punishment or reward). Consequently the national identity which derives from this will not easily find a place for the non-Welsh within Wales or its definition of Welshness, since in this model religious identity, land and cultural purity co-implicate each other. The interpenetration of the land and language is a statement of an attractive historical ideal – but it does not necessarily describe the *realpolitik* of the present. An over-eulogizing of the 'essential' Wales, the largely homogeneous society of Preseli and Carmarthenshire, does not do justice to the disparate experiences of nationality which may coexist within the same geographical territory. For Bachelard, home is the model and basis of all experiences of place. Conflicting interests immediately arise in response to this emotional definition: is there any way in which Welsh traditions of land and nation may find a place for non-Welsh people, and vice versa? In modern Wales as in modern Israel, and many other states, can a place be homeland for more than one nation? Does any one claim on land have ontological or chronological primacy? Issues of absolute or relative meaning are echoed in questions of cultural 'purity' or pluralism. Are such tensions bound to end in impasse? The concepts of Trinitarian-informed perichoresis, and Waldo's insistence on immediacy and the specific come to our aid in these potentially difficult issues.

The fact that perichoresis was originally applied to the relationships of Christ reveals the internal flow of the nature of love, as a dynamically maintained union constantly in search of a healthy equilibrium. Love – and all interpenetrative relationships – demands constant attention and sensitive readjustment. The Wales-Israel tradition has often tended towards essentialist, self-sufficient notions of nationality, stressing the static elements of national distinctiveness, and understanding cultural 'purity' as a turning back of the clock. More modern understandings stress the dynamic, constantly changing nature of culture, in a global vision of aleatoric influences. Biblical Israel sees land as both divine blessing and human task. Since all that was true of the land is centred and transfigured in the person of Christ, then an incarnational spirituality of culture, place and nationality sees that both divine gift and human action, constancy and change, responsibility and rights are necessary for the perpetuation of various levels of human identity, and of place as place.

The linguistic manifestation of this interpenetrative relationship of change and constancy is dialogue. The possibility of dialogue is created by and in its turn creates openness and a willingness to be challenged and to change. Waldo's insistence on brotherhood stresses holding in balance the common humanity of all, with the specific, the local, the disparate – an insight repeated in the popular modern proverb 'think globally, act locally'. Global brotherhood involves and can only become a reality (rather than a non-committed pious liberalism) in local encounter and dialogue. If a Christian spirituality of place is to take the person of Christ as its model, then incarnationality demands attention to the specifics of one's own 'here-and-now', including the nationality and cultural traditions of the place one currently lives in, whatever one's origins. This involves not only a process of responsibility. The other half of the dialogue demands attention to the specific rights as well as responsibilities of all inhabitants of a place. To do less than to balance rights with responsibility is to live incompletely.

An awareness of the fullness of meaning of an individual place is a good starting-point for the expression of local spiritualities of place. Much of what has been written about place in this book considers place primarily as a rural reality, given that such has been the specific context of Wales. Only in the work of Gwenallt has attention been paid to industrial life. The possible results of an acritical and wholesale application of the model of other places, times and peoples include Romanticist reductions, cultural appropriation and a resultant lack of attention to the potential holiness of one's own particular place and time. What can legitimately be applied are the deeper understandings which underlie the manifestations of particular local spiritualities. An incarnational spirituality will tend towards the sacramental, seeing the divine and the human, the spiritual and the material, variously united in place. The implication of all this is that an authentic sense of place, if there is to be *adnabod*, demands several different levels of dialogue: between the various peoples who currently inhabit a neighbourhood or a national territory; between the present inhabitants, and the social traditions of past inhabitants; between those who live in a place and those who live outside. And for Christians, at least, a sense of place must involve dialogue with God.

Within the Welsh spiritual tradition, questions of place and national identity are engaged in intimate dialogue with each other. The academic discipline of spirituality is likewise by its very nature dialogic, since it attempts an internal encounter between different fields of study. But another definition of 'spirituality', namely the lived religious experience, also involves an external, existential encounter with non-religious worlds and ideas. In the concepts of place and nation, many different realities come together, in potential harmony or chaos, and there remain many possible dialogues in which Welsh spiritual traditions may be a partner, including conversations with other spiritual traditions, both Christian and non-Christian, and secular understandings of place and nationality. In these dialogues, a Chalcedonian understanding of the interpenetration of potentially warring elements illuminates the fact that the outside, the strange, the divergent and the unfamiliar, are not threats to purity, but complement and help widen the perception of the truth.

The idea of 'place' stresses only certain aspects of land. Throughout this book, I have considered place mostly in the light of its human significance, but a whole field of dialogue between spiritual and political ideas and ecological considerations remains to be explored: how, for example, might synchronic and diachronic understandings of society challenge and be challenged by a concern for the biological environment? Another field for exploration is that of the physical landscape and demographics of spirituality. The Christian spirituality of place I have tried to explore in this book emphasizes historical and social aspects of land, stressing that it is awareness that creates a sense of place. Out of a religious distaste for paganism, these notions shy away from any superficial essentialist understandings of place. Also fuelling them is a political distaste for colonialist assumptions that people with differing cultural and social awareness can or do partake of the same experience of place. But the material realities of land inevitably affect all human identity and spirituality, whatever the origins of the people who live there: the small scale and dramatically varied nature of Welsh land has inevitably made it easier to discover the macrocosm at work in the microcosm of Wales. Other spiritualities have made local geographical features central to their religious experience – the Australian Aborigines, the Apache, are just two examples. The question then arises of whether particular types of landscape – plain or mountain, forest or desert, rural or urban – foster particular religious experiences, and if so, what is their universal import?

Other areas of ongoing dialogue include internal Welsh issues. The long-held understanding of the Welsh as a religious nation has undergone change, but there are strong signs that this particular synthesis of Church and nation may at last be coming to an end. In place of monolithic definitions of national characteristics, a greater plurality of possible Welshnesses is arising, of which the religious is only one. Dialogue between secular and spiritual partners as to the nature of nationality will help to ensure that such newly emerging identities find expression.

In all of these conversations, perfect agreement will remain an ideal and a horizon – but the process of encounter will itself open up new horizons. Benedictine monks traditionally make a commitment to *conversatio morum*. The discipline of dialogue and the religious process of moral conversion are both dynamic processes, in which the static element is the constant willingness to listen and to evolve into true, better, and more beautiful expressions of identity. The aim of dialogue is not to forge uniformity out of divergence, but to create and nurture harmonious growth. And we can only create dialogue out of a strong sense of our own specific identity.

For the time being, Welsh spiritual traditions continue to live and to change. It is my fervent hope that the next century will see the development of a more inculturated Welsh Catholicism, one which is more aware of all of the treasures of Welsh spirituality. I hope also to see the development of an ecumenical Welsh spirituality, which is more aware of its place in the wider community of faith. In a spirituality of place and nation, all Welsh Christians may find things old and new. Twentieth-century Welsh Nonconformists especially have inherited the Welsh-Israelite tradition, with its riches and its poverty. In a biblically based, historically engaged spirituality of nationhood, these Welsh Christians may find much they can identify with. Sacramentalist Christians in Wales – Anglicans, Catholics and the few Orthodox – have the gift of a strong sense of church, but have frequently suffered historically from a vitiated sense of national identity. They will be able to identify strongly with sacramentalist understanding of individual places in the riches of the Catholic-local tradition but may also see the sacramentality of the nation. In both traditions, *pars pro toto* understandings can see Wales and Welshness as processes of perpetual creation, looking outward in universal engagement with a wider church and a more all-inclusive humanity. United in their concerns for the Kingdom within Wales, and for Wales within the Kingdom, the conversation – and conversion – of these faith traditions can bring together faith and works, creation and salvation, contemplation and action, responsibilities and rights, Wales and the world.

Notes

Notes to Chapter 1: Mapping the terrain

1 Belden C. Lane, *Landscapes of the Sacred: Geography and Narrative in American Spirituality* (Mahwah, NJ, Paulist Press, 1988), 130.

2 In conversation with me, 21 June 1994.

3 I have invented this label with a certain trepidity, perfectly conscious of a danger of baptizing into membership of the Catholic Church those whose work lies in this tradition – something which Saunders Lewis could have been accused of in his writings on say, Ann Griffiths and Pantycelyn, and which represents something resembling religious colonialism. Karl Rahner's theology of 'anonymous Christianity' to describe other religions is a similar expression of this tendency. I do not by this term wish to suggest that every poet who writes in praise of his local neighbourhood is a Papist in disguise! On the other hand, I also believe that the religious roots which underpin this literary tradition may well lie in a latent, unconscious and residual Catholicism.

4 In conversation with me, 21 June 1994.

Notes to Chapter 2: Laying the firm foundations

1 The title of D. Densil Morgan's book on J. E. Daniel, itself a quotation from Gwenallt's poem on the same author.

2 Mircea Eliade, *The Sacred and the Profane: The Nature of Religion*, tr. William R. Trask (New York, Harcourt Brace and World Inc., 1959), 20ff.

3 Geoffrey Lilburne, *A Sense of Place: A Christian Theology of the Land* (Nashville, TN, Abingdon Press, 1989).

4 On Newtonian space, see R. Glen Coughlin, 'Some considerations on Aristotelian place and Newtonian space', *The Aquinas Review*, 1, 1 (1994, Santa Paula, CA), 1.

5 Lane, *Landscapes*, 15.

6 Ellen Ross, 'Diversities of divine presence: women's geography in the Christian tradition', in J. Scott and P. Simpson-Housley (eds.), *Sacred Places and Profane* (New York, Greenwood Press, 1991), 93–114.

7 Walter Brueggemann, *The Land: Place as Gift, Promise and Challenge in Biblical Faith* (Philadelphia, Fortress, 1977).

8 Yi-Fu Tuan, 'Sacred space: explorations of an idea', in *Dimensions of Human Geography: Essays on Some Familiar and Neglected Themes* (Chicago, University of Chicago Department of Geography, 1978), 84–99.

9 Yi-Fu Tuan, 'Geopiety: a theme in man's attachment to nature and to place', in David Lowenthal and Martyn J. Bowden (eds.), *Geographies of the Mind: Essays in Historical Geography* (New York, Oxford University Press, 1976), 11ff.

10 Gaston Bachelard, *The Poetics of Space*, tr. Maria Jolas, with an introduction by Etienne Gilson (New York, Orion Press, 1964), 3ff.

11 This evaluation through imagery is the same tool as I use in assessing the theological import of the poetry of Gwenallt and Waldo Williams.

12 Bachelard, *Poetics*, 5.

13 Lane, *Landscapes*, 25.

14 Quoted in Lilburne, *Sense of Place*, 26. This bears interesting comparison with attitudes towards mountains in nineteenth-century Welsh literature and landscape paintings. Ioan Bowen Rees's 'Landscape and identity', *New Welsh Review*, 25 (Summer 1994), 17–26, quotes O. M. Edwards: 'Wales is a land of mountains . . . Its mountains explain its love of independence . . . A land of mountains . . . forms the character of those whom come to it.' Peter Lord's excellent article on Welsh landscape painting, 'Tir y Cymry: Golau newydd ar hen ddelwedd' (The land of the Welsh: new light on an old image), *Taliesin*, 89 (Spring 1995), notes that in the nineteenth century, Welsh landscape was felt to be a symbol and cause of the honour of its being the nurturing place of the Methodist 'saints', noting the prevalence in art and literature of the combination of the mountainous landscape of Wales and its high degree of public religiosity.

15 Keith H. Basso, ' "Stalking with stories": names, places, and moral narratives among the Western Apache', in D. Halpern (ed.), *On Nature: Nature, Landscape, and Natural History* (San Francisco, North Point Press, 1986), 95–11. For further details on the moral behaviour which particular places evoke for the Native American, see Leslie Marmon Silko, 'Landscape, history and the Pueblo imagination', ibid. 83–94.

16 Bruce Chatwin, *The Songlines* (London, Cape, 1987).

17 Lilburne, *Sense of Place*, 36–7.

18 The insights of Edward Said's classic study of colonial European attitudes towards Asia, *Orientalism* (London, Routledge & Kegan Paul, 1978), may easily be applied to English attitudes towards

Celticity. See also Peter Lord's concise study, 'A Celtic muddle', in *Gwenllian: Essays on Visual Culture* (Llandysul, Gomer, 1994).
19 Lane, *Landscapes*, 190–1.
20 Ibid., 191.
21 Jonathan Z. Smith, *Map is Not Territory: Studies in the History of Religions* (Leiden, E. J. Brill, 1978), 101.
22 Ibid., 2.
23 Ibid., 110.
24 Eliade, *Sacred and Profane*, 32ff.
25 Yi-Fu Tuan, 'Sacred space', 90.
26 Philip Sheldrake's *Spirituality and History* (New York, Crossroad, 1992), 201ff., discusses different types of spirituality which are fostered by specific attitudes towards place, two of which seem applicable to Wales: a 'catholic' type where 'God is essentially *present* and revelation is bound up with specific context, priesthood, cult and holy places', and a 'city of God' spirituality where 'the context for transformation is one special place, inner or outer, to the exclusion of others – this place is a reflection of the Kingdom of God in a privileged way . . . [T]he classical expression [of this is] monasticism, which seeks to build a kingdom community.' In the light of this, and given the importance of monasticism in Celtic Christianity in general and in Welsh political and cultural history up until the dissolution of the monasteries, this suggests that Welsh spirituality contains a quasi-identification not only with the Church, but specifically with monasticism. Medieval ideas of the cloister as *paradisum* are echoed in nineteenth-century writings on Wales as a moral, Protestant paradise: in both cases the place is made holy by the holy lives of its inhabitants which contrast with the *saeculum* which lies beyond their borders.
27 Brueggemann, *The Land*, 52.
28 Ibid., 93.
29 A problem identified in Lilburne, *Sense of Place*, 66.
30 Ibid., 57.
31 Quoted in W. D. Davies, *The Gospel and the Land: Early Christianity and Jewish Territorial Doctrine* (Berkeley, University of California Press, 1974), 368.
32 On the development of the Holy Land as a Christian concept, see Robert L. Wilken, *The Land called Holy* (New Haven: Yale University Press, 1992).
33 *15 Hom. in Cant.*
34 Lilburne, *Sense of Place*, 101–2.
35 Wolfhart Pannenberg, *Human Nature, Election and History* (Philadelphia, Westminster, 1977), 50.

36 Ibid., 54.
37 The Eusebian vision of history is espoused by Gildas, who sees the Christian Britons as inheritors of Roman culture and destiny.
38 Pannenberg, *Human Nature*, 68.
39 Ibid., 74.
40 Quoted in ibid., 77.
41 Lane, *Landscapes*, 110.
42 Pannenberg, *Human Nature*, 89.
43 Ibid., 92.
44 Ibid., 95.
45 Ibid., 96–7.
46 William Pfaff, 'Nationalism and identity', *The Way*, 34 (January 1994), 6–16.
47 Ibid., 6.
48 Ibid., 15.
49 Ibid., 12.
50 Isaiah Berlin *The Crooked Timber of Humanity: Chapters in the History of Ideas* (New York, Knopf, 1991).
51 Ibid., 235.

Notes to Chapter 3: Standing in the breach

1 From Saunders Lewis's 'Vineyard' speech. See chapter 4.
2 See Geraint H. Jenkins, *Religion, Language and Nationality in Wales* (Cardiff, University of Wales Press, 1990).
3 See Prys Morgan, 'Welsh national consciousness: the historical background', in W. J. Morgan (ed.), *The Welsh Dilemma* (Llandybïe, Christopher Davies, 1973), 14–35. Prys Morgan, 'From a death to a view: the hunt for the Welsh past in the Romantic period', in Eric Hobsbawm and Terence Ranger (eds.), *The Invention of Tradition* (New York, Cambridge University Press, 1983).
4 See Derec Llwyd Morgan, *The Eighteenth Century Welsh Religious Revival* (London, Epworth, 1988). Also R. Tudur Jones, 'The evangelical revival in Wales: a study in spirituality', in J. Mackey (ed.), *An Introduction to Celtic Christianity* (Edinburgh, T. & T. Clark, 1989). 'Nonconformism' denotes the 'chapel religion' of Wales, that is, most varieties of Protestantism, but not including the Anglican Church in Wales.
5 Geraint J. Jenkins, *Cadw Tŷ Mewn Cwmwl Tystion:Ysgrifau Hanesyddol ar Grefydd a Diwylliant* [Keeping House in a Cloud of Witnesses: Historical Essays on Religion and Culture] (Llandysul, Gomer, 1990), 54.

6   Gwyn Alf Williams, 'Twf hanesyddol y syniad o genedl yng Nghymru' [The historical growth of the idea of the nation in Wales], *Efrydiau Athronyddol* (1961), 35.

7   R. Tudur Jones, *Ffydd ac Argyfwng Cenedl* [Faith and National Crisis], 2 vols. (Swansea, Tŷ John Penry, 1982), vol. 1, 89.

8   Respectively, Evan Williams and David Davies, two nineteenth-century Nonconformist ministers, quoted in Peter Lord, 'Tir y Cymry' [Land of the Welsh], *Taliesin*, 89 (Spring 1995).

9   Quoted in Geraint Gruffydd, 'Ein hiaith a'n diwylliant' [Our language and culture], *Cylchgrawn Efengylaidd* (March 1979), 82.

10 Quoted in R. Tudur Jones, 'Yr Eglwysi a'r Iaith yn Oes Victoria' [The Churches and the Welsh Language in the Victorian Era], *Llên Cymru*, 19 (1996), 165.

11 Ibid., 165.

12 R. Tudur Jones, *Ffydd ac Argyfwng Cenedl*, 224.

13 Ned Thomas, *The Welsh Extremist: A Culture in Crisis* (London, Victor Gollancz, 1971), 23.

14 A younger generation of historiographers and non-Christian nation-alists eloquently critique such unilateral notions. See for example John Davies, *A History of Wales* (London, Penguin Books, 1994) and Gwyn A. Williams, *When was Wales?: A History of the Welsh* (London, Penguin Books, 1985).

15 Glanmor Williams, 'Fire on Cambria's Altar: the Welsh and their religion', in *The Welsh and Their Religion: Historical Essays* (Cardiff, University of Wales Press, 1991), 102.

16 Ned Thomas, *Welsh Extremist*, 60.

17 Emrys ap Iwan (Robert Ambrose Jones), *Y Ddysg Newydd a'r Hen* [The Old and New Teachings], in *Homilïau* [Homilies], vol. 2 (Denbigh, Gee, 1903), 107.

18 Quoted in R. Tudur Jones, 'The evangelical revival', 246.

19 John Saunders Lewis (1893–1985) – Catholic convert, dramatist, literary critic and historian, poet, university lecturer, one-time prisoner for the first modern act of Welsh political protest, founder of Plaid Cymru and the inspiration of language activism from the 1960s onwards – is without doubt the most significant Welsh figure of the twentieth century. No account of Welsh nationalism would be complete without taking into account his many contributions. In his Catholicism and his aristocratic stance, however, Lewis stands apart from the mainstream: his understanding of Wales and his philosophy is notably more sophisticated and European than that of most of his contemporaries and compatriots. His writing does not stand generally in the line which I am attempting to trace, but is rather a continuation of late medieval and Renaissance humanism, touched

by neo-scholasticism and the philosophy of Action Française. For these reasons this book does not include a substantial study of Lewis.

20 See Brueggemann, *The Land*, 93–6, on inheritance as a land notion.

21 *Torri'r Seiliau Sicr: Detholiad o Ysgrifau J. E. Daniel* [Making the Firm Foundations: A Selection of the Writings of J. E. Daniel], with a foreword by D. Densil Morgan (Llandysul, Gomer, 1993), 74.

22 Ibid., 34.

23 This view is challenged by J. R. Jones: 'The family has been considered as part of the "land" in which personality is rooted and from which it draws its nourishment . . . There is a vague comparison between the nation and the family as national and original form of organic intercourse. But it is not enough to establish the spiritual significance of the nation on its similarity to the family, since there are also differences between the two. The family is based on sexuality and reproduction. It also has a spiritual function of being the personal nurturing-place of people. But we must have more than a small circle of intercourse for the handing-on of culture. We also need a society or a world which will be the theatre for creating culture.' J. R. Jones, *Cristnogaeth a Chenedlaetholdeb* [Christianity and Nationalism], (n.pl., n.d.), 15.

24 Daniel, *Torri'r Seiliau Sicr*, 76.

25 Gwynfor Evans, 'Gwleidyddiaeth a'r genedl' [Politics and the nation], in Dewi Eirug Davies (ed.), *Gwinllan a Roddwyd* [The Vineyard that was Given] (Llandybïe, Christopher Davies, 1972), 89. The Welsh Independent chapels own a theology of church which is resoundingly Congregational. Together, they form one of the larger of historical Welsh Christian denominations.

26 Daniel, *Torri'r Seiliau Sicr*, 86.

27 Ibid.

28 Rt. Revd G. O. Williams, 'Christianity and nationalism', in W. J. Morgan (ed.), *The Welsh Dilemma – Essays on Nationalism in Wales* (Llandybïe, Christopher Davies, 1973).

29 Gwynfor Evans, 'Gwleidyddiaeth a'r genedl', 201.

30 Herder is quoted approvingly by J. R. Jones: 'It was the work of Providence to separate out Peoples from each other, not only by forests and mountains and the extremes of climate . . . but also by something much more effective, namely differences in language and the specificity of national character and tendencies, so that the work of the oppressive Powers might be rendered more difficult and that humankind might not be pressed into the jaws of one Trojan Horse of a world-wide state.' J. R. Jones, *Prydeindod* [Britishness] (Llandybïe, Christopher Davies, 1966), 1.

31 Gwynfor Evans, 'Gwleidyddiaeth a'r genedl', 94. Cf. G. O. Williams,

'Christianity and nationalism', 59: 'If I am to pay serious regard to the Christian understanding of creation, I am bound to affirm that national cultures are too important to be discarded as though they were an impediment to human history . . . The way to become more involved with the human community in general is to enter as deeply as I can into my own particular heritage, and use this as a means of appreciating cultures other than my own, learning respect for their distinctiveness and responding to them with sympathy and understanding. It cannot be by accident that a very small country like Wales has produced far more that its share of outstanding pioneers and servants of international relations. There is an inborn understanding of what it means to belong to a poor and exploited people whose roots go down to an ancient and still living past.'

32 Dewi Watkin Powell, 'Etholedigaeth a'r genedl gymreig' [Election and the Welsh Nation], in E. Stanley John (ed.), *Y Gair a'r Genedl* [The Word and the Nation], (Swansea, Tŷ John Penry, 1986).

33 Ibid., 191–2.

34 Ibid., 192.

35 Ibid., 197.

36 Ibid., 199.

37 Ibid., 196.

38 R. Tudur Jones, 'Christian nationalism', in P. J. Ballard and D. H. Jones (eds.), *This Land and People: A Symposium on Christian and Welsh National Identity* (Cardiff, Collegiate Centre of Theology, 1979), 75.

39 Ibid., 79.

40 Ibid., 80–1.

41 Ibid., 86.

42 Ibid., 84.

43 Ibid., 89. Cf. *Catechism of the Catholic Church*, no. 2239: 'It is the *duty of citizens* to contribute . . . to the good of society in a spirit of truth, justice, solidarity and freedom. The love and service *of one's country* follow from the duty of gratitude and belong to the order of charity.' (My italics.)

44 R. Tudor Jones, 'Crist: Gobaith Cenedl' [Christ: The Hope of the Nation], in Dewi Eirug Davies (ed.), *Gwinllan a Roddwyd* (Llandybïe, Christopher Davies, 1972), 110.

45 D. R. Thomas, 'Cenedligrwydd a Chrefydd' [National identity and religion], *Efrydiau Athronyddol* (1961), 41.

46 J. Gwynfor Jones, 'Nation, language and religion: the historical background', in Ballard and Jones (eds.), *This Land and People*, 18.

47 G. O. Williams, 'Christianity and nationalism', 61.

48 Ned Thomas, *Welsh Extremist*, 29, 32 and 64.

194 *Sacred Place, Chosen People*

49 J. R. Jones, *Gwaedd yng Nghymru* [A Cry in Wales] (Swansea, Cyhoeddiadau Modern Cymreig, n.d.), 1.
50 *Prydeindod*, 12.
51 J. R. Jones, *Cristnogaeth a Chenedlaetholdeb* [Christianity and Nationalism] (n.pl., n.d.), 6.
52 J. R. Jones, 'Y Syniad o Genedl' [The Idea of a Nation], *Efrydiau Athronyddol* (1961), 5.
53 J. R. Jones, *Ac Onide* [But If Not] (Llandybïe, Dryw, 1970), 159–60.
54 *Cristnogaeth a Chenedlaetholdeb*, 7.
55 *Ac Onide*, 85.
56 'Y Syniad o Genedl', 12.
57 *Ac Onide*, 170.
58 *Prydeindod*, 13.
59 Ibid., 9.
60 Quoted in R. Tudur Jones, 'Cenedlaetholdeb J. R. Jones' [J. R. Jones's Nationalism], *Efrydiau Athronyddol* (1971), 26. R. Tudur Jones proudly points out that this idea is found in Welsh literature two centuries before Fichte, in the works of the Puritan John Penry.
61 A reference to Waldo Williams's poem 'Cymru'n Un'. See Chap. 6.
62 *Prydeindod*, 3.
63 Ibid., 67. Another example of the continuing Welsh identification with the Jews is Saunders Lewis's note that his play *Esther* was inspired by Racine's play of the same name: 'Between my time and Racine's there lay Hitler's attempt . . . to destroy the Jewish nation utterly . . . And I could not forget that my own nation too was being wiped out, just as efficiently, though not in such obviously diabolical ways.' Quoted in Thomas, *Welsh Extremist*, 97.
64 Jer. 32: 15, quoted in J. R. Jones, *A Raid i'r Iaith ein Gwahanu?* [Must Language Keep us Apart?] (Aberystwyth, Cymru Fydd, 1967; reprint, Aberystwyth, Cymdeithas yr Iaith Gymraeg, 1978), 24.
65 Ned Thomas, *Waldo Williams* (Gwasg Pantycelyn: Caernarfon, 1985).
66 Ibid., 69.
67 Gwenallt's lyric, 'Cymru' (Wales). See Chap. 5.
68 From Saunders Lewis's 'Vineyard' speech. See Chap. 4.
69 *Cenedlaetholdeb J. R. Jones*, 31–2.
70 *Prydeindod*, 12.

Notes to Chapter 4: Extra Cambriam nulla salus
1 The classical scholastic dictum that salvation is gained only within the confines of the Catholic Church I have applied, tongue-in-cheek, to Wales.

2 Miranda Green, *Dictionary of Celtic Myth and Legend* (London, Thames and Hudson, 1992), 22.

3 Ibid., 182.

4 Miranda Green, *The Gods of the Celts* (Gloucester, Alan Sutton, 1986), 16.

5 Robert W. Hanning, *The Vision of History in Early Britain from Gildas to Geoffrey of Monmouth* (New York, Columbia University Press, 1966), 48. Cf. the function of place as moral mnemonic (p. 22) and Hobsbawm's observations on the power of image in the shaping of a nation.

6 See Elissa Henken, *National Redeemer: Owain Glyndŵr in Welsh Tradition* (Cardiff, University of Wales Press, 1996).

7 For what follows I depend largely on Hanning.

8 Hanning, *Vision of History*, 27.

9 Ibid., 39.

10 Ibid., 39.

11 *Gildas' 'The Ruin of Britain' and Other Works*, ed. and tr. Michael Winterbottom (London, Phillimore and Co., 1978). All references to *De Excidio* are to section divisions. *De Excidio*, 20. 3.

12 Ibid., 1. 7.

13 Ibid., 93. 4.

14 Ibid., 97. 1.

15 Ibid., 22. 3.

16 Ibid., 21. 2.

17 Ibid., 83. 2.

18 Ibid., 70.

19 Ibid., 3.

20 See A. C. Sutherland, 'The imagery of Gildas' *De Excidio Britanniae*', in M. Lapidge and D. Dumville (eds.), *Gildas: New Approaches* (Studies in Celtic History, 5; Woodbridge, Boydell Press, 1984), 157–88.

21 *De Excidio*, 8.

22 Ibid., 24. 4.

23 Ibid., 40. 2.

24 Ibid., 24. 2.

25 Ibid., 3. 1.

26 Ibid., 11. 1.

27 Ibid., 4.

28 Ibid., 23.1.

29 Winterbottom, Introduction, 3.

30 Phil. 3: 20.

31 *De Excidio*, 110.3.

32 See Ann Griffiths, 'Rhai agweddau ar y syniad o genedl yng

nghyfnod y cywyddwyr, 1320–1603' [Some aspects of the concept of nation in the period of the court poets, 1320–1603], Ph.D. thesis, Aberystwyth, 1988.

33 The efforts of Giraldus Cambrensis to secure ecclesiastical independence from Canterbury for the see of St David's are witness to this.

34 Derec Llwyd Morgan, *Charles Edwards* (Caernarfon, Pantycelyn, 1994), 1. I am deeply indebted to this full study of Edwards. See also his monograph, *Canys Bechan Yw: Y Genedl Etholedig yn ein Llenyddiaeth* [For She is Small: the Chosen Nation in our Literature] (Aberystwyth, Prifysgol Cymru, 1994).

35 Derec Llwyd Morgan, 'Y Beibl a Llenyddiaeth Gymraeg' [The Bible and Welsh Literature], in J. Geraint Gruffydd (ed.), *Y Gair ar Waith* [The Bible at Work] (Cardiff, University of Wales Press, 1988), 33.

36 Morgan, *Charles Edwards*, 11.

37 Ibid., 11.

38 Richard Davies, 'Epistol at y Cembru' [An Epistle to the Welsh], in Garfield H. Hughes (ed.), *Rhagymadroddion 1547–1659* [Forewords and Introductions to Welsh Religious Books, 1547–1659] (Cardiff, University of Wales Press, 1951), 22.

39 Ibid., 18. This concept of the Anglican Church was not necessarily original to Davies: both Archbishop Matthew Parker and the Welsh humanist William Salesbury had corresponded with Davies about the idea. See 'Deddfwriaeth y Tuduriaid a statws gwleidyddol yr iaith' [Tudor legislation and the legal status of Welsh], in Geraint H. Jenkins (ed.), *Y Gymraeg yn ei Disgleirdeb* (Cardiff, University of Wales Press, 1997), 145.

40 Morgan, *Charles Edwards*, 25.

41 In translating the citations from *Y Ffydd Ddi-Ffuant*, I have followed Edwards's use of typefaces, to indicate where a biblical citation begins. Edwards's Bible was the 1620 revision of the 1588 translation. I use the English Authorized Version, as an almost direct parallel to the Welsh translation in terms of period and translation style. The Welsh of the 1620 translation has as rich and antique a patina as the English of the Authorized Version.

42 Charles Edwards, *Y Ffydd Ddi-Ffuant: sef Hanes y Ffydd Gristianogol a'i rhinwedd* [The Unfeignèd Faith: Namely the History and Virtue of the Christian Faith], facsimile edn. ed. with an introduction by G. J. Williams (Cardiff, University of Wales Press, 1936), 196–7.

43 Edwards, *Y Ffydd Ddi-Ffuant*, 153.

44 Edwards, *Y Ffydd Ddi-Ffuant*, 182.

45 Ibid., 'At y darlleydd' [To the reader], unpaginated introduction to *Y Ffydd Ddi-Ffuant*.

46 Robert Owen Jones, *Hir Oes i'r Iaith: Agweddau ar Hanes y Gymraeg*

a'r Gymdeithas [May the Language Live Long: Historical Aspects of Welsh Language and Society] (Llandysul, Gwasg Gomer, 1997), 10–11.

47 *Y Ffydd Ddi-Ffuant*, 405.
48 Ibid., 150. Edwards is reflecting here the ancient myth, deriving from Geoffrey of Monmouth, that Brutus founded Britain after the Trojan wars.
49 Ibid., 214. The myth that Gomer, son of Japheth, son of Noah, was the founder of the Welsh nation, had already been propagated by Welsh humanists.
50 Ibid., 'At y darlleydd'.
51 Ibid., 208. In this excerpt, Edwards unshamefacedly substitutes 'Wales' for the 'Jacob' of Amos 7: 2.
52 Ibid., 209.
53 Ibid., 211.
54 Morgan, *Charles Edwards*, 31.
55 Edwards, *Y Ffydd Ddi-Ffuant*, 214.
56 See Peter Lord, 'Tir y Cymry', *Taliesin*, 89 (Spring 1995), 55ff.
57 See Chap. 3 n. 18.
58 Quoted in Harri Pritchard Jones, *Saunders Lewis: A Presentation of his Work* (Springfield, Il., Templegate Publishers, 1990), 101.
59 Cf. Yi-Fu Tuan's notion of geopiety, discussed in Chap. 2.
60 Harri Pritchard Jones, *Saunders Lewis*, 60–1. I have slightly emended this translation.
61 Ibid., 60.
62 Morgan, *Y Beibl a Llenyddiaeth Gymraeg*, 112.
63 Ibid., 84. Morgan is referring to the fact that biblical place-names are quite frequent in Wales, yet another typologically inspired link of geography with religion.
64 *Blodeugerdd o'r XIX ganrif* [A Nineteenthth-century Anthology], ed. Bedwyr Lewis Jones (Aberystwyth, Cymdeithas Llyfrau Ceredigion, 1978), 57.

Notes to Chapter 5: A kingdom of priests
1 Quoted in J. E. Meredith, *Gwenallt: Bardd Crefyddol* [Gwenallt the Religious Poet] (Llandysul, Gwasg Gomer, 1974), 11.
2 Man must choose, choose between living
And chemical death, between civilization and suicide.
Our God is the rural God; he is not an industrial God:
He does not remain within factory, laboratory and atomic reactor.
'Jezebel ac Elias' [Jezebel and Elijah], in Gwenallt, *Gwreiddiau*

[Roots] (Llandysul, Gomer, 1959), 85. All translations of Gwenallt's poems are mine unless otherwise noted.

3 Where Deirdre's beauty and song once were,
   CúChulainn's bravery and the warriors of Finn,
   Came the English forces with their steel and fire
   To rip open the valley and to rape the hill . . .

   . . . Like a hidden spring Finn's spring flowed
   Growing to a flood in the centuries' turning
   Till it has become in our days a bold river, warlike in its course;
   Its rush brought freedom and peace,
   And the barbarians are swept into the sea.

   'Iwerddon' [Ireland], in Gwenallt, *Ysgubau'r Awen* [Sheaves of the Muse] (Llandysul, Gomer, 1938), 34.

4 Bobi Jones, 'Gwenallt', in *Crist a Chenedlaetholdeb* [Christ and Nationalism] (Bridgend, Evangelical Press of Wales, 1994), 96.

5 'Y Ddaear' [The Earth], *Y Coed* [The Trees] (Llandysul, Gomer, 1969), 38.

6 See Chap. 2, for the difference between 'place' and 'space'.

7 'Rhydcymerau', English translation from *Oxford Book of Welsh Verse in English* (Oxford, Oxford University Press, 1977), 200.

8 'Cwm Tryweryn', *Gwreiddiau*, 39.

9 'Cymru' [Wales], *Gwreiddiau*, 46.

10 Ibid., 45.

11 *Ysgubau'r Awen*, 70.

12 Ibid., 84.

13 Ibid., 25.

14 *Gwreiddiau*, 46.

15 'Ar Gyfeiliorn' [Lost], *Ysgubau'r Awen*, 27.

16 'Dewi Sant' [St David], *Eples* [Leaven] (Llandysul, Gomer), 64.

17 'Yr Esgob William Morgan' [Bishop William Morgan], *Gwreiddiau*, 51.

18 'Eglwys y Pater Noster' [The Church of the Pater Noster], *Y Coed*, 53.

19 Quoted in Meredith, *Gwenallt*, 139.

20 'Pechod' [Sin], *Ysgubau'r Awen*, 78.

21 Ibid., 78.

22 'Cymru' [Wales], *Ysgubau'r Awen*, 70.

23 'Cymru', in *Oxford Book of Welsh Verse in English*, 201–2.

24 Bobi Jones, 'Gwenallt', 112.

25 Ned Thomas, *The Welsh Extremist* (London, Victor Gollancz), 62ff.

26 Gwenallt in conversation, quoted in T. Emrys Parry, 'Ystyried "Ysgubau'r Awen" ', *Ysgrifau Beirniadol* (March 1969), 262.

27 'Yr Eglwys', *Ysgubau'r Awen*, 79.

28 'Sul y Pasg' [Easter Sunday], *Gwreiddiau*, 113.
29 'Ynys Cyprus' [Cyprus], *Gwreiddiau*, 53.
30 Jonathan Z. Smith, *To Take Place: Toward Theory in Ritual* (Chicago, University of Chicago Press, 1987), 88ff.
31 'Dewi Sant' [St David], *Eples*, 63.
32 'Catholigrwydd' [Catholicity], *Y Coed, 26.*
33 'Y Capel yn Sir Gaerfyrddin' [The Chapel in Carmarthenshire], *Gwreiddiau*, 47.
34 'Noswyl yr Holl Eneidiau' [All Souls' Eve], *Gwreiddiau*, 10.
35 'Sir Benfro' [Pembrokeshire], *Eples*, 67.
36 'Oberammergau,' *Eples*, 71.
37 *Ysgubau'r Awen*, 85.
38 'Cartrefi'r Gweithwyr' [Workers' Homes], *Gwreiddiau*, 48.
39 'Dewi Sant', *Eples*, 63.
40 'Y Tipiau' [The Tips], *Gwreiddiau*, 57.
41 'Cymru,' *Oxford Book of Welsh Verse in English*, 201.
42 'Prosser Rhys', *Eples*, 33.
43 Keith Basso, ' "Stalking with stories": names, places, and moral narratives among the Western Apache,' in D. Halpern (ed.), *On Nature: Nature, Landscape, and Natural History* (San Francisco, North Point Press, 1986), 110ff.
44 'Morgannwg' [Glamorgan], *Gwreiddiau*, 57.
45 'Sir Forgannwg a Sir Gaerfyrddin' [Glamorgan and Carmarthenshire], *Eples*, 24.
46 'Llywelyn Ein Llyw Olaf ' [Llywelyn Our Last Prince], *Gwreiddiau*, 37.
47 'Yr Iddewon' [The Jews], *Y Coed*, 72.
48 'Y Wal Wylofus' [The Wailing Wall], *Y Coed*, 57.
49 'Cymru', *Oxford Book of Welsh Verse in English*, 202.
50 'Y Cymun' [Communion], *Y Coed*, 60.
51 'Bethlehem', *Y Coed*, 44.

Notes to Chapter 6: Apocalypse of tradition
1 Tony Bianchi, 'Waldo and Apocalypse', *Planet*, 44 (August 1978).
2 Waldo published only one volume of work, *Dail Pren* [Leaves of the Tree], apart from a co-authored book of poems for children. I have used *Cerddi Waldo Williams* [The Poems of Waldo Williams] (Newtown, Gregynog Press, 1992) as the source for this study, and all footnotes refer to this volume.
3 Quoted in James Nicholas (ed.), *Waldo: Cyfrol Deyrnged* [Waldo: A Tribute](Llandysul, Gwasg Gomer, 1997), 225.
4 Bobi Jones, *Cyfriniaeth Gymraeg* [Welsh Mysticism] (Cardiff, University of Wales Press, 1994).

5   From Waldo's Statement as a conscientious objector to the Tribunal in Carmarthen, 12 February 1942, published in *Y Traethodydd* (October 1971).

6   Bianchi, 'Waldo and Apocalypse'.

7   Bobi Jones, 'Ein cerdd genedlaethol gyntaf' [Our first national poem], *Barddas*, 190 (February 1993), 12ff.

8   See Chap. 4 on the psychology of exile in Gildas.

9   Bobi Jones, *Cyfriniaeth Gymraeg*, 248.

10 Ned Thomas, *Waldo* (Cyfres Llên y Llenor; Caernarfon, Pantycelyn, 1985).

11 John Rowlands, 'Waldo Williams, bardd y gobaith pryderus' [Waldo Williams, poet of anxious hope], in Nicholas, *Waldo: Cyfrol Deyrnged*, 206.

12 This translation draws on Waldo's own, printed in James Nicholas, *Waldo Williams* (Writers of Wales series; Cardiff, University of Wales Press, 1975) and that of Joseph Clancy, *Twentieth Century Welsh Poems* (Llandysul, Gwasg Gomer, 1983).

13 Bianchi, 'Waldo and Apocalypse', 9.

14 'Y Tŵr a'r Graig', *Cerddi Waldo Williams (CWW)*, 27.

15 *CWW*, 40.

16 'Plentyn y Ddaear' [Child of the Earth], *CWW*, 33.

17 'Tŷ Ddewi', *CWW*, 10.

18 Tr. Nicholas, *Waldo Williams*, 36.

19 Robert Rhys, *Chwilio am Nodau'r Gân: Astudiaeth o Yrfa Lenyddol Waldo Williams hyd 1939* [Searching for the Notes of the Song: a Study of Waldo Williams's Literary Career up to 1939] (Gomer, Llandysul, 1990), 121. I have drawn extensively on his detailed study of 'Tŷ Ddewi'.

20 Ibid., 124.

21 Nicholas, *Waldo Williams*, 38–9.

22 'Cymru'n Un', tr. Nicholas, *Waldo Williams,* 4, slightly emended.

23 *CWW*, 58.

24 Bedwyr Lewis Jones, 'Waldo Williams: triniwr daear Dyfed' [Waldo Williams: tiller of Dyfed's soil], in Rhys, *Waldo Williams*, 178.

25 John Rowlands, 'Waldo Williams', 206.

26 Thomas, *Waldo*, 67.

27 'Cwmwl Haf' [A Summer Cloud], tr. Gwyn Jones, *Oxford Book of Welsh Verse in English* (Oxford, Oxford University Press, 1977), 218.

28 Ibid.

29 'Wedi'r Canrifoedd Mudan' [After the Silent Centuries], tr. A. Conran, *Welsh Verse*, 291. Since this book was written, Tony Conran has published *The Peacemakers*, translations of selected poems by Waldo, along with a valuable introduction to the poet's work.

30 'Y Tŵr a'r Graig', *CWW*, 28.

31   Quoted in Dyfnallt Morgan, 'Waldo Williams: thema yn ei waith' [A theme in the work of Waldo Williams], in Rhys, *Waldo Williams*, 248.
32   John Rowlands, 'Waldo Williams', 248.
33   'Yr Iaith a Garaf' [The Language I Love], *CWW*, 3.
34   'Cymru a Chymraeg' [Wales and Welsh], *CWW*, 59.
35   'Yr Heniaith' [The Old Language], *CWW*, 60.
36   'Cymru a Chymraeg', *CWW*, 59.
37   'Yr Heniaith', *CWW*, 60.
38   'Heb Deitl' [Untitled], *CWW*, 77.
39   'Bydd Ateb' [There will be an Answer], *CWW*, 65.
40   Tr. Nicholas, *Waldo Williams*, 56.
41   'Cwmwl Haf', *Oxford Book of Welsh Verse*, 56.
42   Nicholas, *Waldo: Cyfrol Deyrnged*, 177.
43   Berdyaev's influence on Waldo shows itself in this emphasis. Bianchi notes ('Waldo and Apocalypse', 12) the parallels between Waldo and 'the marriage of the mystical and the political in the work of Russian writers at the turn of the century, who frequently embraced some form of cultural nationalism, whilst prophesying the imminent reconciliation of violently conflicting forces in a new "sobornost" – that quality of being gathered together which they regarded as the chief value embodied in the Russian people'. On the concept of Holy Russia, see pp. 41–2.
44   Pp. 68–9.
45   Litany of Loreto.

Note to Epilogue

1   From Saunders Lewis's 'Vineyard' speech.

Select bibliography

Allchin, A. M., *Praise Above All: Discovering the Welsh Tradition* (Cardiff, University of Wales Press, 1991).

Allchin, A. M., *Celtic Christianity: Fact or Fantasy?* (Bangor, Wales, University of Wales Press, 1993).

Allchin, A. M., *God's Presence Makes the World: The Celtic Vision Through the Centuries in Wales* (London, Darton, Longman and Todd, 1997).

Armes Prydein [The Prophecy of Britain], ed. Sir Ifor Williams and tr. Rachel Bromwich (Dublin, Dublin Institute for Advanced Studies, 1982).

Bachelard, Gaston, *The Poetics of Space*, tr. Maria Jolas, with an introduction by Etienne Gilson (New York, Orion Press, 1964).

Ballard, P. J. and D. H. Jones (eds.), *This Land and People: A Symposium on Christian and Welsh National Identity* (Cardiff, Collegiate Centre of Theology, 1979).

Basso, Keith H. ' "Stalking with stories": names, places, and moral narratives among the Western Apache', in. D. Halpern (ed.), *On Nature: Nature, Landscape, and Natural History* (San Francisco, North Point Press, 1986), 95–116.

Berlin, Isaiah, *The Crooked Timber of Humanity: Chapters in the History of Ideas* (New York, Knopf, 1991).

Bianchi, Tony, 'Waldo and Apocalypse,' *Planet*, 44 (August 1978).

Brueggemann, Walter, *The Land: Place as Gift, Promise and Challenge in Biblical Faith* (Philadelphia, Fortress, 1977).

Clancy, Joseph, *Twentieth Century Welsh Poems* (Llandysul, Gwasg Gomer, 1983).

Conran, Tony, *Welsh Verse*, tr. with an introduction by Tony Conran (Bridgend, Poetry Wales Press, 1986).

Conran, Tony (tr.), *The Peacemakers: Selected Poems of Waldo Williams* (Llandysul, Gomer, 1997).

Davies, John, *A History of Wales* (London, Penguin Books, 1994).

Davies, Oliver, *Celtic Christianity in Early Medieval Wales: The Origins of the Welsh Spiritual Tradition* (Cardiff, University of Wales Press, 1996).

Davies, Oliver and Fiona Bowie, *Celtic Christian Spirituality* (London, SPCK, 1995).

Davies, W. D., *The Gospel and the Land: Early Christianity and Jewish Territorial Doctrine* (Berkeley, University of California Press, 1974).

Eliade, Mircea, *The Sacred and the Profane: The Nature of Religion*, tr. Willard R. Trask (New York, Harcourt, Brace and World, Inc., 1959).

Halpern, Daniel (ed.), *On Nature: Nature, Landscape and Natural History* (San Francisco, North Point Press, 1986).

Hanning, Robert W., *The Vision of History in Early Britain from Gildas to Geoffrey of Monmouth* (New York, Columbia University Press, 1966).

Henken, Elissa R., *The Welsh Saints: A Study in Patterned Lives* (Cambridge, D. S. Brewer, 1991).

Henken, Elissa R., *Traditions of the Welsh Saints* (Cambridge, D. S. Brewer, 1987).

Henken, Elissa R., *National Redeemer: Owain Glyndŵr in Welsh Tradition* (Cardiff, University of Wales Press, 1996).

Hobsbawm, Eric J., *Nations and Nationalism since 1780: Programme, Myth, Reality* (New York, Cambridge University Press, 1990).

Jones, Gwyn (ed.), *The Oxford Book of Welsh Verse in English* (Oxford, Oxford University Press, 1977).

Jones, Harri Pritchard, *Saunders Lewis: A Presentation of his Work* (Springfield, Il., Templegate Publishers, 1990).

Jones, J. Gwynfor, 'Nation, language and religion: the historical background', in P. J. Ballard and D. H. Jones (eds.), *This Land and People: A Symposium on Christian and Welsh National Identity* (Cardiff, Collegiate Centre of Theology, 1979), 14–21.

Jones, Robert Tudur, 'The evangelical revival in Wales: a study in spirituality', in James P. Mackey (ed.), *An Introduction to Celtic Christianity* (Edinburgh, T. & T. Clark, 1989), 237–67.

Jones, Robert Tudur, 'Christian nationalism', in P. J. Ballard and D. H. Jones (ed.), *This Land and People: A Symposium on Christian and Welsh National Identity* (Cardiff, Collegiate Centre of Theology, 1979), 74–97.

Lane, Belden C., *Landscapes of the Sacred: Geography and Narrative in American Spirituality* (Mahwah, NJ, Paulist Press, 1988).

Lapidge, M. and D. Dumville (eds.), *Gildas: New Approaches* (Studies in Celtic History, 5; Woodbridge, Boydell Press, 1984).

Lilburne, Geoffrey, *A Sense of Place: A Christian Theology of the Land* (Nashville, Abingdon Press, 1989).

Llywelyn, Dorian, 'Inculturation and the Catholic Church in Wales', *Priests and People* (October 1991).

Lord, Peter, *Gwenllian: Essays on Visual Culture* (Llandysul, Gomer, 1994).

Mackey, James P., *An Introduction to Celtic Christianity* (Edinburgh, T. & T. Clark, 1989).

Morgan, Prys, 'Welsh national consciousness: the historical background', in W. J. Morgan (ed.), *The Welsh Dilemma* (Llandybïe, Christopher Davies, 1973), 14–35.

Morgan, Prys, 'From a death to a view: the hunt for the Welsh past in the Romantic period', in Eric Hobsbawm and Terence Ranger (eds.), *The Invention of Tradition* (New York, Cambridge University Press, 1983).

Nicholas, James, *Waldo Williams* (Cardiff: University of Wales Press, 1975).

Pannenberg, Wolfhart, *Christianity in a Secularized World*, tr. John Bowden (New York, Crossroads, 1989).

Pannenberg, Wolfhart, *Human Nature, Election and History* (Philadelphia, Westminster, 1977).

Pfaff, William, 'Nationalism and identity', *The Way*, 34 (January 1994), 6–16.

Phillips, Dewi Z., *J. R. Jones* (Cardiff, University of Wales Press, 1995).

Ramanathan, Suguna and Fernando Franco, 'Universality and identity', *The Way*, 34 (January 1994), 17–27.

Rees, Ioan Bowen, 'Landscape and identity', *New Welsh Review*, 25 (Summer 1994), 17–26.

Rees, Ronald, 'Landscape in art', in University of Chicago Department of Geography, *Dimensions of Human Geography: Essays on Some Familiar and Neglected Themes* (Chicago, University of Chicago Department of Geography, 1978), 48–68.

Ross, Ellen, 'Diversities of divine presence: women's geography in the Christian tradition', in Jamie Scott and Paul Simpson-Housley (eds.), *Sacred Places and Profane Places: Essays in the Geographics of Judaism, Christianity and Islam* (New York, Greenwood Press 1991), 93–114.

Saunders, Scott Russell, 'Rediscovering our sense of place', *Notre Dame* 22, 4 (Winter 1993–4), 36–41.

Schama, Simon, *Landscape and Memory* (London, HarperCollins, 1995).

Scott, Jamie and Paul Simpson-Housley (eds.), *Sacred Places and Profane Spaces: Essays in the Geographics of Judaism, Christianity and Islam* (New York, Greenwood Press, 1991).

Sennett, Richard, *The Conscience of the Eye* (New York, Knopf, 1990).

Sheldrake, Philip, *Spirituality and History: Questions of Interpretation and Method* (New York, Crossroad, 1992).

Sheldrake, Philip, 'Spirituality and history: keeping the conversation going', *Christian Spirituality Bulletin*, 1, 1 (Spring 1993), 8–10.

Shepard, Paul, *Man in the Landscape: A Historic View of the Esthetics of Nature* (College Station, TX., Texan A&M University Press, 1961).

Silko, Leslie Marmon, 'Landscape, history and the Pueblo imagination', in D. Halpern (ed.), *On Nature: Nature, Landscape, and Natural History* (San Francisco, North Point Press, 1986), 83–94.

Smith, Jonathan Z., *Map is Not Territory: Studies in the History of Religions* (Leiden, E. J. Brill, 1978).

Smith, Jonathan Z., *To Take Place: Toward Theory in Ritual* (Chicago, University of Chicago Press, 1987).

Stephens, Meic (ed.), *A Companion to the Literature of Wales* (Cardiff, University of Wales Press, 1986).

Thomas, Ned, *The Welsh Extremist: A Culture in Crisis* (London, Victor Gollancz, 1971).

Thomas, Patrick, *Candle in the Darkness* (Llandysul, Gwasg Gomer, 1993).

Tuan, Yi-Fu, 'Sacred space: explorations of an idea', in University of Chicago Department of Geography, *Dimensions of Human Geography: Essays of Some Familiar and Neglected Themes* (Chicago, University of Chicago Department of Geography, 1978), 84–99.

Tuan, Yi-Fu, 'Geopiety: a theme in man's attachment to nature and to place', in David Lowenthal and Martyn J. Bowden (eds.), *Geographies of the Mind: Essays in Historical Geography* (New York, Oxford University Press, 1976), 11–39.

Tuan, Yi-Fu, *Topophilia: A Study of Environmental Perception, Attitudes and Values* (Englewood, NJ, Prentice-Hall, 1974).

Wilken, Robert L., *The Land called Holy* (New Haven, Yale University Press, 1992).

Williams, Rt. Revd G. O., 'Christianity and nationalism', in W. J. Morgan (ed.), *The Welsh Dilemma: Essays on Nationalism in Wales* (Llandybïe, Christopher Davies, 1973), 56–62.

Williams, George W., *Wilderness and Paradise in Christian Thought* (New York, Harper and Brothers, 1962).

Williams, Glanmor, *Religion, Language and Nationality in Wales* (Cardiff, University of Wales Press, 1990).

Williams, Glanmor, 'Fire on Cambria's Altar: the Welsh and their religion', in *The Welsh and their Religion: Historical Essays* (Cardiff, University of Wales Press, 1991).

Williams, Glanmor, 'Medieval Wales and the Reformation', in James P. Mackey (ed.), *An Introduction to Celtic Christianity* (Edinburgh, T. & T. Clark, 1989), 206–36.

Williams, Gwyn A., *When was Wales?: A History of the Welsh* (London, Penguin Books, 1985).

Winterbottom, Michael (ed.), *Gildas' 'The Ruin of Britain' and Other Works* (London, Phillimore and Co., 1978).

Index